# HASAN MUSTAPA

"*Hasan Mustapa* is a fascinating presentation of an extraordinary Indonesian scholar who was deeply engaged with Sufi thought during the height of the colonial era. Mustapa's firm grounding in local culture is balanced by a cosmopolitan spirituality, as revealed here for the first time in English. This richly documented study will be appreciated by anyone interested in modern Muslim thought."

Carl W. Ernst
William R. Kenan, Jr., Distinguished Professor of Religious Studies
The University of North Carolina at Chapel Hill

"This fine collection of articles covers various aspects of the life and work of the great Sundanese man of letters, scholar of Islam, mystic and colonial official Haji Hasan Mustapa (1852–1930). In addition to enhancing our knowledge on this remarkable man, it also forms a most welcome contribution to the current Indonesian debate on the place of local culture within more uniform and universal understandings of Islam. Well-conceived and varied in content, the book is a great pleasure to read."

Nico J.G. Kaptein, Leiden University

"This book is the first to comprehensively discuss the roles of Hasan Mustapa as mystic, poet and member of the traditional religious elite. Hasan Mustapa has frequently been misunderstood by the generations that followed him, often being viewed as a blasphemous mystic. This book will correct this impression. It will encourage scholars and non-specialists alike to think more seriously about the relations between Islam and Sundanese culture. It is not an exaggeration to say that this book sheds new light of great value for the study of Islam in Indonesia."

Jajang Jahroni, Syarif Hidayatullah State Islamic University, Jakarta

# HASAN MUSTAPA

## ETHNICITY AND ISLAM IN INDONESIA

EDITED BY JULIAN MILLIE

MONASH University
Publishing

Monash University Publishing
Matheson Library and Information Services Building
40 Exhibition Walk
Monash University
Clayton, Victoria 3800, Australia
www.publishing.monash.edu

Monash University Publishing brings to the world publications which advance the best traditions of humane and enlightened thought.

Monash University Publishing titles pass through a rigorous process of independent peer review.

http://www.publishing.monash.edu/books/hm-9781925495553.html

Design: Les Thomas

Cover image: Artwork by Kendra H. Paramita, used with permission of TEMPO.

Series: Vernacular Indonesia
Series editor: Julian Millie (Monash University)



**National Library of Australia Cataloguing-in-Publication entry:**

| | |
|---|---|
| Title: | Hasan Mustapa : ethnicity and Islam in Indonesia / Julian Millie, editor. |
| ISBN: | 9781925495553 (paperback) |
| Subjects: | Mustapa, Hasan, R., 1852-1930 |
| | Sundanese literature--Islamic influences. |
| | Islam--Indonesia--21st century. |
| | Islamic renewal--Indonesia. |
| | Ethnicity--Religious aspects--Islam. |
| | Islam and politics--Indonesia. |
| Other Creators/Contributors: | |
| | Millie, Julian, 1967- editor. |

Printed in Australia by Griffin Press an Accredited ISO AS/NZS 14001:2004 Environmental Management System printer.

# CONTENTS

# LIST OF ILLUSTRATIONS

**Image A: Hasan Mustapa**
Image originally published in *Bijdragen tot de Taal-, Land- en Volkenkunde van Nederlandsch-Indië* 101 (1942).

# FOREWORD

Martin van Bruinessen

This book is a long overdue tribute to a most remarkable man of letters, religious official, mystic and vernacular ethnographer *avant la lettre*, who has been undeservedly almost forgotten outside his native Priangan. Haji Hasan Mustapa was a towering figure of the late nineteenth and early twentieth century who embodied a rich composite of Islamic scriptural knowledge, Sundanese literary and mystical tradition, and the *adat* or customs of highland West Java. In international academic circles, little is known of him apart from his collaboration with Snouck Hurgronje in Aceh as well as Java or his authorship of a comprehensive inventory, at Snouck's prodding, of Sundanese *adat*. In Indonesia too, he has never received wide recognition of his qualities as an intellectual giant bridging tradition and modernity, *adat* and Islam. This may be due at least in part, as Julian Millie has suggested elsewhere, to his association with Snouck Hurgronje and the Dutch colonial project, but some of Snouck's other associates (Sayyid Usman, Hoesein Djajadiningrat) have not been relegated to similar oblivion. Another factor no doubt is that Hasan Mustapa expressed himself exclusively in Sundanese or Arabic, and that his poetry was most appreciated in Sundanese aristocratic (*menak*) circles, who in Indonesia's Independence struggle supported the Pasundan state rather than the Sukarno-Hatta Republic and have been politically marginalised ever since. Later Sundanese literary figures, most notably Ajip Rosidi, have made efforts to generate a revival of interest in Hasan Mustapa, and among Sundanese intellectuals and academics there has been an ongoing if minor tradition of engaging with his writing and religious ideas. Broader recognition has not yet been forthcoming, but I venture to suggest that Haji Hasan Mustapa's work is potentially of contemporary relevance. Among the different responses to globalisation and resistance to Westernisation and Arabisation of Indonesian cultures there is a renewed interest in what some have glossed as *Islam Nusantara* (Archipelagic Islam), discourses and practices that are genuinely Muslim as well as authentically Indonesian. Haji Hasan Mustapa was definitely an authoritative and inspiring representative of *Islam Nusantara.*

My own encounter with Haji Hasan Mustapa and his religious ideas took place more than thirty years ago. I was living in Bandung and making efforts to become an anthropologist of Indonesian Islam. My research project was about economic marginalisation and Islamic radicalisation, but I soon became more interested in the various Sufi orders and Sundanese mystical movements in which some of my respondents were involved. Travelling through West Java and spending nights in various Islamic schools and places of pilgrimage, I thought I could discern a distinct Sundanese spirituality, which found expression in esoteric movements and local cults such as *Perjalanan* and *Sunda Wiwitan* but also in formal Muslim religiosity in West Java. A chain of holy graves and other sacred sites, stretching from Pamijahan on the south coast, Cirebon in the northeast and Banten in the west to pilgrimage sites closer to Bandung visited by my respondents, appeared to mirror the gradual penetration and indigenisation of Sufi teachings, mostly associated with the *Syattariyah* Sufi order. The concepts of divine emanation in seven grades of Being (*martabat tujuh*) and of man as an imperfect but perfectible manifestation of divine and prophetic attributes, expressed in oblique terms and suggestive diagrams in *Syattari* manuscripts, were embraced by Sufi orders as well as ostensibly non-Islamic esoteric movements. So was the idea that religion has different levels of understanding and obedience, the exoteric level of *syariat* (Ar: *shari'ah*), i.e. formal obligations and literal meanings, and the esoteric level of a higher reality or *hakékat* (Ar: *haqiqah*). The devotional repertoire of Sundanese spirituality includes pilgrimages to holy graves, self-purification in nightly bathing ceremonies, and various exercises to connect with the spiritual forces surrounding us.

The *Darul Islam* (*The Abode of Islam*) movement, which had aimed to establish a state based on the Shariah instead of the secular nationalist ideology of Pancasila, consisted of Islamist hardliners but was at the same time pervaded by this Sundanese spirituality. (I acquired a copy of the diary that had been kept by a *Darul Islam* fighter and was surprised by the mystical-magical worldview it revealed.) The *Darul Islam* was militarily defeated in 1962 but has persisted as a number of loosely connected underground networks, which have remained more closely attached to Sundanese Muslim traditionalism than to the Salafism of other Muslim radicals.

At the time of my research in Bandung, the Sundanese spiritual tradition found perhaps its most prominent embodiments in the *Qadiriyah wa Naqsyabandiyah* Sufi order and the cult of Abdul Qadir Jailani (which Julian Millie later studied). And, as said, it had many other manifestations: in other Sufi orders, mystical cults, esoteric spirituality groups, and the everyday religiosity of ordinary village and urban neighbourhood communities. The only Muslim group that fiercely rejected this Sundanese spirituality and its devotional practices was the puritan reformist movement *Persis* (*Persatuan Islam*, The Islamic Association). There was a small *Persis* congregation among my neighbours; their puritan attitude isolated them from the rest of the community, who spoke of them as having broken away from a common cultural heritage.

In fact, one of my key informants, Oemar Soeraatmadja, had in his youth been an active member of *Persis*, but following an encounter with a charismatic mystic teacher, D.S. Roekman, he had a conversion experience, became Roekman's acolyte, and helped him to organise his disciples into a Sufi association, *Paguyuban Mistik Islam Rasa Tunggal* (The Mystical Islamic Collective of the Foremost Feeling), and acted as his exegete, explaining the master's Sundanese mystical teachings in terms of the Sufi tradition. ('In *Rasa Tunggal*, I represent *syariat*, and Roekman *hakékat*,' he said.) Pak Oemar introduced me not only to Roekman but also to several other representatives of the Sundanese spiritual tradition, ranging from orthodox Muslims to self-consciously heterodox *kebatinan* (inner spirituality) followers. Pak Oemar was also, I believe, one of the first to speak to me of Haji Hasan Mustapa and mention that he was praised by the orthodox as well as the heterodox as a man of deep knowledge, an authority of *syariat* as well as *hakékat*.

In one of our first discussions on Sufism and different levels of understanding, Pak Oemar hinted at the deeper meaning of the Muslim creed (*shahadah*) he had begun to grasp thanks to his teacher Roekman: at the *syariat* level, the prophet Muhammad was a historical figure in Mecca, distant from us in time, place and culture, but at the deeper level of *hakékat*, Muhammad is a spiritual entity that we can only know in and through ourselves. The devotions *Rasa Tunggal* taught included interiorising exercises for connecting with the latter True Muhammad. This resonates with well-known concepts of metaphysical Sufism, *wahdat al-wujud* (Unity of Being) and *haqiqah Muhammadiyah* (Muhammadan Reality). It is also reminiscent of the well-known anecdote of Haji Hasan Mustapa's challenging and confounding his learned colleagues over the true meaning of the Muslim creed (which is narrated by Julian Millie in the first chapter of this book).

Haji Hasan Mustapa was not interested in having many disciples and followers. Among orthodox Muslims there is no school of thought directly traceable to him. The self-described followers whom I did meet and could interview were older, Dutch educated men, who had been associated with the group *Galih Pakuan* (Heart of Pakuan) and belonged to the heterodox end of the spectrum. Ema Bratakoesoema was a prominent promoter of Sundanese culture and the martial arts – I first met him through my martial arts contacts and later found out that several Sundanese intellectuals owed their higher education to their having been adopted by him. He had also sponsored the recent publication of one of Haji Hasan Mustapa's works, *Gendingan Dangding Sunda Birahi Katut Wirahmana* (1976). Oemar Soeraatmadja, who was his relative, suspected that Ema had tampered with the text to have it conform better to his own project of a not-so-Islamic Sundanese revival. (That was not Oemar's only suspicion: he also believed that Wangsaatmadja, Haji Hasan Mustapa's scribe in the latter part of his life, made his own adaptations and changes in the texts he was dictated and may even have passed off some of his own writing as Mustapa's. Wangsaatmadja had been active in the Theosophical Movement before he met Hasan Mustapa, and Oemar believed some of the later works show an influence of Theosophy.)

Ema Bratakoesoema and Djajasupena, the men from whom I heard most about Haji Hasan Mustapa, told me they had in fact been closer to a follower and close friend of his, Ajengan Bangkonol ('the religion teacher of Bangkonol'). Bangkonol, whose personal name was Abdul Hafid, had spent many years studying the exoteric and esoteric sciences of the *pesantren* (Islamic boarding school) tradition as an itinerant student in East Java and Madura and was well-versed in Islamic law as well as the invocation of supernatural support in healing and the martial arts. He led a small mosque and *pesantren* in the village of Cibangkonol, to the west of Bandung, and not long after Haji Hasan Mustapa's appointment as the chief Islamic official of Bandung the two men met. Hasan Mustapa questioned Abdul Hafid about the true meaning of the *shahadah* – the question referred to above and in Millie's first chapter. In a sudden flash of enlightenment, Abdul Hafid saw the old certainties on which his life had been based shattered and knew he had to make a radical break. He started behaving very eccentrically – 'like a madman,' Djajasupena said; but the eccentricities resembled those of some other holy men (*wali*) in Java. Abdul Hafid smashed the mosque's *bedug* to pieces (the large wooden drum used for marking the times of prayer) and sent the students in his *pesantren* home. 'He did not want to sell lies anymore,' Djajasupena explained; having grasped the *hakékat* of God's and Muhammad's existence, he no longer cared for the *syariat*. He left his house and wandered about, avoiding human company and spending the nights in a hut in the paddy fields, where he was visited by a mysterious guest from the spirit world. From that time on he would speak in his sleep, or go into a trance when awake and speak words that were only partly intelligible but foretold events that were to happen.

Abdul Hafid later resettled in the city of Bandung, where he remained known by the name of Ajengan Bangkonol, although he had abandoned his village and position as a teacher. He became one of Haji Hasan Mustapa's closest friends, as well as father-in-law to Wangsaatmadja, Hasan Mustapa's scribe. Ajengan Bangkonol and Wangsaatmadja, who survived Hasan Mustapa by many years, appear to have had a significant impact on the reception of the latter's ideas in self-consciously syncretistic upper class circles and may have downplayed the orthodox dimension of his religious views.

This was at least what I gathered from a conversation with Wangsaatmadja's youngest son Tjitjih, the only of his children who was seriously interested in Haji Hasan Mustapa's religious thought (and who kept a large though incomplete collection of his works). He told me that his father had come to Bandung from Subang as a schoolteacher in the early 1920s. With his background in Theosophy, he was fascinated when he heard the story of Ajengan Bangkonol's enlightenment and eccentric behaviour. This had in fact been what motivated him to approach Haji Hasan Mustapa and volunteer to become his scribe. He also sought Ajengan Bangkonol's company, gained his confidence and married his daughter, and remained close to him after Hasan Mustapa's death.

I told Tjitjih that I was interested in the genealogy of Sundanese esoteric movements and wondered whether Hasan Mustapa might have been the crucial link connecting the earlier *Syattariyah* Sufi tradition with these movements. Tjitjih strongly objected to this suggestion and insisted that, unlike his own grandfather Ajengan Bangkonol, Haji Hasan Mustapa always firmly remained within the boundaries of orthodox Islam. He was a master in expressing Islamic thought and concepts in the Sundanese language, but he never accommodated Sundanese pre-Islamic ideas in his religious worldview, Tjitjih insisted. He had an intellectual interest in heterodox beliefs and practices and described some in his book on the *adat* of the Sundanese, but always made his disagreement clear. He never dabbled in magic or recited mantras and formulas to call upon spirits, as Ajengan Bangkonol used to do and Tjitjih himself (like many young Sundanese) did in his youth. Tjitjih clearly felt protective of Haji Hasan Mustapa's legacy and did not want him to be associated with esoteric spirituality; he wanted him to be remembered as a Muslim intellectual. He was convinced that copies of Haji Hasan Mustapa's work that had been deposited in the National Museum were deliberately destroyed, and was concerned lest radical puritans might attempt to wipe out his work altogether.

I never had the chance to become more deeply involved in Hasan Mustapa's work. I never mastered Sundanese language and culture sufficiently to understand his poetry with its rich metaphors, or even the prose texts edited by Wangsaatmadja. Moreover, the vicissitudes of academic life steered my work into another direction. I remained convinced of the importance of Haji Hasan Mustapa's work to understanding the spiritual tradition of Indonesian Islam, and I have always wanted to return to it later in life. It is gratifying to see that his work has now been made more accessible with this important volume. It is the first time that we have now a major work by Hasan Mustapa in English translation, along with some helpful essays on the man and his work.

This book is an important contribution to scholarship about Haji Hasan Mustapa, and Julian Millie is to be congratulated for presenting this interesting figure for the first time to an international audience. He has put together a judiciously chosen set of essays that highlight various aspects of Haji Hasan Mustapa's religious thought and literary production. Pride of place is given, after Millie's introductory chapter, to a key work in Hasan Mustapa's oeuvre, which discusses the mystic path in Islam. The translation and annotation of this text alone are major feats. This is followed by an analysis of this work by Hasan Mustapa's leading exegete, Ahmad Gibson Albustomi, and a study of the Sufi doctrine of the seven grades of Being in Hasan Mustapa's poetry by Jajang A. Rohmana. These chapters clearly establish his place as a major representative of metaphysical Sufism embedded in its Indonesian cultural context. Among the other chapters we find a thoughtful essay by Ajip Rosidi, the senior Sundanese literary author and intellectual who has played a major role in reassembling Hasan Mustapa's oeuvre and transmitting his heritage as a man of letters and religious thinker to younger generations. It is good to see this early essay now in English translation.

The remaining chapters deal with various other aspects of Haji Hasan Mustapa's life and work: his attitude towards the colonial government, his attachment to Sundanese culture and his efforts to harmonise Islamic content and Sundanese form, the literary technique and use of various verse forms in his poetry. Together, the chapters of this book also constitute a good overview of the contemporary reception of Hasan Mustapa and his work by Sundanese intellectuals and academics. I have thoroughly enjoyed reading this book and wish it a large readership.

# CONTRIBUTORS

**Julian Millie**

Julian Millie is Associate Professor in the Anthropology program of Monash University. His first book, *Bidasari: Jewel of Malay Muslim Culture*, was a study of Islamic romance in the Malay language. His second, *Splashed by the Saint: Ritual Reading and Islamic Sanctity in West Java*, was based on a period of field research over fourteen months during which he attended an Islamic intercession ritual in West Java. Since then, Millie has continued to work in West Java, focusing mainly on Islamic preaching and the interactions between sub-national and national Islamic spheres.

**Ahmad Gibson Albustomi**

'Kang Gibson' teaches philosophy of religion in the *Usul al-Din* Faculty at the Sunan Gunung Djati State Islamic University in Bandung. He obtained his PhD in Religious Studies from the same institution. He has been active in the Bandung-based philosophy study group known as the *Yayasan Pasomoan Sophia*, and is an active contributor of articles on Islam and society to various media.

**Mufti Ali**

A native of Banten, Mufti undertook undergraduate study in the Shariah Faculty of Banten's Sultan Maulana Hasanuddin State Islamic University, where he currently works as lecturer and head of the Centre for Research and Community Service (LPPM). Between 1998 and 2008 he undertook postgraduate studies in the Faculty of Theology at Leiden University, in the Netherlands. In November of 2008 he successfully defended his thesis entitled *Muslim Opposition to Logic and Theology in the Light of the Works of Jalal al-Din al-Suyuti*. From 2007-2015 he was director of the research division of the Centre for the Study of Banten History and Culture (Laboratorium Bantenologi). He has published a number of articles in academic journals.

**Martin van Bruinessen**

Martin van Bruinessen is Emeritus Professor in the Department of Philosophy and Religious Studies at Utrecht University. He carried out his first fieldwork among the Kurds of Iran, Iraq, Turkey and Syria in the mid-1970s. Between 1982 and 1994 he spent altogether nine years in Indonesia, in research and teaching on Islam-related subjects. He has frequently revisited both regions for shorter periods of field research. His most recent, book-length publication on Indonesia is the edited volume *Contemporary Developments in Indonesian Islam: Explaining the 'Conservative Turn'* (ISEAS, 2013), published in Indonesian as *Conservative turn: Islam Indonesia dalam ancaman fundamentalisme* (Mizan, 2014).

**Jajang A. Rohmana**

Jajang A Rohmana currently lectures at the Sunan Gunung Djati State Islamic University in Bandung. He was awarded his PhD title in 2013 at the same university for his dissertation on Qur'anic exegesis in West Java. In 2015, Jajang received the National Lecturer Achievement Award from the Indonesian Ministry of Religious Affairs. He has published many articles on Sundanese Sufi and Qur'anic studies, including several on Mustapa's works.

**Ajip Rosidi**

Ajip Rosidi has published many books in Indonesian and Sundanese containing his original poems, essays, short stories and criticism. Throughout his career, this autodidact has been an advocate for Sundanese culture, and has pioneered programmes for the preservation of the sub-national cultures of Indonesia more generally. He has completed many research projects on Sundanese arts, literature and culture, including his massive transcription project of the Sundanese bardic genre, *pantun* (1970s). His monumental body of written work includes the first encyclopedia dedicated to a sub-national Indonesian culture, the *Ensiklopédi Sunda* (2000), and his 1989 volume on Mustapa has opened the door to subsequent academic approaches to the man and his work. Ajip has won many awards and honours, including two national literary awards for poetry (1955-1956) and prose (1957-1958). In 2011, Ajip was awarded a Doctorate *Honoris Causa* at Padjadjaran University, Bandung. His autobiography, *Hidup Tanpa Ijazah* was published in 2008.

**Ruhaliah**

Ruhaliah was born in Bogor, West Java, and completed her PhD in 2006 at Padjadjaran University in Bandung, West Java. Her dissertation research involved the philological study of the verse narrative of Amir Hamzah. Included amongst her research experience is a lengthy period working with microfilms of Mustapa's verse works, transliterating them into Roman script. She teaches in the Sundanese Language and Culture program at the Indonesia University of Education, Bandung.

**Asép Salahudin**

Asép Salahudin earned his PhD degree from Padjadjaran University in Bandung. He now lectures in the Arts and Literature Faculty at Pasundan University, and is Dean of the Shariah Faculty at the Latifah Mubarakiyyah Islamic Institute at the Suryalaya religious school in Tasikmalaya, West Java. He regularly contributes articles to local and national newspapers, including the national daily *Kompas*.

**Hawé Setiawan**

In 2014 Hawé was awarded his PhD degree in the Faculty of Visual Arts at Bandung's Institute of Technology (ITB) for his dissertation entitled *Representation of the 19th Century Priangan Landscape in the illustrations of Franz Wilhelm Junghun*. He now lectures in the Arts and Literature Faculty of Pasundan University in Bandung, and has a weekly column in the newspaper *Pikiran Rakyat*. He is a prolific writer whose writings have appeared in Indonesian, Sundanese and English in a wide range of media and publications.

# ACKNOWLEDGEMENTS

Dr Hawé Setiawan was my co-traveller in the journey of translating *The Teachings of Our Islamic Inheritance*. This was a demanding task during which we were continually challenged by Mustapa's imagination and intelligence. Hawé's knowledge of Sundanese, his commitment to this project, and general good humour made this experience a pleasant and edifying one. The gracious support of Téti Nurherliyati is also acknowledged.

Dédé Syarif gave tremendous support to the organisation of the original conference from which these papers emerged (January 2009), and assisted in a number of ways during the editing process.

Financial support for the research leading to this book was provided by the Australian Research Council through its Discovery Grant program (DP1094913, *Glocalisation and sub-national Islams in Indonesia: neo-traditionalism, localism, and the commemoration of local Islamic legacies*). The original conference was funded by a new appointees grant from the Monash University Faculty of Arts. I am grateful to all the support given by the Faculty of Arts and its dean of the time, Professor Rae Frances, as well as its current dean, Professor Sharon Pickering.

Acknowledgement is gratefully expressed to *Hamdard Islamicus*. Chapter Five was originally published in Vol. XXVII, No. 4 of that journal.

I am grateful for the assistance and support of Universitas Islam Negeri Sunan Gunung Djati, Bandung, and its rector of 2009,

Prof Dr Nanat Fatah Natsir, for hosting the gathering at which these chapters were originally presented.

I acknowledge the assistance given in various forms by Nico Kaptein, Swati Parashar, Ajip Rosidi, Jujun Junaedi, Penny Graham, Dadang Kahmad, Iip Yahya, Neneng Khozanatu Lahpan, Peter Riddell, Bambang Q. Anees, Alfathri Adlin, Dadang Kahmad, Helmi Siregar, Marieke Bloembergen, Margaret Coffey and Antje Missbach.

I acknowledge Atep Kurnia's assistance in bibliographical matters, as well as the generosity of TEMPO media in allowing permission for use of the cover image. Martin van Bruinessen kindly wrote the foreword and provided images from his private collection. Nathan Hollier's enthusiasm for the project and advice on issues connected with the publication were valuable, as was the report provided by an expert reviewer, which led to substantive improvements to the book. I am grateful to Stuart Robson and Rabin Hardjibrata for their assistance with translation.

Julian Millie
Clayton, February 2017

*Chapter 1*

# HASAN MUSTAPA AND THE SUNDANESE

Julian Millie

> One custom remains to be described. A pregnant woman, especially if she is pregnant for the first time, will receive from the ritual specialist or the midwife an amulet packaged in a waist-wrap called a *kendit*. The amulet consists of ginger, some grasses, and a little incense. It might contain ten or twenty cotton threads, in which knots have been placed by someone while listening to a reading of the verses telling about [the saint named] Sheikh Abdulkadir. People make a knot for each new episode, as many as 40, 50 or 100. People like to make armbands or wristbands out of these threads for children, who wear them to avoid stomach worms. A pregnant woman will wear it in a waistband. According to custom, she starts to do this when she is in her seventh month. (Moestapa 1913: 19-20)

These words were my first introduction to the Sundanese Islamic scholar, colonial official, ethnographer, preacher, mystic and poet Hasan Mustapa (1852-1930). I found them in a descriptive book about Sundanese tradition that Mustapa wrote around 1910 in response to a request from a Dutch colleague. When I encountered this book, in 2002, I was studying in the Dutch city of Leiden, preparing to go to Bandung, the capital city of West Java, to do field research about the ritual Mustapa describes in the excerpt: the verbal performance of a text describing the wondrous deeds of the famous saint, 'Abd al-Qadir al-Jaelani. Of all the writings about this ritual that I had read during my preparation in the Netherlands, Mustapa's was the only one to mention the knotting practice. This impressed me because although a number of scholars had written about the global popularity of 'Abd al-Qadir as intercessor, not many had produced obervations of actual performances of the ritual.

Not long after, I was privileged to be welcomed at performances of this ritual in many Muslim households in Northern Bandung. I sat beside people as they did exactly what Mustapa had described. As the singer commenced each new episode in the performance, a participant in the ritual would loop a length of cotton string around his toe and tie a knot in it. As the knots accumulated, the string formed a wristband that would later be worn by a child. I still have one of these wristbands stored away.

Mustapa's observations about the knot-tying reveal two aspects of the man. The first is the range of roles he filled, and the demanding competencies implied by them. He wrote the ethnographic work cited above at a time when very few natives of Indies societies had turned a scientific gaze on the lifeways of their own communities, and even fewer had produced such lengthy works (the book has 199 pages). His relationships with colonial officials were instrumental in his production of the work, but this does not devalue his achievement. Apart from being an ethnographic writer he was also recognised during his lifetime as an Islamic visionary. In thousands of stanzas of Sundanese verse, he expressed a characteristic Islamic worldview in which concepts from the Islamic canon were combined in novel ways with the language and symbolic repertoire of the Sundanese. He also served as colonial official in the Netherlands Indies government, developing close relationshps with agents of the Dutch government, and dedicating himself to the service of the government through official roles in Aceh and Bandung. (This dedication is remembered ambivalently in the present). In all these roles, Mustapa showed not only talent and ability, but also a remarkable facility for crossing social, religious, political and ethnic boundaries.

The second aspect of Mustapa revealed in his observations about the knot-tying is his compassion towards Muslims engaging with everyday life in colonial Netherlands Indies. In his adulthood, Mustapa was among the most learned Muslims of the Indies, having spent a combined total of thirteen years studying in Mecca. His knowledge of the Islamic sciences was deep. But that deep textual learning never determined the scope of his vision, and his status as a learned man did not determine the nature of his engagement with his fellows. Although the knot-tying custom is not found in the Islamic canon, it was not outside the range of Mustapa's inclusive vision. For him, the things that farmers and labourers believed to be proper observances were not signs of inadequate Islamic knowledge, but things to be dignified through careful and respectful attention. In a number of his works, such as the one translated below in Chapter Two, he mentions the mid-wife alongside the Islamic teacher as a figure of spiritual and social authority. And the ethnographic book was not the only writing in which Mustapa dealt with Sundanese Islamic convention; his speculative, philosophical and mystical writings are drenched in the linguistic and symbolic worlds of the Sundanese.

This compassion is one of the reasons for which Muslims of West Java have begun to find new meanings in Mustapa and his work in recent years. When I was attending the 'Abd al-Qadir intercession ritual in Bandung in 2002-2003, the world was becoming angrier. Muslim terrorists were causing suffering to innocent Muslims and non-Muslims. Western military coalitions were throwing the full might of the latest military technology against vulnerable Muslim populations. These occurences affected relations between religious groups in West Java. Muslim society in the province had always included tensions between rivalling segments, but these global developments were causing anger and frustration that strengthened existing antagonisms. Borders between West Java's religions and Islamic segments were becoming battle-lines, rather than positive signs of the rich diversity of the region.

For younger Sundanese, Mustapa's legacy provides responses to this tension in forms that are authentically Islamic as well as authentically Sundanese. They see that Mustapa formulated ways of being religious that avoid some of the problems stemming from the hardening of group identities. They like the way that Mustapa encourages people to live in many worlds, to avoid singularity, to understand social constraints and aspire to transcend them. Because of the novel meanings these people are identifying in Mustapa and his work, it is a good time to pay closer attention to them. In January 2009, a group of academics, activists and writers gathered in Bandung, the capital of Indonesia's West Java Province, to discuss the work, life and legacy of Hasan Mustapa. The publication of this book is an outcome of that meeting. It has two goals, intending firstly to provide an introduction to the man and his work for readers of English, and secondly, to explore the emerging meanings these are creating in contemporary West Java and Indonesia. All chapters, bar the first and last, are written by scholars and activists belonging like Mustapa to the Sundanese ethnic group.

CHAPTER 1

## The Sundanese

Indonesia is an ethnically diverse country, but the world at large knows little about the country's internal diversity. The chapters that follow are directly concerned with sub-national Indonesia, and specifically with one of its ethnic groups, the Sundanese. This group is currently the second largest ethnicity in the Republic of Indonesia, after the Javanese. At the time of writing, approximately 37,000,000 Indonesians self-identify as Sundanese.[1] Most of these people live in the western part of the island of Java, in the province of West Java. Before Sukarno announced Indonesia's independence in 1945, this province was also called Pasundan (the Land of Sunda). The province neighbouring West Java to the west, Banten, also has a large population of Sundanese.

Most Sundanese are bilingual, speaking Sundanese as well as the national standard, Indonesian. Like the Indonesian language, Sundanese belongs to the Malayo-Polynesian branch of the Austronesian family. There are currently no precise statistics concerning the number of people who speak Sundanese, but the figure is presumably close to the number of people identifying as Sundanese (37,000,000). The oldest surviving expression in Sundanese is an inscription found in Bogor that dates back to the early 14th century (CE), although Sundanese polities existed in the region long before that time. A number of Sanskrit inscriptions, found mostly in the Bogor region, date back to the fifth century (CE). These inscriptions tell of King Purnawarman and his kingdom, Tarumanagara. In

1 This figure is based on the figures for ethnic self-identification generated from the 2000 national census (see Suryadinata et al 2003). In that census 15.41% of Indonesians identified as Sundanese.

most historical accounts, Tarumanagara is mentioned as the oldest Sundanese kingdom.[2]

The late nineteenth century saw the rise of West Java's capital city, Bandung. This city became a thriving centre for commerce, government and service industries. The Netherlands Indies government as well as private actors invested heavily in its architecture and planning, giving it a 'colonial' ambience which persists in the present. The first president of Indonesia, Sukarno, studied in Bandung, and developed his nationalist politics in discussions with other like-minded figures there. The city was the focus of the world's attention in 1955 when Sukarno chose Bandung as the site for the Asia-Africa conference. For the last three decades of his life, Hasan Mustapa lived in Bandung, enjoying the company of Dutch as well as Sundanese elites.

In the material sense, life is hard for most Sundanese. The region is prosperous because of its manufacturing, service industries and food production, but the vast majority of Sundanese get by with very basic resources. According to official Indonesian statistics, only 10 percent of West Javanese live in poverty, but the test behind this statistic admits only the very poorest to the category: a person is only recognised as being poor when their monthly income is below 30 US dollars.[3] For the numerically massive communities living in such materially impoverished conditions, Islam is a source of individual and collective resilience.

---

2 Accounts of pre-modern Sundanese history include Ekadjati (1984) and Noorduyn and Teeuw (2006).

3 It is almost impossible for a single person to live independently on such an income. According to the minimum wage levels determined by the West Java government, the minimum monthly wage for the Province in 2017 was to be US $142 per month.

### The Sundanese and Islam

Muslim influence was first felt in the ports of the western part of Java in the first decades of the sixteenth century. At around the same time, Portugese and Dutch traders also began to conduct commerce in the region. Yet West Java was not colonised at this time by Europeans but by the Javanese Mataram Kingdom. From the seventeenth century onwards, Sundanese elites became strongly influenced by Javanese court culture. Sundanese language, custom and social hierarchy bear the traces of this contact into the present.

The Sundanese enthusiastically embraced Islam, to the point where almost 98 percent of Sundanese currently self-identify as Muslim. This population dislays much Islamic diversity, and includes Islamic minorities such as (very small numbers of) Shi'ite and Ahmadiyyah Muslims. The vast majority follow the sunni current. As is the case with most Indonesian Muslim communities, the Shafi'i school is considered authoritative in legal matters.

Islamic routines and symbols give a distinctly Islamic texture to public and private life in most West Javanese communities. For example, Sundanese customarily hold Islamic education in very high regard. In present day West Java, all children receive at least a basic education in reading the Qur'an. In recent history, the Province's population have shown preferences for Islamic political causes. After President Sukarno announced Indonesia's independence in 1945, West Java was one of the regions in which a rebellion unfolded, motivated to a significant degree by Islamically-based opposition to the new republic. Apart from that, since the first Indonesian election of 1955 West Javanese voters have regularly given strong support to candidates of Islamic parties such as the Prosperous Justice Party (PKS) and the United Development Party (PPP).

In order to understand Mustapa's life and the meanings being made of his legacy, some knowledge of West Java's Islamic public sphere is necessary. West Javanese Muslims are highly supportive of a public sphere in which Islamic symbols and norms are prominent, yet because of the Province's Islamic diversity, it is never possible for a satisfactory consensus to be reached about the role of Islam in public life. It is the norm for activist groups to demand, sometimes aggressively, that public life in West Java, already very Islamic, be made more Islamic. Contemporary examples include: activist demands for restrictions on operating hours of entertainment venues, especially during the fasting month; opposition to the establishment of non-Muslim places of worship in the Province; public campaigns against concepts for collective life such as pluralism and liberalism, which are interpreted as being corruptive of Islamic norms; public programs for the eradication of minorities such as the numerically small Ahmadiyyah and Shi'ah communities; and activist support for public morality programs containing provisions that potentially restrict women's freedoms and cultural practice (see Hasyim 2007, Mudzakkir 2008, Crouch 2014, Millie and Hindasah 2015). Government responses to such demands generally disappoint those who vocalise them, but the demands are energetically expressed and sometimes create conflict.

Disputes such as these have been and always will be part of public life in West Java, and have earned the Province a particular reputation. Indonesian groups monitoring religious conflict in the country usually cite West Java as the province with the lowest level of religious freedom and tolerance (e.g. Wahid Institute 2014: 25-26). Yet such evaluations need to be understood alongside a number of qualifications. First, reports by monitoring organisations such as the

Wahid and Setara Institutes never factor demographic conditions into their reports, basing conclusions on raw numbers of incidents of religion-based conflicts. In fact, West Java's population is by a considerable margin the highest of any Indonesian province (in 2010 it was 43,053,732). In 2014, its population density of 1301 people per square kilometre made it the most densely populated of Indonesia's provinces.[4] A more sensitive demographic treatment would quite possibly see the Province removed from its position as the most conflict-ridden Province. Second, without trivialising the problems created by aggressive activist projects of public Islamic advocacy, the level of religion-based physical violence in West Java is very low.

**Hasan Mustapa: A brief biography**

Mustapa was born in 1852 and raised in a Sundanese family belonging to the minor nobility during a time of intense commercial exploitation of West Java by the Dutch.[5] Hasan Mustapa's father was descended from elites of Parakanmuncang, and held the official position of *camat*, meaning he oversaw the administration of an area below the level of regency (*kabupaten*). He had authority over an important tea-planting region in Cikajang, Garut. Mustapa's mother was the daughter of a nearby *camat*, and claimed descent from Garut nobility. Like many other families belonging to indigenous elites, this one had good relationships with the Netherlands Indies government. The colonial administration worked in close cooperation with local Indies elites to achieve its goals in economic and governmental

4 These figures are sourced from Indonesia's Central Body of Statistics: www.bps.go.id/linkTabelStatis/view/id/1267

5 Bibliographical writings about Mustapa include Wangsaatmadja (1932), Kartini et al (1985), Rosidi (1989), and Jahroni (1999). I have relied upon these sources in preparing the biography found here.

affairs. Close cooperation with the colonial government was to be an ongoing feature of Mustapa's life.

His upbringing in a rural centre left its marks in his mediations of Islam, including the major work translated in this book (*The Teachings of Our Islamic Inheritance*). Mustapa's deep knowledge of the different names and properties of plants at varying stages of their life cycles equipped him with a range of symbols and metaphors that he would use as vehicles for Islamic expressions in later life. The stages of the life of the coconut, for example, or the various parts of the *kawung* (sugar palm) tree and their usages, all appear frequently in his works. Sundanese myth, lore, foodways, idiomatic expression, and popular Islamic tradition have left their traces in many of his works, along with the performance genres through which these were given meaning by Sundanese Muslims.

His early education was a religious one, obtained in the Islamic schools of Garut.[6] It is possible that he was also taught for a while in the home of the Dutch planter and government adviser K.F. Holle, against the wishes of his father, who wished to take him on pilgrimage to Mecca. Apparently, Holle was wishing to support the boy, in whom he saw academic ability. Whatever the case, his father took him to Mecca for the first time at the age of eight or nine. This was the first of three trips to the Holy Land, which added up to around thirteen years' of residence there.

The Dutch orientalist and adviser to the colonial government, Christiaan Snouck Hurgronje (1857-1936) met Mustapa in 1884 or 1885 when the latter was studying and teaching in Mecca.[7] Snouck

6 Mustapa gave an account of his education in his work *Istilah* (Rosidi 1989: 48-49) and in Wangsaatmadja (1932). See also Rohmana (2013).

7 Scholars have expressed doubt about the dates of Mustapa's stays in Mecca, and whether he met Snouck Hurgronje there (see Rosidi 1989: 54-56; Koningsveld 1990:

Hurgronje's book on Mecca notes about Mustapa that 'in his [Mustapa's] house [in Mecca], one always found after sunrise and in the afternoon, several dozens of Javanese and Sundanese, listening to his words' (Snouck Hurgronje 1931: 268). If his early years were spent immersed in the Islamic conventions of rural West Java, his experience in Mecca exposed him to the scholastic traditions of the global Islamic heritage. Mustapa's Islamic creativity was heavily determined by both experiences, and this combination signals the level of difficulty encountered by those wishing to interpret his writings. Not many readers have sufficient Islamic learning to recognise the Islamic concepts underpinning a work such as *The Teachings of Our Islamic Inheritance*. At the same time, only Sundanese readers will have sufficient knowledge of Mustapa's symbolic repertoire to interpret his figurative language.

The relationship Mustapa established with Snouck Hurgronje would determine the future path of Mustapa's life. After he returned to West Java from Mecca, perhaps because his father refused to continue supporting him there (Ronkel 1942: 315), he commenced teaching in the mosque of the Garut Regency. In May of 1889, Snouck arrived in Batavia, and met up with Mustapa not long after that. Between 1889 and 1891 Mustapa was Snouck Hurgronje's travelling partner and research assistant during the Dutchman's research into Islam in West and Central Java (Ronkel 1942; Laffan 2011). Mustapa's assistance enabled Snouck Hurgronje to enjoy deep access to Javanese Islamic society. These travels provided rich material for Snouck Hurgronje's subsequent writings.

---

LI-LIV; Jahroni 2000: 109). Nevertheless, Snouck Hurgronje states clearly that he met Mustapa in Mecca (see Kaptein 2014: 191). Furthermore, in the first person recollections found in Wangsaatmadja (1932: 59-60), Mustapa recounts meeting 'Doktor Senoek' in Mecca during his third visit there.

Snouck Hurgronje continued to influence Mustapa's life when he recommended Mustapa for two successive appointments as *hoofd-penghulu*, this being the government-appointed Islamic official responsible for the administration of personal Islamic law at the administrative level of Residency. The first post (1893-1894) was in Kota Radja, Aceh, now known as Banda Aceh. In a letter written to recommend Mustapa for the post of the *hoof-penghulu* of Kota Radja, Snouck Hurgronje vouched for Mustapa's reliability and accountability to the colonial government, describing him as a candidate 'for whose sound knowledge I am prepared to answer, and of whom I believe that if we were to employ him, in the long run he could prove to be of good service as the *hoofd-penghulu* of Kota Radja' (Gobée and Adriaanse 1965:131). In 1895 he commenced the same appointment in Bandung. He continued in this position until his retirement in 1918.

Mustapa's personal loyalty to Snouck Hurgronje was strong: he served as his interpreter and chaperone in Java; he dutifully acted as Snouck's informant while in Aceh, giving Snouck Hurgronje weekly updates on the situation there (Jahroni 1999: 24-29); he ventured religious opinions favourable to the colonial presence (Ali, this volume); he sent manuscripts to Snouck Hurgronje in the Netherlands for his collection; he even arranged a marriage for him, which although compliant with Islamic law, was clearly understood by Snouck Hurgronje as a relationship of concubinage (Koningsveld 1985:119); and Mustapa wrote his best known work, his ethnography of the Sundanese (Moestapa 1913), in response to a commission from the government, offered in support of its effort to promote indigenous law and custom (*adat*) above Islamic law.

Mustapa's loyalty to the Indies government attracted negative critiques during his lifetime. In an extraordinary series of attacks launched upon him in the first years of the twentieth century, Mustapa was confronted with two defining features of his life and work – his closeness with the colonial government and his highly individualistic religious outlook (Rosidi 1989; Laffan 2011; Kaptein 2014). Anonymous letters circulated in late 1902 pointing out his privileged relationship with the Dutch, and attacking the correctness of his religious expressions. Also in late 1902, an Egyptian newspaper published a letter bearing these accusations, framed as an illustration of the suffering of Muslim peoples under colonial rule. It alleged Muslims were being pitted against each other by the colonial government. It describes a man, referred to as the 'Bandung Devil', who had agreed to take on the position of *hoofd penghulu* in Aceh for personal gain at the expense of the followers of his own religion, and was subsequently rewarded by the colonial government with the same position in Bandung (Rosidi 1989: 435; Laffan 2011: 168-169).

The attacks on Mustapa's Islamic teachings followed the contours of disputes that had long existed between learned Muslims of maritime Southeast Asia. His Islamic conceptions drew heavily on two controversial doctrines, the *Unity of Being* and the *Seven Grades* (see Chapter Four below).[8] In simple terms, orthodox scholars objected to some versions of these doctrines on the grounds that they tended to erase or blur the distinction between Creator and creation. To the West Javanese Islamic establishment, such pantheism was and still is a

8 General discussion of these doctrines and their resonances for Islamic scholars of maritime Southeast Asia can be read in Zoetmulder (1995), Van Bruinessen (1995) and Riddell (2001).

highly sensitive topic. The most famous attack on Mustapa was made by the Batavia-based scholar and publisher, Sayyid 'Uthman bin Aqil (1822-1914). 'Uthman published his critique of Mustapa in 1903 in a book entitled *The protection of religion against the incitements of those who mislead* (see Kaptein 2014: 92-194). Kaptein's brief summary of 'Uthman's critique indicates that it originated at least in part from sensitivity about the need to maintain distinctions between Divinity and creation. 'Uthman accused him of holding to a doctrine called *Ilmu Peyakinan* (The Science of Convincing) (Kaptein 2014: 193). For Muslims of West Java, this term points to teachings outside the established canon. (I have not encountered an instance of Mustapa using the term).

'Uthman corresponded with Mustapa, asking him for copies of the writings that had led people to make complaints to him. Mustapa wrote a letter in reply that tells us much about his writing practice, and his ambivalence concerning public orthodoxy:

> 'Forgive me, I regret that I haven't sent anything, because I am unable to do so. In fact, I do not write or compose anything at all for other people. It is true that I have spoken in public, in accordance with the harmonious positions that I have reached in my own personal adherence to the teachings of Muhammad. When I speak in public, I use poetic language when talking about religious faith and creed, and I have shaped these subjects into a number of poetic stanzas. Some of my listeners have written these down, making them into booklets. Some people approve of those writings, but others reject them. I have no desire to conflict with those who do not approve of them, and nor do I wish to accommodate those who are envious of them. At this time I have none of those poetic notes upon me. If I had them, and you were to request them, I would certainly send them, but not so that they could be corrected by you or the reverse, for Allah the Almighty

> Adjudicator has firmly forbidden that kind of deed!' (quoted in Rosidi 1989: 434).[9]

This attack on Mustapa, along with his response, reveals an important background for understanding the man and his work. Mustapa was a figure of Islamic authority in a society where religious differences motivated public conflict. Ideological and theological disagreements were and still are causes of serious disputation in the West Javanese public sphere, and the pressure to conform to a public orthodoxy is strong.[10] Critics of Mustapa felt confident that by publishing doubts on the correctness of his Islamic conceptions, he would become a figure of suspicion in the eyes of many in the community.

But in retrospect, it seems Mustapa was willing to appear as an opponent of public orthodoxy. He deliberately positioned himself in opposition to formal, static conceptions of Islam. In his verses, he actively resists centred meaning, all the while urging contextual and shifting interpretations.[11] He shows a disregard for ontological and epistemological certainty, preferring to highlight ongoing essences manifest in changing forms (Millie 2014). His verses make frequent reference to the inadequacies of religion in its formal aspects (see Jahroni 2000:108). Late in his life, he expressed a desire to be known as *Bagawan Sirna Dirasa* (Sund.: The ascetic lost in feeling) (Wangsaatmadja 1932: 64). In the West Javanese

---

9 This text is my translation of Josef CD's translation into Sundanese of one of Mustapa's Arabic letters. Mustapa wrote a lengthy defence in Arabic entitled *The Disharge of the Obligation to Douse the Flame*, partially translated into Sundanese by Josef CD in Rosidi (1989: 438-467).

10 For perspectives on contemporary intra-Islamic conflict in West Java see Muzzaki (2006) and Riyadi (2012).

11 Many expressions of this kind are found in the translation contained in Chapter Two below. For example, 'Faith cannot be realised by words, for faith must be felt, which means it is never the same for all, for each person has his own faith according to his own feelings.' (Rosidi 1989: 284).

context, the embrace of such a title indicates a disregard for the Islamic establishment, and the exchange with 'Uthman indicates that this establishment included at least some people who were willing to publically censure him. Nevertheless, Mustapa's work had at least one enthusiastic audience, and that was the Theosophical movement, which thrived in Bandung during the 1920s. According to Ryzki Wiryawan (2014:66), 'Aside from the question of whether Mustapa actually had any connection to Theosophy, his mystical writings appeared to have been favourites amongst the members of the *Galih Pakuan* (Heart of Pakuan) Lodge'. The key agent behind this popularity was M. Wangsaatmadja, a primary school teacher whom Mustapa met in 1923. Wangsaatmadja acted as Mustapa's scribe during the latter period of his life. He was actively involved in the *Galih Pakuan* lodge, where he delivered talks about Sundanese mysticism (Wiryawan 2014; Rosidi *et al*, 2000: 226-227).

**Image B: Wangsaatmadja (d. 1961) was Mustapa's scribe from 1923 to 1930.**
(From the collection of Martin van Bruinessen).

Mustapa's disregard for a stable public orthodoxy comes out clearly in anecdotes that still circulate about him. Some of these anecdotes were preserved and circulated by the members of the *Galih Pakuan*. The anecdotes reveal a person who had no fear of public disputation, and in some cases relished conflict with a clerical class that relied upon representational certainty and doctrinal fixedness as foundations for its authority. According to one anecdote, after Mustapa's return to West Java from Mecca, he summoned the Islamic scholars of Bandung to a meeting. I quote Rosidi's version of the story:

> At the meeting, Mustapa was saying all kinds of extraordinary things, and many of the scholars were beginning to consider him as an 'eccentric'. It is said that Mustapa asked the gathered scholars, 'What is the *shahadah*?' [the Muslim creedal affirmation]. Some of the scholars [*ulama*] were offended to be asked this. Even little children know this! But nevertheless, they replied by reciting the creed. And they were more offended when he asked, 'What does it mean?'
>
> But when the scholars translated the *shadahah* literally, 'I testify there is no God other than Allah, and I testify that Muhammad is Allah's messenger', Mustapa continued by asking, 'But when did you meet with Allah? Or with the Prophet?'
>
> The scholars looked at each other. After all, who had ever met with Allah?! Mustapa continued, 'If you make this testimony without having met Allah, isn't that a false testimony? If you make a false testimony, not to mention about Allah, but even about the village head...' (Rosidi 1989: 9)

Stories such as this reveal a person who was unreliable in his affirmation of the formal aspects of religion, and for this reason, people were wary of associations with him. The Sundanese writer, editor and political leader, D.K. Ardiwinata (1866-1947) was the first chairman of the Hasan Mustapa Remembrance Committee (*Comite Mendak*). On taking up this role, he received many letters from people asking why he had agreed to do so when Mustapa's Islam was so unorthodox. In the introduction to the Committee's first publication, Ardiwinata went to some lengths to explain that his admiration for Mustapa was based not on the latter's Islam, but on his speaking abilities, knowledge of Sundanese language and tradition, and the sharpness of his intellect (Wangsaatmadja 1932: 1-7).[12]

It was around the time of the Egyptian letter and subsequent attacks, that is to say in the early years of the twentieth century, that his lengthy mystical verses (Sundanese: *guguritan*) began to appear in writing. This occurred more as a result of the efforts of others than his own, for Mustapa's works were transcribed and published by his followers. An important but as yet unresolved question about these followers is whether they understood themselves to be part of a sufi order (Arabic: *tariqah*). The question can be framed in two ways. First, did Mustapa consider himself to be a link in the chain of teachers belonging to one of West Java's many sufi orders? Jajang Rohmana argues in the affirmative below in Chapter Four, locating Mustapa specifically within the *Syattariyah* order (see also Jahroni 1999: 277). Another framing of the question would ask: did Mustapa have pupils who might consider themselves to be in a guru-master relationship with him? Rosidi doubts this, pointing for evidence to Mustapa's statement that he 'never accepted students' (*tara ngamuridkeun*) (1989: 6). Yet there are reasons for thinking that he played the role of guru to disciples. First is the unmistakeable 'guru' voice adopted by Mustapa in a number of his works. This voice

---

12 Despite these sentiments, the Remembrance Committee went on to publish Mustapa's mystical works, including the one translated in Chapter Two of this book.

appeared in Mustapa's works not through Mustapa's own preference, but through the editing and publishing efforts of his followers, who structured his writings to convey the impression of a guru-disciple relationship. A further proof is the reference to 'Our Sheikh' in the opening pages of the Comite Mendak edition of *The Teachings of Our Islamic Inheritance* (see also Rosidi 1989: 246-248). A final indication is the unverified story that the soles of his feet were photographed and the resulting images distributed to his disciples. Pijper quotes an old follower of Mustapa who stated the meaning of these reproductions to be: follow my footsteps (Pijper 1977: 91).

Mustapa's literary activity continued after his retirement as *hoofd penghulu* of Bandung in 1918, to the point where he claimed to have 'written' more than 20,000 stanzas. Wangsaatmadja was an important agent in this writing process. He was attracted to Mustapa's speech, ideas and personality, and became his scribe and informal secretary. He explained much later to Ajip Rosidi that he would accompany Mustapa, who by that stage of his life had retired from public office, as he visited friends. People would ask Mustapa questions while Wangsaatmadja noted down his answers. Wangsaatmadja transformed these notes into manuscripts and books. Much of Mustapa's work owes its survival to the efforts of this man (Kartini et al 1985: 38; Rosidi 1989).

Mustapa died in January of 1930. The members of the *Galih Pakuan* continued to study and publish his works up until it became inactive after 1960. In the year after his death a commemorative committee (*Comite Mendak*) was formed, led by cultural and civic leaders of Bandung, which also published a number of works. The Remembrance Committee and *Galih Pakuan* have been crucial to the preservation of Mustapa's legacy. As noted, during his life, Mustapa paid no attention to the protocols of writing and publication followed by Sundanese writers of his time (see Ruhalia in this volume). He submitted little material to the regular channels of publication, but relied on his followers to store, copy and distribute his works in manuscript form. Fortunately, these groups continued this endeavour after his death. Financial support for some of the group's publications was provided by R.A.A. Wiranatakoesoemah (1888-1965), a one-time Regent of Bandung and Foreign Affairs Minister of the Republic of Indonesia.

Mustapa's distinctiveness has to some extent been recognised by the Indonesan state. A street in Bandung is named after him, and in 1977 he was awarded a Presidential honour as a notable regional literary figure. Yet as I argue below in Chapter Ten, remembrance of Mustapa in the Republican era has faced a number of impediments. It is significant, then, that in recent years his name and work have begun to be more frequently cited. Ahmad Gibson and Asep Salahudin, the writers of Chapters Three and Eight respectively, have cited Mustapa heavily in prominent contributions to public polemics over recent years. The Nalar Institute, a civil society organisation based in Jatinangor, to Bandung's east, has made Mustapa a focal figure in its profile, printing T-shirts inscribed with Mustapa's verse. Tisna Sanjaya, one of the most successful of West Java's younger artists, paints couplets from Mustapa's verses into his large canvasses. In its edition of 16 September, 2012, the national current affairs magazine, *Tempo*, published an 11-page feature on the man and his work. The chapters to follow explore the reasons for his re-emergence in West Java and Indonesia, and give an impression of Mustapa's work from the religious and literary perspectives. They also open a discussion about the nexus between ethnicity, citizenship and Islamic identity in contemporary Indonesia.

## Sources cited

Bruinessen, Martin van
1995 *Kitab kuning: Pesantren dan tarekat: Tradisi-tradisi Islam di Indonesia.* Bandung: Mizan.
Crouch, Melissa
2014 *Law and Religion in Indonesia: Conflict and the Courts in West Java.* Oxon: Routledge.
Ekadjati, Edi
1984 'Sejarah Sunda', in Edi Ekadjati (ed.) *Masyarakat Sunda dan Kebudayaannya.* Jakarta: Grimukti Pasaka, 75-124.
Gobée, E and C. Adriaanse
1965 *Ambtelijke adviezen van C. Snouck-Hurgronje, 1889-1936*, Vol. X. 's Gravenhage: M. Nijhoff.
Hasyim, Syafiq (ed.)
2007 *Pluralisme, sekularisme dan liberalisme di Indonesia: Persepsi kaum santri di Jawa Barat.* ICIP: Pondok Indah.
Jahroni, Jajang
1999 *The life and mystical thought of Haji Hasan Mustapa (1852-1930).* Thesis submitted for the Master of Arts Degree in Islamic Studies at INIS/Leiden University.
2000 'Haji Hasan Mustafa (1852-1930) as the great Sundanese mystic', *Kultur: The Indonesian journal for Muslim cultures* 1:1, 105-140.
Kaptein, Nico
2014 *Islam, colonialism and the modern age in the Netherlands East Indies. A biography of Sayyid ' Uthman (1822–1914)*, Leiden/Boston: Brill.
Kartini, Tini, Ningrum Djulaéha, Saini K.M. and Wahyu Wibisana
1985 *Biografi dan karya pujangga Haji Hasan Mustafa.* Jakarta: Pusat Pembinaan dan Pengembangan Bahsa/Departemen Pendidikan dan Kebudayaan.
Koningsveld, P. Sj. Van
1985 'Snouck Hurgronje: moslim of niet?' *Tirade* 29, 98-128.
1990 'Pengantar: Nasehat-Nasehat Snouck sebagai Sumbar Sejarah zaman Penjajahan', in E. Gobée and C. Adriaanse, (eds), *Nasihat-Nasihat C. Snouck Hurgronje semasa kepegawaiannya kepada Pemerintah Hindia Belanda 1889-1936*, INIS: Jakarta, XI-LXXIII.
Laffan, Michael Francis
2011 *The makings of Indonesian Islam. Orientalism and the narration of a sufi past.* Princeton and Oxford.
Millie, Julian
2014 'Arriving at the point of departing: Recent additions to the Hasan Mustapa legacy', *Bijdragen tot de Taal-, Land- en Volkenkunde* 170:1, 107-112.
Millie, Julian and Linda Hindasah
2015 'Regional Aspects of the Indonesian Ulama Council's Ideological Turn', *The Asia Pacific Journal of Anthropology* 16:3, 260-281.
Moestapa, Hadji Hasan
1913 *Bab adat2 oerang Priangan djeung oerang Soenda lian ti éta.* Batawi: Kangdjeng Goepernemen.

Mudzakkir, Amin
2008 'Politik Muslim dan Ahmadiyah di Indonesia Pasca Soeharto: Kasus Cianjur dan Tasikmalaya', Unpublished paper presented at Seminar Internasional Kesembilan, Politik Identitas: Agama, Etnisitas, dan Ruang/Space dalam Dinamika Politik Lokal di Indonesia dari Asia Tenggara, di Kampoeng Percik, Salatiga.
Muzzaki, Akh
2006 'Accusations of blasphemy: are recent fatwa evidence that moderate Islam is a myth?' *Inside Indonesia* 85: Jan-Mar 2006. www.insideindonesia.org/accusations-of-blasphemy.
Noorduyn, J. and A. Teeuw (eds and translators)
2006 *Three Old Sundanese Poems*. Leiden: KITLV.
Pijper, G.F.
1977 *Studien over de Geschiedenis van de Islam in Indonesia 1900-1950*. Leiden: Brill.
Riddell, Peter G.
2001 *Islam and the Malay-Indonesian world: Transmissions and responses*. London: Hurst.
Riyadi, Hendar
2012 'The Islamic Worldview Behind Cikeusik', *Inside Indonesia* 107: Jan-Mar. www.insideindonesia.org/the-islamic-world-view-behind-cikeusik
Rohmana, Jajang A.
2013 '*Asmarandana ngagurit kaburu burit*: pengalaman didaktis kepesantrenan Haji Hasan Mustapa (1852-1930)', *Jumantara* 4:2, 45-81.
Ronkel, Ph. S. van
1942 'Aantekeningen over Islam en folklore in West- en Midden-Java, uit het Reisjournaal van Dr c. Snouck Hurgronje', *Bijdragen tot de Taal-, Land- en Volkenkunde* 101, 315-339.
Rosidi, Ajip
1989 *Haji Hasan Mustapa jeung karya-karyana*. Bandung: Penerbit Pustaka.
Rosidi, Ajip, Edi S. Ekadjati, Dodong Djiwapradja, Embas Suherman, Ayatrohaedi, Nano S., Atik Soepandi, Komaruddin Sastradipoera (eds)
2000 *Ensiklopedi Sunda: Alam, manusia, dan budaya termasuk budaya Cirebon dan Betawi*. Jakarta: Pustaka Jaya.
Snouck Hurgronje, C.
1931 *Mekka in the latter part of the 19th century: Daily life, customs and learning of the Moslems of the East-Indian-Archipelago*, translated by J.H. Monahan. Leiden: Brill.
Suryadinata, Leo, Evi Nurvidya Arifin and Aris Ananta
2003 *Indonesia's Population; Ethnicity and Religion in a Changing Political Landscape*. Singapore: ISIS.
Wahid Institute
2014 *Laporan tahunan kebebasan beragama: Berkeyakinan dan intoleransi*. Jakarta: Wahid Institute.

Wangsaatmadja
1932 *Boekoe dongeng djeung sadjarah djr. Hadji Hasan Moestapa*. Bandoeng: Comite Mendak/Dachlan-Bekti.
Wiryawan, M. Ryzki
2014 *Okultisme di Bandoeng Doeloe: Menelusuri Jejak Gerakan Teosofi dan Freemasonry di Bandung*. Bandung: Khazanah Bahari.
Zoetmulder, P.J.
1995/1935 *Pantheism and monism in Javanese Suluk Literature*. Edited and translated by M.C. Ricklefs. Leiden: KITLV Press.

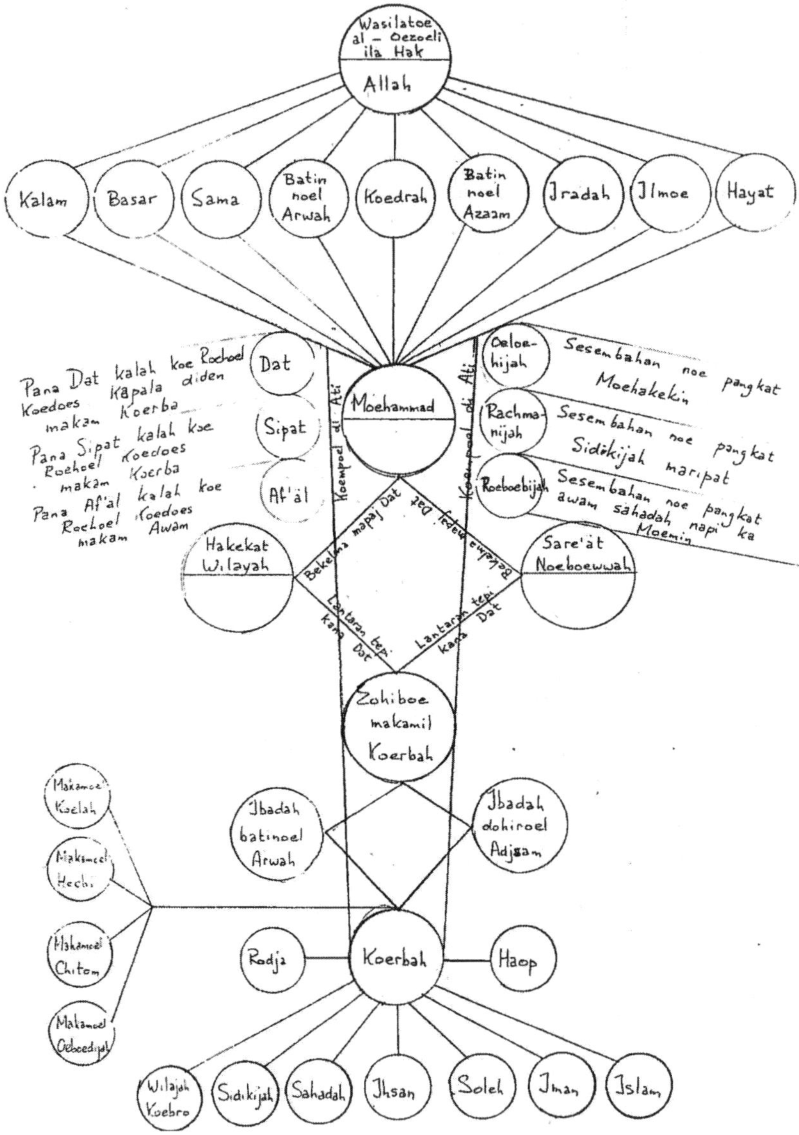


**Image C: A diagrammatic impression of Mustapa's teachings.**
(Copied by Martin van Bruinessen from a privately owned original.)

Chapter 2

# THE TEACHINGS OF OUR ISLAMIC INHERITANCE

*Gelaran Sasaka di Kaislaman*

Hasan Mustapa

*Translated from Sundanese by Julian Millie and Hawé Setiawan*

## Introduction

> After reading *The Teachings*, I [Ajip Rosidi] was overcome by a desire to perform my worship [*salat*] and carry out other injunctions of Islam, things I had never done before that point. Why was that? In fact, in the book there is not one line that invites or instructs us to pray or fast. Perhaps it was because of the poetic way it conveys the stages of faith and its great wealth of beautiful images. These caused me to feel an urge that I had never before experienced. (Rosidi 1989: 16)

The work translated in the following pages is Hasan Mustapa's imaginative exposition on the Islamic faith, the self and social life. It is considered to be one of Mustapa's major works, and is the only one to have stimulated the production of a full-length interpretation, namely the work of Ahmad Gibson Albustomi (b. 1965) republished below in Chapter Three. Its linguistic texture reflects Mustapa's familiarity with the symbolic resources of two environments. The first environment is conveyed in the text's representations of the foodways, wisdom, agricultural practices, ways of speaking, etiquette, social hierarchies, mythology, folklore, and philosophy of the Sundanese people of West Java. These define the expressive texture of the work. The other environment is that of the itinerant Islamic scholar. Mustapa acquired a deep reserve of Islamic knowledge through lengthy study in West Java and Mecca. Mustapa was not the first Islamic writer from the Indies to merge local particularity with Islamic univeralism: *The Teachings of Our Islamic Inheritance* enables us to locate Mustapa in the lineage of sufi-inflected body of speculative Islamic thinking, expressed mostly in Javanese, that scholars have called the *suluk* literature (see Zoetmulder 1995).[1]

Two bodies of Islamic doctrine are primary references for *The Teachings*. The first is the doctrine of the Divine essence and attributes. This body of doctrine, which deals with the nature of Divinity, creation and the relation of human subjects to these, has been shaped by contributions from some of the greatest thinkers of Muslim tradition, most notably Al-Hallaj (858-922), Al-Ghazzali (1058-1111) and Ibn Al- 'Arabi (1165-1240).[2] Many Sundanese in Mustapa's time and in the present have some familiarity with the doctrine through their study of basic theological texts with titles such as 'The Twenty Attributes' (Sund: *Sipat Dua Puluh*).

In *The Teachings*, that doctrine appears within a second doctrinal schema, of a mystical nature, in which the Muslim subject proceeds through a series of stages, totalling seven. Believers acquire attributes of Divinity as they pass through these stages. As explained by

---

1 In Javanese, *suluk* means the body of verse concerning Islamic mystical themes. In Arabic, it refers to the mystical observances of the *salik* (traveller along a path).

2 A representative account of this intellectual lineage is Montgomery Watt (1962).

Albustomi and Rohmana in the chapters to follow, Mustapa's mystical scheme seems most indebted to the Persian scholar 'Abd ul-Karim al-Jili (1365-1406?), whose formulation of the Perfect Man doctrine of his master, Ibn Al-'Arabi, has made him famous to the present day.[3] The idea of Divinity as something that descends upon the seeker in the form of Divine attributes famously belongs to Ibn al-'Arabi, who expressed it in his massive work the *Meccan Openings* (*Al-Futuhat Al-Makkiyah*). Chittick's account of Ibn al-'Arabi's system is highly apt for *The Teachings*: 'God created man in the form of his names [...] all humans display [in latent form] the basic attributes of life, knowledge, desire, power, speech, hearing, and seeing [...] in each stage of the journey, man acquires certain divine attributes which prepare him for acquiring more' (Chittick 1989: 274-275).

As noted already, other Muslim scholars of the Indonesian Archipelago had already written expositions of this spiritual trajectory.[4] A classic statement of this teaching from the Javanese *suluk* literature is Sheikh Ragayuni's advice to his pupils in the *Serat Centini*: 'My two children, the ultimate truth of *ngélmu* [knowledge] is this: the essence of God is our essence, God's attributes are our attributes, God's names are our names, God's works are our works' (Zoetmulder 1995: 216). This conception has been opposed by some Islamic scholars, and Mustapa himself was singled out for criticism on this point. In a work published in 1903, the Batavia-based scholar and publisher Sayyid 'Uthman (1822–1914) criticised Mustapa's

3 The concept of the Perfect Man is not a dominant aspect of Mustapa's teachings. Nevertheless, a number of features of Mustapa's work are central in Al-Jili's scheme: the ascending/descending pattern taken by the Divine Essence as it manifests in creation, the concept of returning to the Absolute, and the interdependence of pairs such as servitude/Lordship and Beauty/Majesty (see the summary of Nicholson (1921)).

4 Drewes summarises a number of texts describing the process in which human subjectivity is pushed aside by Divine attributes (Drewes 1969: 17-32).

works because 'they made the attributes of the One who must be worshipped (*sifat al-ma'bud*) equal to the attributes of the worshipper (*sifat al-'abid*)' (Kaptein 2014: 193). It was possibly *The Teachings* that compelled 'Uthman to make this critique. Yet 'Uthman's criticisms overlook what we consider to be the real achievement of *The Teachings*, and that is Mustapa's creative and sympathetic contextualisation of Islamic concepts in the everyday world of his listeners. As Albustomi argues in the following chapter, *The Teachings* describes a Muslim's journey not only through the acquisition of attributes, but also through a social environment that is distinctly Sundanese.

**The translation**

A reader of *The Teachings* should bear in mind that Mustapa's followers admired him amongst other things for his brilliant linguistic expression. Admiration of this kind was no doubt a motivation for the person or people who put *The Teachings* into writing, for they have not shied in the least from the challenge of capturing Mustapa's imaginative expression in its full length and detail. This effort is most clear in the seventh, longest stage (Oneness), which is rich in extended metaphors. These make the text exciting and imaginative, and indeed, the stage becomes something of a roller-coaster ride because of its dramatic range. At the same time, we found some of these metaphors difficult to interpret and to convey, and struggled to give coherence to a number of passages.

Mustapa included many idiomatic Sundanese expressions, proverbs and sayings in *The Teachings*, in many cases marking them with words such as 'As the Sundanese say…' or 'The Sundanese expression is…'. Apart from these proverbs and axioms, Sundanese convention is also clear in the frequent use of patterned and rhyming prose, in many places resembling the rhythmical prose of the Sundanese bardic performers (Kartini et al 1985: 60-61). Mustapa constantly sacrifices syntactic integrity in sequences of patterned phrases that follow one another without heed to punctuation or conjunction. We have tried to convey the energetic succession of phrases, but due to the many difficulties we encountered in translating this text, have not attempted to preserve their rhyme and alliteration. We have only structured our translation as verse in the small number of examples where whole stanza forms feature in the text.

In order that Mustapa's work be intelligible against the background of the Islamic learning that underpins it, we have used italics to mark the Arabic terms that refer to the two bodies of Islamic doctrine described above. By italicising these terms we hope also to highlight the thematic continuity that is a structural feature of all stages of *The Teachings*. Mustapa sometimes uses equivalent Sundanese terms for these concepts, and in those instances, we have not italicised our translation. The italicised terms are described in the following explanatory paragraphs (Mustapa has 'Sundanised' these words by expressing them in accordance with Sundanese orthography. As a result, the forms below differ slightly from the commonly accepted Romanisations of these Arabic terms):

### *Uluhiyah* and *kauluhiyahan*

We translate the Arabic term *uluhiyah* as Divinity, meaning the Divine essence that sets Allah apart from created beings. Mustapa also uses the term *kauluhiyahan*, that is *uluhiyah* affixed with the Sundanese affixes *ka–* and *–an*, translated here as *Divineness*. This has the effect of presenting the substantive in an expansive sense, that is to say, all things connected to Divinity.

## *Ma'ani*

(Arabic: sing. *ma'na*, plur. *ma'ani*) In the doctrine of the attributes and essence, *ma'ani* designates a category of attributes: power, will, knowledge, life, hearing, seeing and speech. According to one celebrated definition, the *ma'na* (lit. meaning) is the connection between the attribute and the self-subsisting essence (Al-Fudholi 2009:116). The term is complex in its Islamic philosophical meanings as well as in Mustapa's imaginative adaptation. It seems to us that Mustapa's interpretation is to some degree idiosyncratic. Based on our reading of *The Teachings*, we tentatively offer the following definition: in Mustapa's scheme, *ma'ani* are those elements of the Divine essence that humans can acquire – through acquisition of the Divine attributes – over the course of the stages described in the work. Mustapa invests the *ma'ani* with many capabilities: *ma'ani* are things brought on by the senses and feeling (263), and even form the essence of feeling (280); they have the nature of Divinity (266); humans can acquire them (271); *ma'ani* were the cause of the birth of the prophet Muhammad (272); and the soul is a product of *ma'ani* (278). Due to the difficulty we have encountered in finding a suitably equivalent English term, we have decided to retain it in the Arabic form in which it appears in the source text.

## *Rububiyah/'Ubudiyah*: Lordship/Servitude

This pair of oppositions is a paradox that accompanies the believer's progress through the stages of *The Teachings*. The accumulation of attributes does not lead the Muslim upwards and out of the condition of being a servant (Arabic: *'abd*). Rather, the servant will ideally find perfection in servanthood. Mustapa does not always use the Arabic terms to convey this opposition, frequently preferring the Sundanese equivalent, *kapangéranan* (lordship)/ *kaabdian* (servitude).

### *Jamaliyah/Jalaliyah*: Beauty/Majesty

The vicissitudes of human life are rationalised as an opposition found within Allah's attributes. Some of these bring pleasure and goodness, but Allah also has attributes that belong to a distant, magnificent, overwhelming sovereign. These latter attributes are *majesty*. Allah's attributes of gentleness, mercy and beauty are attributes of *beauty*. Mustapa emphasises that the servant's movement through good and bad experiences are movements between these categories of attributes.

### *Sipat/Dat*: Attribute/Essence

This is basic Islamic theology. Although Allah is considered singular in essence (*dat*), the Qur'an ascribes many capabilities, qualities and attributes (*sipat*) to Allah. The opposition between *attribute* and *essence* expresses this tension between oneness and plurality: the true singularity of Allah is in the *dat*. The plurality of Allah's manifestations are *sipat*.

### *Hayat* (life), *élmu* (knowledge), *iradat* (will), *kudrat* (power), *basar* (sight), *kalam* (speech), *sama'* (hearing).

These are the attributes of *ma'ani* (see above) through which the Muslim acquires Divinity.

**The source text**

The source text for this translation is the text appearing between pages 246 and 290 of Rosidi (1989). Numbers in square brackets refer to the pages of that text. Rosidi's source was the text published in 1937 by the 'Remembrance Committee' (*Comite Mendak*) which organised celebrations of Mustapa's death anniversary and the publication of works by him. The 1937 publication was almost certainly based on a version in the collection of manuscripts held by Mustapa's second secretary, Wangsaatmadja. Its publication was sponsored by R.A.A. Wiranatakusumah, the then Regent [*Bupati*] of Bandung (Kartini *et al* 1985: 38-39). Rosidi's edition omits seven and a half pages appearing before the commencement of the text proper.[5] We also omit those early pages, but include here some important material found within them. The following appears on page 7:

> I begin to write at 2 o'clock on Saturday 7 Rajab 1317 of the Hijrah of the Prophet SAW [November 11, 1899], tracing these expressions of the feelings[6] of our beloved sheikh, Haji Hasan Mustapa the son of Usman, the Chief Panghulu of Bandung, compiled from his honour's handwritten notes. (Mustapa 1937:7)

We learn from this that the text translated here was not put into writing by Mustapa himself, but by a follower, and that he was one of a number of followers who revered Mustapa as a spiritual teacher. The existence of this pupil-guru relationship is confirmed on page 6, where Mustapa is referred to as 'our master and shaikh' and the 'shaikh of the shaihks of the law [*sariat*], the way [*thoriat* (sic)] and the genuine truth [*haqekat*]'. There is no mention in these seven pages of any specific sufi organisation or institution.

Apart from this information, the seven introductory pages contain some supplications, diagrams and some brief exposition of the doctrines of the attributes and other ideas. These seven pages flit over many topics, and are confusing to read. They have an unclear relation with the clearly structured text commencing on page 7. For these reasons, we have followed Rosidi and omitted those pages from the translation. All footnotes have been added in the translation process.

---

5 Ajip Rosidi generously sent us a copy of those seven pages from the *Comite Mendak* edition of 1937.

6 'Expressions of the Feelings' is a translation of *penjeupahan raosna* (the chewed quid of his feelings).

In closing, we point out that Mustapa structured the first five of the seven stages as two contrasting monologues. The left column expresses the recalcitrant voice, while the voice of the right column succeeds in ascending through the stages of *The Teachings*. The relations between these monologues are analysed in the commentary of Ahmad Gibson Albustomi, which appears below in Chapter Three. The final two stages are narrated in a single voice.

* * *

## Submission [*Islam*]

[249] When born into the feeling of Submission, under the influence of Iblis from the left, we are in ignorance, guided by proofs that appear at the time: 'What should we do? Is it a good thing to practise Submission, or not? But the result is just the same, a person who practises doesn't benefit from it, but is at best under the command of other people, and suffers physically as he carries out something that doesn't bring any reward, but actually harms him: his physical welfare is damaged. One's property is expended without any benefit. And all this is done for the elders and gurus and clerics, only because we wish to avoid giving them any resistance, and because we remain blinded by their auras. As a consequence, one's wealth is reduced, one's prestige is demeaned, one's enjoyment of comfort turns to suffering, and all this without reward. In fact, what we humans seek is profit and comfort. Furthermore, the elders keep on telling us about things that have no proof,

[249] When born into the feeling of Submission under the influence of Divine Sovereignty from the right, we ask, 'Is it better to practice one's faith or not? But the result is the same either way, a person who practices it never obtains a benefit, a person who doesn't practice it doesn't suffer any loss or misfortune. The voice of the heart says: 'Aaah! It's better to observe it because of the sayings of the old people and one's relatives, and when one is willing to practice Submision, one will be in harmonious accord with the people of one's own community, and in this way earn praise as a 'good person'; as someone who pays proper attention to the old sayings. And no disaster will befall a person who simply follows obediently; wrong, right, it's all up to the old sayings, for it is not wrong for someone to carry out their duty by rendering service to the old sayings, it's impossible to get into trouble for this, because one doesn't wish to be degraded or fatigued, or to lose in a material way.

saying this act will be praised by Gusti Allah,[1] that it was a saying of Allah's messenger, that it is found in the Qur'an, was brought by the angel Gabriel. Then they describe the final day, the irrefutable destiny of its comfort or discomfort, and tell us that these are from Almighty Allah. But in fact, those things are like that if one believes, but they are just the same if one doesn't believe, especially when the things being described are not visible to the eye, nor audible to the ear, nor felt by the feelings, they become even more unnecessary. [250] But even if we ourselves were to encounter or feel something special in such things, there would be no need to make mention of them, because the old people keep repeating these things, having already heard them from someone else. If there were visible signs of benefit for those who believe, and of harm for those who don't, then in that case it would be sensible to choose the one that provided benefit.'

This stage is not progress, but is in fact a reversal to unbelief, away from giving service with one's body, away from giving service with one's heart. If this stage is ignored, the deities will provide hindrance later at the station of Faith. [Iblis says] 'Feel it for yourself, and if not found here, perhaps it will be found somewhere else, for it is only your recalcitrance that has led you to ignore an exhortation to something pleasant. Feel it for yourself, and you will wander back here for the rest of your life.'

1 *Gusti* is a term of address used towards a superior, the equivalent to the English 'Lord'.

We don't expect anything in return, we just perform the duties mentioned in the old sayings.' At this point we do not yet know of the hereafter, are not yet afraid of its tortures or desirous of its rewards. This is the beginning of sharing feeling with feeling; by now one has already heard the old sayings that convey the injunctions of Gusti Allah that are written in the holy book, and has heard the religious teachers retelling the statements of Allah's messenger, and things from the Qur'an, brought by Gabriel. After this, belief creeps up on one, and perhaps the old people are correct when they use the expression 'the flower becomes the fruit'. Aaah! One should simply believe. Believe in Allah, because of the stories about Him; believe in angels, for they brought the Qur'an, or so they say; believe in the holy book, for Allah's messenger brought the Qur'an; believe in the final day, because of the stories about it; believe in the certainty of its delights and hardships that affect the body and the heart, because all of that comes from Almighty Gusti Allah. Moreover, those stories do not go beyond those things, and although they come from the old people, and tell of things to be experienced in the future, one should simply believe them, for no matter how good it is for a person to deny the truth of what the old people say, they have nevertheless travelled widely and had many experiences.'

At this point, one has arrived at the stage called Submission with the body, Belief with the heart. A person soon rises from here to the station called Belief.

## Belief [*Iman*]

[251] When we step onto the stage called Belief, in the grip of Satan's influence from the left, we ask, 'What's the point? It is all clear. What is the benefit for those who practice? For those who believe? I have not yet met a person who refused to observe their religion and suffered for it, who didn't believe and was placed under pressure. It was not the case that their hardships increased, their status worsened, or they suffered greater loss to their material wealth. As for showing awe and respect for their elders and relatives, they achieved that by pretending. As it happens, I myself frequently pretend in this way, but like a child I avoid my parents and relatives in gatherings out of fear that they will find me there. I affirm the truth of what the old people say, but only when I am asked about it. That's enough. Do not exhaust yourself by making sacrifices that are necessary to follow the path set out in what the old people say, but make them now and then only, for there are many other things that must be done, and one's lot in life is to search for happiness: perhaps the old people and relatives will forgive this, and won't force us to the point of fatigue in body not to mention heart. As for me, I am exhausted either way, out of breath from seeking approval, because I will not get back what I put in. And what is the proof of it?

The old people say: 'Gusti Allah created me.' Because of this, I give observance, both to Gusti Allah and to the old people, so that they will say I am of good character.[252] The old people say: 'Gusti Allah ordered the angel Gabriel to bring the Qur'an to Allah's

[251] When we step onto the stage called Belief, our insight illuminates under the Divine Sovereign's influence from the right, and a greater resolve sinks into our feelings: 'I truly must believe in what the old people say, my body must carry out all their commands, my physical self must avoid all their prohibitions, lest I be despised and cursed in public. I truly must believe in what the old people say, that I was created by almighty Allah, who ordered forth Allah's messenger, ordered the angel to bring the Qur'an, to be put in writing by the scholars. The old people do not say just any old thing. I just perform my duty, hoping that proof will appear in the long term. As good as it would be to meet such proof while not yet believing, to receive the command while not practicing it, it is better that I first believe in what the old people say before I come across proof of it, to carry out the command before I understand it, rather than being in a state of anxiety. The things the old people say may be very lengthy but they are not all lies, for as long as I have been practicing Submission with the body, my power and efforts have not been exhausted, so there will be no loss to myself or to other people. I don't want to ask for a reason as to why I must or must not, out of fear the old people will answer: 'Don't wish for everything at once, for everything to be perfectly clear, that's taboo!!' [252] It is better to simply believe in what people say, and the future will reveal the loss or gain. But I have already sensed that rather than being harmed, my friends and relatives do not hate me for practicing Submission, and many of them love me

envoy.' I don't care, for if one believes it, it could well have happened like this, but if one doesn't believe in it, it could well have happened like that all the same. As for whether things will prove to be as people say, take it easy, and simply learn as you go, about observing Submission with the body and believing with the heart, because the proofs can be seen by the eye, heard by the ear and felt by the heart, and these are more important than exerting oneself from now on for ever. I make observance, but only now and then, because I believe the things people say only in order to be noticed by the people saying them. The old people say: 'Gusti Allah gave us His book to be read by His followers, these were brought by the messengers.' And perhaps it really was like that, but it doesn't have to be in writing for one to believe. And as for the perfection that is Allah's, what's the point of being impressed by that? For Allah still exists, just as people say, so what's the point of being impressed by His perfection? The same goes for the perfection of the messenger, you don't have to be impressed by that, for the messenger nevertheless existed, just as people say he did! Just to believe is a good thing, and you will be called a believer.'

This is the stage where one breaks out in a sweat, and wants to climb up the steps, but feels dizzy. It's better to go back than forward, because if we persist in following the intuitions from the divine sovereign, Iblis will snarl: 'Get lost if you don't want my advice! Feel it, if you don't succeed here, you may succeed there! You will not stop because of your stubbornness, wherever you succeed, because you will certainly pass by here again during your life.'

for it, and what's more, the old people say that it was Allah who created me, so just believe it! It was impossible that I came into being by myself. When they say Allah commanded the angel Gabriel as his delegate, just believe it, for it is proper that only a person of greatness should give many orders: when they say that he ordered the scribes and clerks of my own race to practice Islam through the body of Allah's messenger, and to practice faith through the heart of Allah's messenger, then that was in order that he be imitated. The old people say: 'Gusti Allah sent the Book, brought by the Prophets, to be read by his nations, to be translated by the races who have received an intuition of knowledge of the Book.' Just believe it! The old people say: 'There will be a final day.' Just believe it, for it is certain that after tomorrow comes the day after, but it is impossible that there be no end to it. The old people say: 'Your final destiny of comfort or discomfort is from Gusti Allah.' Just believe it, because you aren't forced to wish for comfort, even in earthly matters, and the afterlife hasn't yet been experienced. It is better that we now make a habit of practicing all those Islamic things that are obligatory for individuals, and avoid the things that are forbidden. I do not think about the afterlife, but just wish to be praised in this earthly world, and am consistent in my belief in the things people say, so I can keep on practicing Submission with my heart and body, and practicing Belief with my soul. The existence of Allah must be completed with his twenty attributes, his personal attire. The existence of the messenger must be completed with his four attributes, so one authority is in Allah, and one authority is in the messenger, the substance for Allah's perfection. In my opinion, it would be strange if this perfection were illuminating me alone. Gusti Allah is to be served; Allah's messenger is to be emulated.'

At this stage, we wish to ascend to the stage of Virtuousness; to be called a Virtuous person.

## Virtuous [*soléh*]

[253] When one steps on to the stage of Virtue, darkness descends because of the influence of Iblis from the left. 'Ah! I have practiced Submission for a very long time, following the things the old people say, believing in what they have to say; but now I have come of age, I am already mature. Furthermore the old people are no longer here, and the ones who still are cannot give orders to me. It is time for me to have my own thoughts. I wish to practice Submission, but just to the extent where it doesn't interfere in my life, in my status, and in my work. I will go on giving observance, for perhaps it will give help just when I am being strangled by difficulties, and perhaps I should keep holding on to the words used for asking the Most Holy Gusti Allah for wellbeing, because the old people say that Allah is the one who gives help, who provides for his servants; from whom shall I seek these things if not from Him? But because I am a human being, I still need the assistance and involvement of my fellow humans. Even though I obey Gusti Allah, if my fellow humans do not approve, then the consequences can cause difficulty for me, so I must give in equal parts to both. But rather than seek further trouble, and add to one's difficulties, it is better to

[253] When one steps onto the stage of Virtue, one's heart becomes further enlightened under the influence of Divine Sovereignty from the right side, which sinks into the heart: 'Oh! My father, my mother, and all the old people no longer exist, only my friends remain. It will bring nothing if I practice my Islam, and it will bring nothing if I just abandon it. Believing in the stories of the old people will bring nothing, and so will not believing in them. But ah! I have come so far that it is better to simply continue, so I do not lose out. Perhaps the things I didn't understand in the past will be understood in the present. In the past I observed Islam, but only to be praised by the old people; but now my Islam might be accepted by Gusti Allah. If I continue to do good things, perhaps I will be rewarded by Gusti Allah. After all, my parents said it is Gusti Allah that gives such rewards. If I continue to believe, my desire to know what will happen after that will grow. If I stop and abandon the old people's admonitions just because they are no longer around, I will be very afraid of being tortured by Gusti Allah, for my parents said: 'If you abandon Islam or if you violate its prohibitions or if you cease believing, you will be tortured by Gusti Allah, if not

do it only to the extent that has become the norm in the past. It is better if it is not too drawn out, lest we cause loss to our friends and relatives, and although I myself might be happy, it is because I am living in this world, so rather than think of the benefits in the hereafter, think of the benefits in this world, and rather than fear the misfortunes of the afterlife, fear the misfortunes of this world.

Even though the mystic has already achieved such high knowledge, if he doesn't have money, he will encounter difficulties. But nevertheless I need to think about the rightness or wrongness of my behaviour, so I must have these thoughts! Whenever we are criticised by our friends in life, this is a sign we are doing the wrong thing. Whenever we are praised by our friends in life, this is a sign we are doing the right thing.

To obtain forgiveness from sin, all one can do is repent, but only if there is visible proof of your sin. As for me, I have not yet done something wrong and been criticised by my peers, but in fact I have felt at ease. I will not think of doing things beyond my contemplation, and will not be mindful of things I have never done; even the things I had done in the past were only done because there were people who gave me admonitions, both those who would approve of them, and those who would fault them.'

At this station, progress will be obscured. If we remain inconsistent, it is like believing what the wind says, and we will fall back to the stage of Belief.

in this world then in the hereafter.' So, my fear is for His anger. My desire is for His love. [254] For indeed, the Almighty has the attribute of power when angry, and supremacy when loving. Instead of lessening my practice of Islam as it was practiced in the old days, it is better that I enhance the teaching I have with all the proper Islamic things, enhance it with the recommended things, and in my basic conduct; it is better to develop it so that what I felt in the past to be an obligation becomes a feeling of goodness in the present, but I want to obtain the feeling of being equipped for continually practicing Islam and observing its prohibitions. It turns out that the remedy for carelessness is striving to give one's self this duty, so that if one is cut off from feeling obliged, repentance will occur. There is an expression: one's good or bad fate has been decided from the beginning, and it will never be wrong. But if I am fortunate, then I will prosper: as long as I practice my Submission, my line of destiny will be fortunate; as long as I believe, my line of destiny will be fortunate.

If I do none of these things, and let it all go from now on, then misfortune will follow, and things will become even worse, to the point of deprivation. So why not now? Why later? If my destiny is happiness, then maybe I will regret doing so. But if I had believed as well as observed from the beginning, then maybe all would be free of obstacles; our worldly behaviours will not differ from our behaviour in the afterlife, believing in the world and showing that belief in my behaviour.'

At this point, I ascend to the stage of Goodness, and will be called a person of Goodness [*muhsinin*].

## Goodness [*Ihsan*]

[255] The moment we step up to the stage of Goodness, our souls are in gloom because of the influence of Satan from the left. 'Ah! For a long time we have observed Islam, our souls still resolutely believe in whatever the old people tell us, and even though this has gone on for so long, this has not fatigued us; and even though feeling is still lacking in all this, we should just accept it. Why should I take on further inconvenience and difficulty? Gusti will balance the scales, even for those whose sins are many, for His character is indeed forgiving. Even more towards me, a person who has kept on the straight and narrow for a long time, I won't be regarded too seriously, for I have not yet disregarded the laws of sin, nor broken the rules. Indeed Allah is all-knowing, and certainly knows my failures, for there is no power or strength other than those of Allah. What I look forward to is to achieve goodness, and I have never been a wrongdoer, never experienced doubt. I will never be shaken as long as I feel happy, or for as long as I am in faith. Even if my belief comes under attack and I should lose touch with the divine injunctions, or if from time to time I should fall into doubt, these things will be weighed up by Gusti Allah Himself. Even if I become unsteady when visited by something that causes me to lose touch with the divine orders or to break a prohibition, these things are in Allah's power. If I can do something, it is by His authority, and if I am prevented, it is by His authority. After all, I have neither power nor strength, so how could I have knowledge of these things, [256] of how to act with care, propriety and

[255] At the very moment one steps up to the station of Goodness, one is illuminated under the influence of Divinity from the right. 'Ah, I must hold fast because I am growing old, and what remains left is the observance of Islam with the body, the practice of belief with the heart, that is all there is. In fact, at this point the feeling is not one of increasing heaviness, but of increasing weightlessness, and the impediments do not multiply, but apprehensions become fewer. Free from the old people, free from father, knowledge increases, conviction increases, the sayings will be vindicated, one's actions will yield a benefit. In fact, one should move back from convention, and thereby increase in conviction. For it is indeed clear that our respect and service must be offered to the one who brought us into creation. It would be strange for a creator to have no proof of his creation. It would not make sense to create something that had no sovereignty, and it would not make sense if the creation were not taken care of. Aaaah! It is a great embarrassment: all our acts are being observed, all our movements are being moved. This does not mean that I become complacent. Although I know nothing, He is all-knowing, and even the smallest insects are doubtless within His knowledge. Even more so if I am bad in mind and deed. Even if I cannot improve, the things of the past will not change, and I will fear that my respect will be lessened, and fear that I will be treated carelessly, so it is better that I accept that all my movements and inclinations are doubtless known by Allah. So! [256] This doesn't mean that I can become careless in serving

correctness, and of how to look after myself on my own? If we are careful, we could nevertheless come under attack, and if we are negligent, and if we are careless, we could nevertheless be saved; who can know such things? As for repentance, it is absolutely obligatory, but in my case, only if I had been disobedient from the start. As for resignation, it is absolutely obligatory, but only if I don't have the human characteristic that we are sometimes in comfort and sometimes not. As for believing in Allah, that is absolutely obligatory, but only if all my options are exhausted. As for accepting my fate, that is absolutely obligatory, but only when I am no longer curious. As for being pure-hearted, that is obligatory, but only if I have forgotten how I came into the world, ashamed of human eyes, afraid of human criticism. As for loving the Loving One, this is obligatory, but only while I am not yet convinced that all bounties and hardships are granted by Allah. But it is impossible that Allah will not recompense me in the same way. I will never entertain the belief that goodness comes from anyone else, as long as prosperity does not come from other humans. What I fear is the wrath caused by my declining worship in comparison with the past, my wilful reduction in my faith in comparison with the past, and by my wilful fear of wrath in this world. What I desire is to be granted favour by Gusti Allah in this world first, and even more so in the afterlife.'

At this point our progress is obscured, and in fact we travel backwards. The conditions for advancing are being fulfilled, but I have still not made my choice. On the one hand I am longing, but I still have the thought: What for? the One who is observing me, but it leads me to merely endorse these seven matters, in the hope that they won't be concealed by being trivialised. In the past I was fearful that my outer existence belonged to people, and my inner existence belonged to Allah. I was fearful of being punished with hardship in this world, and even though I feared torture in the afterlife, there was no feeling associated with it: doing the right thing would be pleasing, doing the wrong thing would lead to torture. Scary! But now, I don't mind, I desire to be fearful of His wrath, even without punishment; I desire His favour, even without reward. My wish is only to avoid doing something to bring on His anger, to avoid disobeying the Almighty and being arrogant towards the One observing me. How could such a thing be unseen? How could it not be heard? How could it not be punished...even though there is no difference between the worshipper and the non-worshipper? That is what makes me ashamed, the fact that His anger has never been seen. There is nothing that will prevent us from disobedience other than remembering the things I have been arguing for above.

I see it now! What a sin it was that I forgot this! What a sin for me to have broken off my service! What a sin for me to be put to shame by other people while forgetting that Gusti Allah is watching! Now, all things that come to me and leave me in fact come from Him and go back to Him. I shall put my soul in order, and I shall not trivialise His orders or violate His prohibitions. I wish to avoid all things of that kind. I simply submit to Him! Let me be guided so that I accept all the things that have happened, the pleasant along with the unpleasant, and

If I keep holding a desire for knowledge under the influence of Divinity from the right, Iblis will forbid it, and say: 'Wah! Disaster! If you get that knowledge, you will be in a worse state. Too many things are prohibited. [257] But if you persist, that's up to you! It is inevitable that you will later feel the many ways in which conflicts and separations will arise. If you don't obey me at this point, perhaps you will pay attention to me later, and won't be so harsh towards me. Rather than receiving His wrath later when you already know Him, you are better to receive it in your current condition, and at least you won't be known as a trouble-maker. Indeed, we must be thorough and careful in what we do, and not be careless. Regret always comes too late.'

be completely pure. Let me not serve any other in my deeds, or hold any other reasoning that will move my submission to any other, attributing to it the power to bring something or take it away. As for wrong conduct, and as for sins against Islam, sins in the conduct of the heart, I will definitely not do such things as long as I remain conscious. It may be that a negligence of mine may not be punished, but there must be proper reason for that negligence. I will not tire of it, for it will be sufficient for me to be like that. I am not worthy of the Almighty, who begat me, proved by the fact that I like to receive things from Him without giving anything in return: for a long time I have received His compassion, received mercy and bounties, and it is proper that one who receives compassion should return the compassion, even though I do so with an expectation, being aware that my happiness must have a cause.'

At this point one wishes to ascend to the station of Witnessing and be called a witness. This begins with an urge in the heart, which has a longing to search for it, wishing to attain familiarity with it, fearful of meeting some other which does not provide in the same way.

## Witnessing [*Sahadah*]

[258] At the moment one steps up to the stage of Witnessing under the influence of Iblis from the left: 'Ah! I have gone too far! For such a long time I have grown tired obeying the injunctions of the old people, all the while observing Islam with my body, and believing with my heart in what the old people say, and my firm resolve in this has never failed. But now, I really want my wants, and I really long for my longings, and nothing

[258] At the very moment the stage of Witnessing breaks out in light, just as one steps up, illumination is brought by the influence of Divinity from the right. 'Ah! Earlier, I longed for Him, hoping my love would be returned in love, but now, it really doesn't matter, I still long for Him but not because I want to receive a gift. I still love Him but not for the rice. It doesn't matter, even though I am clapping with one hand without any

stands in the way, for it is clear now that the Merciful needs to be worshipped, and the Compassionate is the place of our service; but as for coming to the point of wanting knowledge of Him, this is neither proper nor appropriate, for I am conscious of my inferiority; my good works are few, and my faith is thin. That would be too much, I fear it is beyond my capability. I am clever at loading myself with stupidity, enriching myself with sinfulness. It is unmistakably clear that I do not know my place! When it comes to being acknowledged by Him, I suppose I have been acknowledged, after all, I am His servant [*abdi*]. But what about my self [*aing*], what is it supposed to do?

At this very moment, I am doing nothing except trivial things. If I had already achieved knowledge, there would be many prohibitions. People may well say that I am flighty, for I let go of the mole while chasing the hornbill, let go of things I was doing in order to go for something else, and let go of the spade to get the shovel, clever but stupid, I brought troubles on myself. The proof of this is that when a noble makes a curse, it affects his equals in the inner circle, not his peasants and lower subjects, for they can just say any old thing, basing their evaluations on ignorance and forgetfulness. It is clear then, that I should know my own place. [259] After I die, I will be in the care of others, but while still alive, we must be aware of ourselves. How ever much we long for someone, it is better if that person longs for us, but what if the person does not? No matter if the gift is from a stranger, the important thing is the gift itself. No matter if I eat without gusto, as long as I get the rice. No matter if I have no response, for as time goes by it becomes clearer that I am sending without any expectation, having concern without any return. Now it is the right time for a fatal encounter in which death is one blow away, wherever it happens, and my heart will not be deceived any more. For a long time I have replied by sending vegetables in response to what I received, but I am not sure whether what I sent Him has been accepted.[2] I am constantly receiving things from there. Once we are already familiar, perhaps I will be able to ask directly for myself whether they have arrived or not. Perhaps my courier hesitated, or fatigued of the task, and the vegetables rotted on the way. No matter if people say I am impudent for asking directly, but that is no problem. What appears so generous from afar would be how much more generous when familiar! In the past, I was happy to receive rice, but now I am happy when I get rice and the feeling of satisfaction. In the past I was glad to receive good health, now I am glad to receive good health and virtue. [259] In the past I was happy to receive nice clothes, but now I am happy to receive good clothes and perfection. In the past I was happy to get a mat and a pillow, but now I am happy to get these and a good sleep. In the past I was happy to receive life, now I am happy to have a sense of belonging. In the past I was glad to have knowledge, now I am happy to have knowledge and practice it. The thing I really want is to meet face to face. I do not want the cananga plant, I only want its flower; I do not want its flower, I just want its perfume; I do not want

2 The sending of vegetables to neighbours is a common expression of Sundanese sociability.

desire, as long as I can just see her. No matter if its shape is flawed, as long as it is good. No matter if I don't feel at ease, as long as I can merely live. No matter if I do not put my knowledge into practice, as long as I have the knowledge. No matter if we are intact, as long as we are noble. No matter if the rice is wet, as long as I get the rice. No matter if the drink has lost its flavor, as long as I drink its fluid. No matter if I miss out on the nectar, as long as I capture the perfume. No matter if I miss out on the perfume, as long as I get the flower. No matter if I miss out on the flower, as long as I get the stalk.[3] In fact for a very long time I have paid attention to my duty, followed all the advice of the old people, avoided breaking the prohibitions, trusted in the things my father said, perpetuated and continued them, and they didn't have to force these on me, whether in happiness or misfortune. When I bravely testified that there is no other to be worshipped, to be respected, to be feared other than Gusti Allah, that was enough, for this was not just any kind of testimony. No one has yet asked: 'How do you know this?' And if they did, the answer would be: 'My father told me!' It would be proper if I loved Him merely because of His bounties. But Gusti Allah, if loved, will love us back, and if not loved, He will still love us. It does not please Him to be longed for.

Doubtless He has no shortcomings. If we want to find Him, that is appropriate, but do not search for visible proof. Our expectation is His love, for I have stated the proof: all bounties are from Gusti Allah. In order that we do not turn away, the cananga's perfume, I only want its nectar. I do not want a gift, I just want the giver; I do not long for rice, if it tastes as if it were wet; I do not want water, if it tastes like fetid palm-wine; I do not covet status, if the status brings pain with it; I do not fear illness, if I feel I am one with the Divine. No matter the pain and fatigue, providing I keep in accord with my heart. No matter if I am not praised, if the praise comes with expectations. No matter if I am not fully provided, if the providing has a vested interest. No matter if I am not asked about myself, if the one asking is flighty of interest. No matter if I am burnt by the sun, as long as I remember coldness. No matter if I am rained on, as long as I remember being burnt by the sun. No matter if I suffer from the pangs of hunger, as long as I think like a student [*santri*]. No matter if I live in deprivation, as long as I remember the hereafter. How could I have the nerve to testify for so long that there is no deity other than Gusti Allah? What if someone asks me: 'How do you know?' Maybe I will only be able to answer with: 'Because the old people said so! Because my father said so!' How could this be believed? How can testimony rely on talk alone? So! [260] Because of this I will persist in telling people that I will not fail in my wish to get real proof. For instance I have been asked: 'How do you know what a chili is like?' I replied: 'Of course I know, for I have tasted that it is spicy!' 'Do you know sugar?' I replied: 'Of course I know, because I have tasted that it is sweet!' 'Do you know salt?' I replied: 'Of course I know because I have tasted that it is salty!' I do not answer: 'Because my father told me!'

3 These are commonly used Sundanese idioms.

Gusti Allah is agreeable with us; [260] I find proof of the existence of the Provider in the way He provides; it signals love, and does not signify hate. No matter that I do not put it into practice, as long as I have the motive to do so; No matter I do not make it manifest, as long as I have the power to do so; No matter I have nothing to gaze at, as long as my eyes are still sharp; No matter I have nothing to listen to, as long as I have my hearing; No matter that I have nothing to say, as long as I can still babble on; No matter if there are no fruits or flowers, as long as there is verdant green; No matter if I do not eat what I grow, as long as I become rich. It is clear that Allah watches over us, and knows all my heart's inclinations, so why should I long for Him? I hunt and hunt for visible proof, what for? Only to be rejected. I am laden with squalor that cannot possibly be accepted. Even if I claimed I could be accepted, my squalor would repulse Him, so why should I want to make up a story for Him? Even if I wanted to, I would end up in error. And if I wanted to, I would have to possess a longing for the desire to come to fruition. I could travel up and down the mountains but it would be impossible for me to be different from other people, for that is not my intention. And what would be the purpose of longing for Him? I could ask Him for things, but He sends me things anyway without being asked. I could ask a question, but what sort of answer would I want? I might receive an answer I did not want. Our desires only cause remorse: regret always comes too late. Aargh! I will hold my position grimly through whatever highs and lows may come my way. I am already this happy at this time, more happy than

The listener (with ears ringing from that long reply) says: 'Wow! Be careful of being swindled! You say that you have no expectation, but look at you shivering in fever all night long, sweating in the heat since daylight just because you hope that it is *beauty* that sends it, and you are infatuated by her beauty.' God forgive us! If I ever meet in person, I will demand to know: Who is it that is obstructing your intention? I want to be sent *beauty*, but what comes is *majesty*.

If it is true that there is someone doing the sending, then just force yourself to receive it: for when I was healthy, sickness came; I wanted to live, but death came; while listening, deafness came; while seeing, blindness came; while chatting away, dumbness came; while remembering, forgetfulness came. If you do not force yourself, you will have a vested interest, longing for the green and fertile, only liking the prosperous things, approving of bounties only, enjoying the profits alone, comfortable with good health, desiring only the sweetness. That would mean worshipping pleasure and comfort, without the unpleasantness, but then who makes the unpleasantness? Who has this attitude? Without doubt this is what is known as a love of *beauty* and an aversion for *majesty*. It is precisely this that forms the constraining wall, a curtain that obscures the message. We will not comprehend while failing to discern, worshipping *beauty* and shrinking from *majesty*, even if we can recognise it, the recognition will come and go throughout the night and day; [261] we discern in the daylight, but this disappears in the evening; we discern on land, but this disappears on the water; we discern on the water, but

I used to be, so why should I want and desire [to know Him]? I don't want any deprivations: that would be even more wrong. [261] I would have a steady gloom in my heart: Aargh! But *whoever seeks something with intent will find it* [Arabic: *man thaloba syaian jiddan wajajadahu*], so go ahead! A gate opens up in front of me, but it is shrouded in mist, obscured.'

At this, Iblis complains: 'Aargh! We've been together for a long time, but now we are parting. Alright, if you resist my affections, that's okay! If you don't receive me here, perhaps you will do so there. He thinks I will not squeeze my way through. He thinks he will not pass through here again. That's okay, he thinks it will not affect him, for we are old friends, the wood might be rotten but it is still teak, and no matter how vicious the tiger, she will not eat her offspring. I will certainly persist. Goodness, the time! Excuse me! Allow me to end this audience with mercifulness [*rahmaniyah*]'. this vanishes on the land. You claimed we could drink from the same well and live together in the same valley. It is not enough at this point to avoid worrying about the sad and the happy, the sweet and the bitter, to not be worried in the day about the night, to not be worried in the night about the day, to not worry about the cold when it is hot, to not worry in the cold about the hot, for when this thing comes, that thing goes: desires come, desires go, replacing each other endlessly.'

At this point we begin to lament: I thought it was a black butterfly / It turns to be a colourful one / Water retreats and flows back / Water flows to a grave / Tomorrow's dusk may not be in daylight / And is glimpsed for but a moment.[4]

At this point there appears an obscure image of the gate at the margins of Truthfulness, the outposts of the divine abode, an abundance of mercifulness [*rahmaniyah*]. We gaze in amazement: Oh my! What is that? I look but cannot see, scared to blink lest it vanishes. I pace back and forth to the nearby square, avoiding the heat under the shade of a flowering tree. I approached it again, it became clearer, and I stand and watch the gate. The approach has five steps, the sixth is the threshold. The gatehouse has seven pillars, and seven windows.

4 The verse structure here resembles the Sundanese *wawangsalan*, which are verses in which the relations between the first and subsequent couplets are not semantic, but are based on sound similarity. The sound pattern of the opening lines alludes to the content or message conveyed in the subsequent lines. Such verses are common in Mustapa's work.

Its chandelier has ninety-nine levels, to which innumerable bright lights have been added. Even the grains of its sands are lovely, the rocks are gleaming. There is not enough ink to describe it in words, not enough pens to write it. Its name is the perfection of *Divinity*, its shade is called the perfection of humanity [*Insaniyah*].

I pause at the threshold, look above and look below. I feel it with my hands. It opens up as I recite [261]: '*May the peace of Allah be upon you.*' Three times. No one answers. I then recite: '*May the peace of Allah be upon you, Oh Prophet, and His mercy and blessings. May the peace of Allah be upon us and upon all His pious servants*'. Then I praise His greatness: '*Allah is great! I turn my face to the One who rules the heavens and earth as a true Muslim, and I am not one of the polytheists.*'[5]

5 Muslims utter this Arabic text in the *salat* (ritual worship). Mustapa includes many Arabic expressions with which his readers/listeners would be familiar because of their use in worship or as everyday expressions (e.g. pages 283, 287-290). In *The Teachings of Our Islamic Inheritance*, Mustapa proposes some striking re-interpretations of the meaning and value of these phrases.

[Editor's note to the reader: the structuring of the text in two contrasting monologues does not continue beyond this point. The remaining two stages, Truthfulness and Oneness, are narrated in a single voice.]

## Truthfulness [*Sidikiyah*]

[263] At the very moment I open the gate to the feeling of mercifulness, under the influence of Divinity, I sense eternity, which means the influence of the feeling, and the gate disappears: Aeeeh! Why does no one reply to my greeting? It turns out the gate is actually an allegory, the ninety nine levels of the chandeliers are actually the beautiful names [*asmaul husna*], some of which are *beauty*, some of which are *majesty*, and some are perfection, along with innumerable names of perfections. The seven pillars are actually the structure of *ma'ani*. The windows are opened by the attributes that depend on *ma'ani* [*ma'nawiyah*]. The threshold is a scale balancing *fear* [*khaof*] and *hope* [*roja'*], and is opened by the key of the scales of precision [*qisthosi'l-mustaqim*]. The five steps are actually the five stages already passed, and the sixth is the threshold of Truthfulness. An abundance of mercifulness: the flowering tree is actually the furtherest lote tree, the fragrant flowers are manifestations of *beauty*, and the ugly flowers are manifestations of *majesty*; the green leaves are manifestations of *beauty*, and the dried leaves are manifestations of *majesty*; the scents of ripe fruits are manifestations of *beauty*, and those of fallen fruits are manifestations of *majesty*. The fruit that comes from ripe flowers does not fall; the flower will not be ugly if the trunk is healthy; the trunk will not be diseased if the tree is alive; the tree will not be diseased if its roots are healthy.

We will not achieve [the station of] Oneness if our Truthfulness is not complete; we will not achieve Truthfulness if our Witnessing is not complete; we will not achieve Witnessing if our Goodness is not complete; we will not achieve Goodness if Virtuousness is incomplete; we will not achieve Virtuousness if Belief is not complete; and we will not achieve Belief if our Submission is not complete.

Where knowledge is concerned, if it is eternal, that is *beauty*. If it is broken, that is *majesty*. It is impossible to be harmonious if our knowledge is incomplete. We will not have knowledge if our request for it is incomplete. We cannot request if our persistence is not complete. We will not persist if we are not consistent. We will not be consistent if our belief is not complete. We will not believe if our observance is not complete. We will not obtain spiritual authority if our gnosis is not complete. We will not have gnosis if there is no *will*. We will not have *will* if there is not rectitude. We will not obtain rectitude if there is no perseverance. We will not have perseverance if there is no affirmation. We will not be able to have affirmation if we don't practice the feeling of it. We will not have *life* without *knowledge*; we will not have *knowledge* if there is no *will*; we will not have *will* if there is no *power*; we will not have *power* if there is no *hearing*; we will not have *hearing* if there is no *sight*; we will not have *sight* without *speech*.

The reception hall is the place for balancing *beauty* and *majesty*. We feel with our feeling, we sense with our senses, this is how I became *ma'ani*, and is the original property of the attributes that depend on *ma'ani* [*ma'nawiyah*], an heirloom from the past, my origin since childhood, [264] *ma'ani* is the place to worship, the dependent attributes [*ma'nawiyah*] belong to the one who serves. We come from there and will return, since the stage of Submission, the origin of mercifulness has been clear.

Good things are *beauty*, and they drop down onto the body and spirit in the world and hereafter.

Unpleasant things are *majesty*, and they drop down onto the body and spirit in the world and hereafter.

*Beauty* makes us happy; *majesty* brings misfortune. The two are actually mercifulness, neither higher than the other, they both are created out of *ma'ani*, arising from the self; the feeling feels, the senses sense.

My goodness! The origins of *ma'ani* have very clear proofs; the proof of *speech* is our words, the proof of *sight* is the eyes, the proof of *hearing* is our ears, the proof of *power* is behavior, the clear sign of *will* is our desire, the clear sign of *knowledge* is our knowing, the clear sign of *life* is our living. The proofs of *speech* are manifest; the manifestation of *sight* is resolve, the manifestation of *hearing* is appearance, the manifestation of *power* is hierarchy, the manifestation of *will* is intention, the manifestation of *knowledge* is familiarity, the manifestation of *life* is remembrance.

It would be strange if something manifest could be neither seen nor heard; it would be strange if something heard did not exist; it would be strange if something created was not intended; it would be strange if what was intended could not be comprehended; it would be strange if comprehension did not come from life, for every living being has comprehension, although a baby is small it can suck; every being that can comprehend will have wants, even small ones, like a baby needs to be clothed; and every want must be undertaken, like a hot and sweaty child needs to be bathed.

Every being that can hear will be visible, although distant, for we are not talking about human hearing. Every being that hears has come into existence, and gives service to its hearing; this is proved by our vision, we can see because of our hearing, we can hear because we have the ability, we have the ability because we have the will, we have the will because we can comprehend, and we comprehend because of our living; this revelation is the feeling of Divinity.

People say it is difficult to search for the feeling of Allahness, that is because the feeling is only an introduction, and if someone has not yet experienced the feeling, he puts stock in the thing's name, and is moved to ask: What are its *attributes*?

For instance, a child wants to taste the thing called 'sweetness', but we could swap it for something else; a sick person wants a strawberry, but we can give him a snack made from flour. When we want revelation of something because of the fact that the thing exists, when we obtain it, even if it is real, we disregard it, for although the thing really exists, it is something new, whereas what we search for is not new but something that exists. When we want revelation of the *attributes* of life, the life we have is disregarded, because even though the life is real, it is new, but what we are searching for is life, not something new. When we want revelation of the nature of knowledge, the knowledge we have is disregarded, because although it is knowledge, it is new, and what we are searching for is knowledge, not new knowledge. When we want revelation of the nature of want, the want we meet is disregarded, because even though it is really want, it is new, and what we seek is want, not a new want. When we want revelation of the nature of hearing, the one we come across is disregarded, because although it is genuinely hearing, it is new, and what we need is hearing, not something new. When we want revelation of vision, the vision we come across is disregarded, because although that vision is real, it is new, and what we seek is vision not something new. When we want revelation of the nature of speech, the one we come across is disregarded [265], because although it is real, it is new, and what we seek is speech, not something new.

In ignorance of the happenng of *ma'ani*, which has the nature of Divinity, I wanted to know this happening, but when it actually happened, I disregarded it. It is good to meet with its *essence*, but what is its *attributes*? It is quite good to meet with its nature, but what are its names? It is quite good to meet a man, but what are his deeds? It is quite good to meet his deeds, but what is his name? But this is knowing the name before the actions, and then, after meeting the actions, asking where the person who did them is! When these are mixed, it is a long process. When we have learnt about the owner of the actions, we are going round in circles. When will we come across the traces of the Lord's *ma'ani*?

If we are not careful and resolute in delving into things that are small and hidden, we will be blocked because of impediments in the person concerned. The most substantial of these is the border posed by *majesty*. This causes us to think that the *attributes* of the Lord are impossible to attain, and we will not realise we are actually experiencing them, and when experiencing them we will attribute them to something else. Not to mention things that take shape of their own accord, which we then go and attribute to Allah. If not like this, when we will find the work of Almighty Allah? But when we force ourselves to explain it, we attribute material things to this or that person, and spiritual things to Almighty Allah. It would be strange if understanding did not materialise, if a need was not fulfilled. It would be strange if ears existed without something to hear, if vision existed without things to be seen; it would be strange for writing to exist without teachings; for a servant to exist without being commanded; for something visible to not be observed; for a thing to be heard to not be listened to; for a task to not be undertaken; for something comprehensible to not be comprehended; for something desirable to not be desired; for life to exist without birth; it is not possible to give orders other than to the servant; to look at something invisible; to listen to something inaudible; perform something that is not to be performed; to comprehend something that is not to be comprehended; to remember something that is not to be remembered. The midwife revealed all of this when she cut my umbilical cord; she did not do this intentionally. Even though she did not understand what she was revealing, she was forced to say it by order of Allah's *speech*. The *speech* is obeyed when the word is received by the ear, the ears send it to the heart, and the heart is pleased to give service. Things in harmony are proof of *beauty*, things in conflict are proof of *majesty*. The *speech* is proved by its materiality, not by the lips, and because it is heard by the body, not because of the ear. Pleasure is the manifestation of *beauty*, unpleasantness is the manifestation of *majesty*. *Sight* becomes real through the eyes, our vision sends to the heart, and it is the heart that orders the body towards the pleasant manifestation of *beauty* and the unpleasant manifestation of *majesty*.

This is the starting point for the heart's conviction. It is expressed through His speech, heard through my ears, and when it arrived in my heart there arose fear and courage, pleasure and unpleasantness, belief and unbelief. All these things are of the Divinity. If something is pleasant, it is a manifestation of *beauty*, if something is unpleasant it is a manifestation of *majesty*. That is why it is Gusti Allah's practice to reveal things not through speech, to see things but not with eyes, to hear things but not with ears, and as for our speaking with Allah, it is not with words, we see Allah not with eyes, and we hear Allah but not with our ears.

I used to think that when stones fell into valleys and water flowed downstream, they were not doing this out of service to Allah's *speech*. But as it turns out, the stone does fall as service, the water does flow in servitude, and fire burns in service. [266] Water sometimes trickles rather than flows, the fire goes out instead of burning; that is because they are prevented from doing so by Allah's *speech*. My business is my business, His business is His! I set my knowledge in competition with His, I set my soul in comparison with His.

God forgive me! I know only His acts, and am not yet convinced by the proof. In the beginning, at the stage of Submission, I knew the names of Allah, which I uttered so I would not forget them. When I became familiar with His acts of *beauty* and *majesty*, I was still thinking that my business was mine, and His business was His. Things came from There to me, and things went to There from me. I knew the names, so they could not be confused, nor could His possessions. If there was a debate on this, I would be a witness. If someone said that something did not belong to Allah, I would say it did, daring even to swear than none other than Gusti Allah could possess it. At this point I worshipped, feeling ashamed by His character. I only knew the clothing, ignorant of the sewing; I only knew the rice, ignorant of its cooking; I only knew the unhusked rice, ignorant of growing it in the terraces; I only knew heat, ignorant of its combustion; I only knew the shade, ignorant of the shelter; I only knew weight, ignorant of its heaviness; I only knew lightness, ignorant of its weightlessness; I only knew breathlessness, ignorant of constriction; I only knew size, ignorant of dimensions; I only knew fear, ignorant of anger; I only knew boldness, ignorant of patience.

Oh! I used to think that *beauty* was singular, and *majesty* was singular. But in fact, they operate in the same way on the same level. The moon shines in the night because of *beauty*; it does not shine at night because of *majesty*; the day is light because of *beauty*, the day turns to darkness because of *majesty*; the coldness of water that eases the thirst comes from *beauty*, the coldness of water that makes one too cold is from *majesty*; I speak because of *beauty*, I am dumb because of *majesty*; I see because of *beauty*, I am blind because of *majesty*; I hear because of *beauty*, I am deaf because of *majesty*; I have knowledge because of *beauty*, I am ignorant because of *majesty*; I live because of *beauty*, I die because of *majesty*; I obey because of *beauty*, I disobey because of *majesty*; I recognise because of *beauty*, I fail to recognise because of *majesty*; I remember because of *beauty*, I forget because of *majesty*; I exist because of *beauty*, I do not exist because of *majesty*; I am capable because of *beauty*, and I am unable because of *majesty*; I am willing because of *beauty*, I am unwilling because of *majesty*. That is why people who recognise each other did not do so beforehand; that is why people who fight know each other beforehand; that is why those who remember were forgetful beforehand; that is why those who forget remembered beforehand.

How could I go so astray? How could I still be spending time distinguishing *beauty* and *majesty*? Allahness is beyond time and place; and don't the two things work together, not one after the other? *Allah's names* are manifested by the *attributes*; *attributes* are manifested by *essence*. If *attributes* are fixed in time; *ma'ani* has its beginning. If the *attributes* have an end, that means they are wandering aimlessly. Perfection cannot be given an end or beginning, or else we turn to something other than Allah. Isn't it clear that cold co-exists with hot, and hot co-exists with cold; capacity co-exists with incapacity; forgetting co-exists with remembering; dying co-exists with living, existing co-exists with not living? [267] There will be no darkness while light reigns, and there will be no light while darkness reigns; there will be no pain while wellbeing reigns; there will be no pleasure as long as pain reigns. As the saying goes: a battle between captives is a war with no end. Not existence versus existence, not non-existence versus non-existence, not the clever versus the clever, nor the strong versus the strong; if it was like that, how could any two things go together, what would become of Allah's oneness? I will not comprehend something like this without a revelation. As the saying goes, we rise in order to descend, for it is clear that I was given birth by my mother, head first; and as I grew up I got to know her; when I die, the feet will go first, as the saying goes, descending before ascending, ascending before descending once more, seeking leave to return to eternity. It is my own fault if I make a trip to misfortune, unable to praise His *attributes* and to replace them with *ma'ani*, for that was already determined in an age other than my own.

All this is made obligatory by the *speech* of Allah, and as a result I say that something exists when it does not, or that something does not exist when it does; if I call something dark when it is light, call something light when it is dark; call something big when it is small, call something small when it is big; call something long when it is short, call something short when it is long; call something narrow when it is wide, call something wide when it is narrow; call something lengthy when it is temporary, call something temporary when it is lengthy; call something initial when it is final, call something final when it is initial; call something alive when it is dead, call something dead when it is alive; call something external when it is inner, call something inner when it is external; call something obscure when it is clear; call something clear when it is obscure. Whose doing is this? Mine! Because *Divinity* is reflected by humanity! Corporeality is reflected by incorporeality! Worldliness is reflected by awareness of the afterlife! Of course the left side will become the right, and the right will become the left; but I insist this is still proven by Allah's *speech*. As it turns out, my right and left feet have been moving in separate directions since I dropped out of the womb. And that pertains to body parts, how much more when we are talking about body and spirit? The world is contrasted with the hereafter! When I dwell in *servitude*, I am reflected in *Divinity*. From the past, our conduct has been turning back to the origin, the head becomes the foot, the foot becomes the head; people say that the outer self is in awe of the approval of others, the inner self is in awe of the Lord of the Universe; the outer repents before other people, the inner before the Lord.

Why do you keep bringing up the Lord? If I was not forced by Allah's *speech*, from childhood I would have loved those who loved me and been in fear of my superiors. As it turned out, my feelings were not formed by my education but by Allah's *speech*. People say: our parents are now gone. Yes, I don't know my mother, or the teachings of my mother and father, just as long as they are not confused with others, the reality of form that generated *ma'ani*. Let it be! By a slow process I came to possess the feeling that the first predecessor will not be born. As it turns out I do not have a mother or father. It is strange that we all make progeny, it is strange that the unborn calf does not have graying hair, it is strange that babies are not born with gray hair, it is strange that the young coconut hasn't grown a seed yet; it is strange that the nut of the sugar palm doesn't have juice; it is strange that children don't precede their parents; it is strange that the past precedes the future; it is strange that we put non-existence before existence; it is strange that we put the worldly life before the hereafter; it is strange that we put evening before morning; it is strange that we put morning before evening. People say: Destiny is fixed from the beginning, and that is why light is preceded by darkness. I feel that the war in captivity referred to above is a new thing, and its cause is that we make captives of ourselves first. [268] I thought that oneness was in the past, but in fact it is strange that things compete to be the first. I thought boldness was all about going to the forest, but it turns out that the heart is a coward; I thought that longing was for other people only, but it turns out that love is only for ourselves. People say we must love each other, but in truth we must love our own selves. The right side of the body must love the left, lest pleasure suffer from a lack of pleasure; the pleasured soul loves its unpleasantness; so then the right side is clearly for a good reputation, and the left side is for disgrace; the right side is clearly the way to heaven, and the left is clearly the way to hell; the right side is clearly the source of familiarity, the left side is the source of misrecognition; so that the right side is the source of a good account of our actions, while the left is clearly the source of a bad record; so that I am bold because I am fearful of others, and I am moving forward, even though it is because others are pulling me. People say this is conflict within one's own self, and without doubt there is such conflict. People are defeated by a lack of *beauty*, and are victorious because of an excess of *majesty*. People say we have a place of origin, and it is true that people come into existence. People say there is a place to go home to, and it is very true that people go home to their own villages. I am ashamed to talk about returning to my place, fearing people are saying that I am a person who feels at home when he is away; I am ashamed to say that I am away from home now, as this is my own village. People say that going back means returning to our place of birth, and that is very true, for after forgetting, we remember. It is said that we wander in our thoughts, but this is not a departure, but only the wandering of the soul. People say we return to Allah's mercy, and even Satan will one day return for we all belong to Allah, everyone feels this way and it is impossible not to, and so we must be mindful, and never omit to do this.

At this point we step up to the stage of Oneness, or the consensus of mutual interests.

## Oneness [*Kurbah*]

[269] Oh my! Oh my! Oh my!

Oh yes! Oh yes! Oh yes!

Where did your *ma'ani* go? Because these are mine.

Where are your *attributes*? Because these are mine.

Where are your Divine acts [*af'al*]? Because these are mine.

I stand in silent relection. It does not feel like day, it does not feel like night, neither hot nor cold, neither sunny nor shady, neither bright nor dark, neither low nor high, neither I nor Him. I vanish, pushed aside by *Divinity*, He disappears, pushed aside by *servitude*; He cannot be called I because He is He, I cannot be called He because I am myself, He cannot properly be called I because He cannot be pushed aside by *ma'ani*, and I cannot be called Him because I am experiencing *majesty*. Let us share these names together, go to the river as one, and live together as one.[6]

6 This final sentence is a string of three Sundanese idioms, all of which express the value of collective harmony.

*Beauty* is of our own making! *Majesty* is of our own making! Wow! Even though we work together, we still speak of ourselves as two, and only then do we say Allahness is manifest. Ih! It should not be like that! Do not forget our beginnings. *Divinity* is the origin of lordship, *servitude* was my name since childhood. These names collapse, but we still pit our feelings against feelings, for we will not be defeated by names. Feel it! Once sticky rice is made into a cake, it is still named sticky rice, the earth in a brick is still called earth, sugar is still sugar when it is in the sugar palm. It is the taste that changes. Before we were not sharing together, but now we share together; in the past we did not share our ups and downs, but now we do. Nowadays, I do not wait to be told by the old people first, for what will be favourable to God will be favourable to me, and what is unwelcome to God will be so to me, even though I will not have made a complaint beforehand. In the past, I turned from my mother to my father, or turned from my father to my mother, but as time passed I consulted at their graves. As more time passed I asked for something from their Allah, and as further time passed I simply arrived at their Allah.

Why do you give priority to your own complaint? Why do you give priority to your supplication? You should feel your *ma'ani*ness by yourself first! If it feels pleasant, our *beauty* will suffer it, if it feels unpleasant, our *majesty* will suffer it. It may be true that all things change over time, but our profession of faith has not changed since time immemorial. It may be true that etiquette and language evolve, and that the forms of Islamic behavior evolve, but the name of Allah has not changed since time immemorial; and we will continue to call the Prophet 'Allah's messenger' until the station of Oneness. There is nothing more to say about the failure in *servitude*, it will not attain [*idrak*] the *essence* of *Divinity*.

[270] Attainment must be discovered, and this discovering should be one of a number of types. For me, there are only five external kinds of attainment:

Aroma; deals with the sense of smell.

Feeling; deals with the sweet and sour.

Vision; deals with images.

Hearing; deals with sound.

Touch; deals with the rough and smooth.

The inner attainments are dealt with by the soul; there are those which are rational, these are dealt with by thinking; there are suppositions, which concern what is supposed; and there is conviction, which deals with proofs.

These things are not in opposition to an encounter with *Divinity*. There can be an encounter even without an encounter, discovery without meeting face to face. The only sign that we can take as proof of the perfection of our status in *Divinity* is our wholeness to our original creation, these can't be mixed up but must stay firm, and then we will know our status is not wrong: I was created from fire, following the fire of *life*; I was created from earth, following the light of *knowledge*; I was created from water, following the light of the *will*; I was created from wind, following the light of *power*; solid and stable in perfect balance, accompanied by love, and awareness, then flying to the essence of *Divinity*; knowledge is born in the attribute of *mercifulness*; the Divine will flows into the sea of visible things; *power* shakes the shoots of *life*. Hence there are various manifestations, their revelations are not the same, they do not replace each other, they have their own independent properties. This is because the shoots of fire and awareness are blown by the wind of *power*, and when they light up the ground, sometimes there is brightness and sometimes gloom, sometimes hot and sometimes cold, sometimes red and sometimes white, sometimes green sometimes blue; depending on the part brought on by *power*. At the point where the water flows in, it is sometimes cloudy and sometimes clear, it is sometimes flowing and sometimes calm, it is sometimes flooding and sometimes receding, when the light of its *life* will diminish. The earth cannot receive it if it is not inclined to obtain *knowledge*, and the two will certainly fail to meet. It is flooded without *knowledge*, illuminated without *knowledge*, blown by the wind without *knowledge*; because of that there is a comparison, the wind in its character as *power* shakes the shoots of *life*, illuminating the breath of the self. It found me as I was remembering that it is certain that my breaths replace each other, the ones coming out and in; while a breath is in or out, it does not change its appearance, and does not feel the same, for it is a part of its *life*, shaken by its *power*, illuminating its *will*, accepted by my conviction, a gift beyond estimation, an accepting that has no end! For this reason, there is no discovery without comparing.

The signs of those who are perfect in their Lordliness are recognised by those who are perfect in their Servitude. Over there is a person in sufficiency [*istighnah*], here is one in want [*iftiqor*], and for this reason we will not discover it while we still hold on to our prejudices.

The *essence* has proof; the fact that I myself have *ma'ani*; I am labelled a living thing, maybe because I was entrusted with *life*, but what is this *life*? Our movements are merely its traces. I have knowledge, I am labelled as a learned man, perhaps because I was entrusted with *knowledge*, but what is this *knowledge*? Red or black is in the eyes, loud or soft is in the ears, bitter or sour is in the taste, stinky or fragrant is in the smell, all of these are the creations of acquired knowledge [*ma'lumat*], the traces of *knowledge* in *ma'ani*; and so, what is this *knowledge*?

[271] I am labelled as a being with will, of course because I have a *will* that will give birth to *power*, and when it has been born, the trace of the *will* shall either depart or sit, and be put into service by the *power*, leaving its traces as its manifestations.

I am labelled as a hearing being, for I have ears; the sound that I hear are merely traces, but what is this thing called hearing? That is *sight* and *speech*; *ma'ani* specified in classification, that is my *selfness*, but its proof is not manifest!

May whatever is in *servitude* be born soon, along with the *ma'ani* of *Divinity*, but this also won't be found, for these will be discovered by not being discovered! This will be a reflection of the essence of *Divinity*. As for manifestation [*tajalli*], that is feeling, the disappearance of the feeling of my own *essence*, made to vanish by *Divinity*, and called the manifestation of the *essence*, the revelation of the feeling of disappearance of everything other than Him. If the *essence* vanishes because of the manifestation of the *essence*, this is part of the Station of Oneness [*Ahadiyat*]. If the *attributes* vanish, because the 'I' is pushed aside by the *attribute* of *Divinity*, it is called the manifestation of the *attribute*, disappearing from mercifulness, and this is a part of the Station of the truthful ones [*shadikin*]. If the divine acts vanish, because the 'I' is pushed aside by the divine acts of *Divinity*, people call this the manifestation of the divine acts, part of the Station of the Commoner, worshipping because of *lordship*, giving service in the form of worship, where the external is greater than the inner, and the body is greater than the spirit. The five steps of that station are completed in *servitude*. *Knowledge* is like earth, it has the character of receiving anything that comes to it. *Will* has the nature of water, flowing wherever it wishes. These two natures are humble, and form the total of seven; the water-course depends on the water, the water depends on the water-course. The *power* gives birth to the intention, swooping down to grab the top of a life, it is manifest in worshipping with the body and the perception of our resolve. The sign of *life* is remembering, dependant on the weight of love, still swooped upon by the wind, and if strong, the *life* burns brighter, but if the wind is slight, it will go out; but with His succour, the faltering flame will be brighter and brighter; the water that is cloudy or receding will be clearer and clearer.

The 'I' was created from four origins, two are felt from below, which are extinct in darkness; two are felt from above, and are extinct in faltering. That is why their characteristics are related, for when a person lies down his recollection is great, but when he stands his forgetfulness is great, and these characteristics remind each other when a person stands and bends down in prayer, then we behold the greatness of the *life* of our *power*, and the *attribute* of *Divinity* becomes manifest; when we prostrate ourselves in solemn prayer, we behold the greatness of the natures of *knowledge* and *will*, and the *attribute* of *servitude* becomes manifest; which weighs more heavily? If the humanness is the heavier, the scales will drop down to that side and will not right themselves; if the *Divinity* is the heavier, we will lose our five senses; and for this reason there is a proverb: our prosperities cannot be exchanged, we cannot compete for our happiness, only then can we say that the *speech* of humanity is perfect, and can share in the origins of our creation; like the status achieved by the Prophet of Allah, he performs divinity by means of remembrance, by his *power*; he performs his servitude by means of his *knowledge*, by means of his *will*. As a consequence, there were no beloved nor kin upon whom he bestowed his *Divinity*, and there has been no one else whose *servitude* can be called more prominent, for he was more perfect both upward and downward than any other, and he became the seal of the prophets before him, and the last exemplar. Let us give service, dear son, give service to the remembrance of the 'I', give service to the *knowledge* of the 'I', give service to the *will* of the 'I', give service to the *power* of the 'I', give service to the hearing of the 'I', give service to the vision of the 'I', give service to the *speech* of the 'I'. It would not be possible for you to give service if the 'I' had no *ma'ani.*

[272] You said we should not have the feeling of being worshipped while worshipping, of worshipping while being worshipped; as much as other people love us it will never be the same as the love we have for ourselves; as much as we are fearful of others, it will never be like the fear we have of ourselves. *Ma'ani* were the cause of the birth of the body of Muhammad, giving an example of perfection by his *servitude* and elevating his *Divineness.* When this spread to his community who had obtained spiritual authority from him, they tried to attain this loftiness from his status of prophethood; when it spread to a teacher who had been the cause of me, the outer dimension was observance with his body, and the inner dimension was conviction of his faith; if the scales weighed more heavily in either direction, this was a sign of misfortune. Their closeness in weight depends on our inclinations, on our preparation at the stage of Witnessing, when we started to follow our Belief, in order to attain knowledge, and after knowing, attaining familiarity, and after familiarity, I wanted to achieve affection; if the knowledge ceases, familiarity has no use, and I will stop giving service to that familiarity, and become more and more indifferent. I will not be knowledgeable just because I know, for knowing alone has no value, and if we know something but forget about it, then forgetting is like non-existence of that thing, and even if it really does exist, there is no value in that existence; existence does not cause shame, its greatness has no value, and the greatness is not something in feeling; if it is glorified it will become glorious, if it is degraded it will be degraded, because the stage of *Divinity* is the reflection of *servitude.* If the *attribute* of *Divinity* is strongly degraded, *Divinity* will have no *attributes*; and if one strives for it along with its *essence*, its Allahness will be lost. If we do not fear Him or feel ashamed before Him, Allah is just an expression; Gusti Allah is made mighty by those who feel their own inferiority; Gusti Allah is made generous by those who feel grateful; Gusti Allah is made fearful by those who acknowledge His power. Even the aristocrat is degraded according to the coarseness of the commoner; richness has no value to those who never ask for anything; and surely knowledge has no value for those who don't want it; and surely remembrance is worthless for those who do not yearn; and isn't familiarity also worthless for those who do not like it? That is why there is a proverb: a taste cannot be felt through words, for our pleasures are not the same, it depends on what we have, and on our own individual feelings. I keep all of this secret not because I cannot explain it, but because I don't know how to describe it.

The name of fire is not hot, the name of sugar is not sweet; the external serves the heart, serving is the following of our feelings, our mother and father are merely a class of people, who come across a duty to love. If I am given life, I am grateful, if I am killed, I welcome it, even though I am subject to authority, I will maintain my joy, giving service since time immemorial, and my motivation to do so depends on my current conviction that I will not forget the four origins, for when I feel their influence, only then do I feel comfortable, for those are my origins: the earth abides in myself, water is destined for movement, wind has the task of shaking things, and fire has the goal of illumination. The ground is derived from water, its bad effect is to make water cloudy; water is derived from wind, its bad effect is to receive the wind; wind is derived from fire, its bad effect is to blow out flames. For this reason people use an idiom, goodness is returned in bitterness, we should remember our origins, the wind makes the light sway, water flows straight in its current, and the earth has the task of encompassing all. In Sundanese, wind means desire, its duty is to shake the soul, and in Sundanese water is motivation, its duty is forced because it is servitude. In Sundanese, earth is knowledge, obliged to watch over the light lest it is replaced by something else, lest it betrays its origins. If the four are not in accord, the limbs of our body will be in confusion.

Allahness is the holding of great power in eternity, hence the proverb: Some shrubs cluster together, while others grow apart. [273] The human heart is beset by challenges, so people abide in solemn resolve, if they fly they land on a figure of authority, feeling awareness that their hearts are captive. In Sundanese: fly up above, fly down below, as long as there is still light; if we wish to fly, it must be with emptiness, to descend we must carry eternity. The Lord is great through surrender [*tanajul*], pleasing to those from below; serving becomes noble through resignation, mindful of something to hold fast to; the teacher becomes great through teaching, the santri becomes noble by curiosity; the rich become noble by generosity; the poor become noble by asking for help; the aristocrat becomes noble through friendliness, the commoners become noble by humility; the king becomes noble through justice, his servant becomes noble through obedience. Divine guidance compels us, even though we are not aware that we are asking for help to someone who we feel is wealthy, or requesting from someone who is capable. That is why when I do wrong, I am troubled by His blame towards me. The humble do not feel humble, the noble do not feel noble. The clever like to complain, frustrated by all those who ask questions, the rich like to complain, frustrated by all those who ask for something. They are not aware of their fault in claiming the property of others; they are not aware of their fault in turning away from their own wealth. Do not let the wall that separates us make us unfamiliar, let us labour together with our neighbours, suffer with our colleagues. Belief is wrapped with external display, in decorum good to look at, in expressions nice to listen to, in close arrangement with the boss, in easy language for our fellows, everything is put in order everywhere, robust of body, giving service side by side, not wanting recognition. A high level to dine at, wanting to be recognised as special, climbing like a concubine, standing out from the others, abandoning social order, in order to amaze others. What they want is pleasure in this world, wanting to trade and exchange for all kinds of things, wanting reward from the demise of others, searching for rare things, which are considered as perfection. Perfection brought by the devil. Wanting big profits from deceiving others, selling divinity for some vegetables, willing for worldliness, forgetting the afterlife; wanting to be known as having favour from Allah, a noble beloved of the Lord, tricking the unmindful, but in fact they are black-faced, only the exemplars remain, the distant prophet and the nearby guru, who became noble through service, not expecting external wealth, resigned to physical hardship, entrusting their faith to Allah. This is Divinity.

The road towards misfortune is oppression, we feel ourselves in comfort and are entranced by deception, through the medium of our five senses; the road ends with falseness that bewilders, with ears deceived by what we hear, and this is regarded as the heaven not to be seen. Eyes deceived by what is seen, feelings deceived by what is felt, smell deceived by what is smelt, and each deceit is as fine as possible, as great as possible, as noble as possible, in order to achieve perfection. Even more so the effect of the satanic heart, as long as it convinces people of unseen things, introduced through spiritual ways, a trickster who opens up secrets, and is able to know the future, like a genie or devil, offering to raise up the victim's station. Like a pan that gets its character from being burnt, he likes to overstate himself, and whenever he meets a friend, he claims superiority over others, knowing things that are hidden, foretelling ages and predicting happiness, describing things that can't be seen, which become manifest only by coincidence, but which cause the careless to believe, wanting their nobility to be recognised, needing to be distinguished, to feel at ease and in comfort, for the 'I' has received its estimation.

People say this or that is a secret of the Lord, but how can it be that the secret is so easily revealed to those who cannot keep it? But Allah is hiding and does not need to be hidden. The secret is in our feelings, and should not be spread around even if we want to do so. There is another thing that I hope for; I want to be enclosed within walls, and not to be given the secret; if I can reveal it openly as if I were with my friends [274], in common ownership, but seeing and hearing secrets better than the others, then the *will* would be realised as knowledge without a guru; *power* is with the Divine, and as a result I would not be able to keep the secret.

Hopefully, if we think ourselves unable to keep a secret, then it shouldn't be given to us, lest we are deceived by our desires and spread it around like a trivial thing. The same signs appear in an infatuated person, he degrades himself in worship, his reason divorces his senses, as if the signs of Divinity were clearly evident, and other people notice this, they see it clearly although the man himself doesn't even feel it; and only when he realises that the beloved does not appear like his own infatuation; he then falls into bewilderment, and seeks her in lament, and once he obtains her he switches to another, and passes her by before he obtains her, and when she is available he says 'she is not the one', if denied he says 'yes she is'; he is prevented by his own conduct, and enclosed by walls.

Why does an infatuation show itself before it can be proved to exist, and become evident before it is announced? In this regard, you should not judge from a position of superiority, for our feelings are not all the same, and the veil is an impediment, the inner is restrained by the outer. When the human consciousness becomes the *essence*, it is concealed by the human consciousness, that is the *essence* of the 'I'. As for the *attribute* of *Divinity*, it is concealed by the *attribute* of the 'I', and as for the names of the *Divinity*, these are concealed by the names of the 'I', and as for the acts [*af'al*] of *Divinity*, these are concealed by the acts of the 'I'. Because of that, people with different feelings never think much over these things, hunting for something they won't find; what is apparent first is preferred, getting relief by an expression: the average man has external knowledge, but the inner is known by the Lord of the Universe; a person's exterior is their own work, their interior is made by the Lord of the Worlds. If these feelings are inverted, the words will be inverted as well, for the words are deep in the feeling, the inner comes before the outer; the external is the work of the Lord of the Worlds, the inner is made by the average man, and so it is harder to think of the outer than the inner.

But it is very true that when people fall into total forgetfulness they become distracted by a primeval human fear of the prophesies of fortune-tellers and the powers of unusual people, by the arrival of the satanic connection, because it is based on familiarity with genies and bewitched beings, unseen by the eyes, and differs from the norm.

These stories appear from a trusted class, who talk like ascetics. The story then rises in credibility by means of a spell, a seduction for the forgetful. But it is already clear that the story is the influence of Satan. As a consequence, the forgetful man will carefully make calculations, as a way of working deceit, and carefully monitor all dangers, with a view to obtaining a benefit, and carefully observes medicine, in order to obtain a remedy. This is never found in the perfect man, but must be found in the sufferer, who eats this afternoon but not in the morning, with too many commitments, who diligently accumulates external things, but runs out before he has filled his own needs. If the story did not come from Satan, the Divine guidance followed by other people would be of prime importance for him, and he would covet his saintliness, and not be prone to all kinds of disturbances which he spreads around profusely. He is deceived by his acquaintances, confused by friendship. In order to destroy himself, he takes in people who believe in him, offers them kindness, more and more people believe in him, and he gets a scholastic veneer. But Satan does not act alone, and the genies do not like to stand out too much in their work; it is better to make humans their agents, tempting the ignorant, deceiving the forgetful.

Those who remain mindful are not seduced, they remember the advice of the old people: don't be easily impressed by others, young men must avoid temptation, don't be quick to anger, protect the ties that bind, [275] weigh things up with due consideration, make thorough accounts, don't be swayed by your passions, for regret always comes too late.[7] Our hopes are for the afterlife, but you are still seduced by this world; the Lord is our goal, but you are still distracted by Satan; our goal is spiritual things, but these are replaced by external things; you say you are setting out on the way of death, but are still in the midst of life. If we succeed in this, we will be left conversing in mercifulness, expressing our innermost soul. It is very true that mercifulness is a perfection, with a Divine nature, without borders, with no limit to the south, no limit to the north, no limit to the east, no limit to the west, no limit above, no limit below. And with all the beings that exist in it, don't show favouritism, or take water from upstream of everyone else, so one can be even in weighing things up.

The external opposes the inner, the inner opposes the outer; the angels oppose the devils, the devils oppose the angels; the body opposes the soul, the soul opposes the body; heaven opposes hell, hell opposes heaven; happiness opposes suffering, suffering opposes happiness; benefit opposes loss, loss opposes benefit, pleasure opposes unpleasantness, unpleasantness opposes pleasure. All possess the same wealth, and are born through their *will*, having no regrets. But they are different, say the forgetful ones, they mention bad things they mention good things, they mention pleasant they mention unpleasant, they worship their preferences, which is the character of humanity. But in the same way, it is not good if we are too occupied in pursuing one, favouring this and ignoring that; pursuing this, but this is not the one, pursuing that, but that's not the one, for there is no end to the search for the *attribute* of *Divinity*, we think we obtain it but the search is not over, it is quieter than quiet, more traceless than tracelessness, spinning with no starting point, coming and going without end. This was proved when I was a child, when I was afraid of my father because of his curses. A father loves his child, thinking it will be returned, a mother loves her child, thinking it will be returned; the mother loves her child, remembering her labor. The cause of worship is belief, and the cause of reward is worship; we believe that something will be sent from There [Allah] because of our willingness to worship. The cause of devotion is belief, and the cause of wanting something is devotion, the cause of familiarity is longing, the cause of intimacy is orderliness, and the cause of service is fear of conflict; the night is caused by the day, the day is caused by the night, the heat is caused by the cold, the cold is caused by the heat; if there is pleasure, it is caused by unpleasantness, if there is unpleasantness, it is caused by pleasure.

Do not go to the right only, for this will make Allah absent from the left!

Do not hunt the left only, for this will make Allah absent from the right!

For this reason, sailors use only the rudder and wheel, if they go to the right

7 This is a string of well-known Sundanese idioms.

they will sink, if they go to the left they will hit coral; the rudder pushes from the back, the wheel follows the rudder; the rudder is for the arrival, the wheel is for the return.

Go ahead! From where are we departing? Where is our destination?

This journey is not about watching time go by, for like it or not, we cannot avoid that; and it is not a questioning of the grave, for each of us has his own. Our journey [*suluk*] must be towards *arrival* [*wushul*], walking along the stages of feeling, a sea with no border, an abundance of mercifulness. For this reason there is a label for the position of Allah's messenger; a mercy for the universe, a gift for Divinity.

[276] Please, my beloved, be watchful! Take the palm to get its juice; take the cane to get its sugar; take the stone to get the diamond; take the indigo plant to get the dye; take the bee to get the honey; take the knowledge to get the taste; take the good works to get eternity.

Watch the needle of the scales carefully! So that they are in balance, like the sailor watches the compass, so the left and right are in harmony.

The soul walks a narrow string, calculate your steps with care, take care of the gravestone's writing, which in Sundanese means the real resolve, the signs of the grave, lest people wrongly place flowers. Conceive of this meaning with your soul! Here is the body, here is the soul, depend on your mother and father, pit your imaginations together! Do not be distracted by the daylight, lest your soul arrive in the twilight; do not focus overly on the evening, lest your soul not arrive till late morning! For these reasons you should be alert towards the intervals of day and night, give equal weight to each, make full and proper accounting, find comfort in between them; at the back we fit a strap, at the front we attach the reins, make the stirrups equal, lest the horse may stumble, lest it suddenly lurch, or as the Sundanese say, make proper accounting, do not put too much weight on one side, too much fear or too much hope. If we fear too much it will lurch, if we hope too much it will be stubborn. If the cart is too close, the horse will refuse, if too far it will be careless.

Don't feel too comfortable at the right, for too long hating the left!

Don't be comfortable at the left, it will make you hate the right!

Do not feel too comfortable with pleasure, it will make you hate the unpleasant!

Do not feel too comfortable with the unpleasant, it will make you hate the pleasant!

A seafarer does not feel at home on the land, and a landlubber does not feel at home on the seas.

City folk are not at home in the village, mountain people do not feel at home in the city.

Do not be unwilling to go to the land, for its attractions are many; do not be unwilling to go to the sea, for it is a place of vast journeying. Do not hate the town, there are many spectacles there; do not be unwilling to go to the mountains, they have many benefits.

Match the external with the external, match the inner with the inner; match the body with the body, match the soul with the soul; match Divinity with servitude, match here with there so there be no conflict between them. Attempt these things before going to Allah, these seven principles for the use of all humanity, if you really wish to be close to righteousness:

1. Recognise those faults which will cause disagreement amongst us;
2. Recognise your obligations to others at all times;
3. Recognise your fear of being hated by people with resentful hearts;
4. Recognise when we should put ourselves at the disposal of others, and know the way to achieve righteousness;
5. Recognise your feelings, and love in your own way;
6. Relish proper conduct, and exclude conduct that brings misfortune to others;
7. A pure heart is not too left or too right, and has intuitions of love in the sweet and the bitter.

If we fail in these, the Lord will not accept us, because these are the amulets of *servitude*. The characteristic of mercy has its amulet in *Divinity*, it is impossible that Allah will not be compassionate towards this, and humanity will not fail in accepting this compassion. [277] That is a mountain and this is a mountain, that is a tree and this is its fruit; that is the ocean and this is the ocean, that is its fish and that is the net.

Do not be averse to the dry months, for this is the part the fishermen love; do not dislike the wet season, for this is the part the farmer loves; do not hold back from giving service, when instructed by one's betters; do not hesitate to attain rank, and be supported by your inferiors; even a sovereign is in need of servants, and a servant is in need of his sovereign. As the Sundanese say: The greatness of a sovereign is his authority over his servants, but he is in servitude when he cannot maintain his performance, and coarsely instructs his inferiors with improper wishes. The servitude of the servant is in obeying the order of his sovereign. The sovereignty of the servant is that he is needed by the sovereign, so that his realm is peaceful, and his sovereignty reigns. Greatness depends on the season, a name is borne by the epoch. Ego again, ego again. But in the beginning there is spiritual motivation, but this name is replaced by foetus, which is replaced by newborn, which is replaced by youth, which is replaced by adulthood, and finally by old age.

The originating *ma'ani* returns once more to *ma'ani*, taking a name according to the journey. To be known by innumerable names signifies Allah again, Allah again. The names by which other people know us are a sign of the ego again, the ego again. Do not shy from being respected in life, but accept affliction from those who offend us; do not shy from a prosperous destiny, the self must accept those who inquire rashly; the feeling of servitude, seen in reflection as a feeling of Allahness, cannot be transferred to someone else. Writing can be read, language can be interpreted, but these do not transfer one's feeling, for the feeling appears of its own accord, differing from person to person, from ego to ego. The feeling cannot be shared, for its expansiveness would be lost; we cannot exchange it amongst ourselves, for that would be erasing a Divine Sovereignty that each of us have in sufficiency. Just fit yourself in! Do not sit tight in the world!

In this way, the rank of *servitude* is face to face with *Divinity*, but there is no right or left in this, and neither is there any high or low, for this is something that is clearly named as the point of mystery [*nuthfah ghaibah*]. For where is the front and back of light? If a beam of illumination has a top and a bottom, this proves it is not light. If one is happy with the obscurity of half-light, this does not mean that illumination is obscured, but that one's heart is in eclipse. Mercifulness is verified when those in obscurity are dazzled by bright light, and those who are illuminated are blinded by a light that is obscured; the short will seek a tall shadow, and those in the light will hide in search of the dark. And so we are split in half, for one must be in daylight to hide from Allah, and one can only be illuminated by Allah in the night. When our eyes are open many obstacles appear, when our eyes are closed there are only a few. The brightness is not as bright, the darkness is not as dark. Knowledge is something for which we must search, but not something to cause wrongdoings; it is good if it enhances the taste of our feeling. For a person who feels authoritative will be in polytheism if the feeling does not come from Allah. Even though one knows there is no power other than Gusti Allah, but has not yet felt this with conviction, then he is holding on to the outer surface rather than the inner.

Now it comes to me! Refine your genealogy from the beginning! My father is desire, preventing me from thinking about solitude, and even more from leaving the outer for the inner, from leaving the world for the hereafter, from leaving the real in search of Allah. My mother is the origin of humanity, preventing me from thinking about other things, from deviating from my own nature. [278] But I have long since followed my mother and father, that was the start of my knowledge of feeling: the outer is the body, the inner is the soul. In the same way, I studied the A-B-Cs of Islam. In actual fact it is the external that we encounter, by using the five senses for coarse and physical things, by using the soul, the product of *ma'ani*, for immaterial things. In their outer forms the body and soul are the same, but the inner forms are the essence of the feeling of life, for the body and the soul have the same holy spirit. Now, these are what become Divine Sovereignty, the spirit of the body, the spirit of the soul. The unseen and the revealed are enclosed by both of them, but their explosion appears in the very feeling of feeling, our ability to accept. Nothing will be manifest is these are not present, there will be no proof of *ma'ani* without them; it is through them that it passes to everybody. This is the clear sign of *Divine*ness; things will be discerned by the feelings as *Divine*ness only when our intuitions move uncertainly in that direction and move back once more, but in truth there is only one, in truth there is only one, and only when we feel all existence as something that is unified, and are aware that this existence is unconditional, and only when we are convinced of oneness without any partner, and do not turn to any others. And we will only discern *Divine*ness when we separate from our parents, but you must not abandon them! Be they good or bad they are still your family, so care for your parents to the extent that it does not harm you. This is clear when we feel cold and we need a blanket, but we felt cold because we had to carry out an obligation; this is clear when our stomach feels thirst so we drink, but we felt thirsty because we became hot doing things we had to do; This is clear when we feed our hungry stomach, which we do in order to perform Allah's injunctions; this is clear when fire burns us and we avoid it, this is clear when water splashes us and we get out of the way, this is clear when we are tired and go to bed, in order that we perform our duties with a sharp mind rather than as if we are sleep-talking; this is clear because a spectacle needs to be seen so we can be mindful of its original maker, but mindful with our hearts not just in words, in order to be in love with the unseen, and not with the deceptive words with which Satan admonishes us, and we can then be in accord with those who claim sanctity.

Be active in bringing your sufficiency [*istighna*] and poverty [*iftiqor*] to other people, and don't rush to the Lord. Do not be in need of what you find in humans, of the rank they have achieved in their servitude, of their failures in *servitude*, for these things will not hold fast if the self reaches out to them. The true character of poverty is *Divinity*. This is the site of *ma'ani*. Mercifulness comes into existence from its heart, *lordship* comes into existence from there; accept it lest its manifestation be overlooked, while you keep on hoping for the blessings given by the Lord, mistakenly thinking this is something you should not actively take on. For I have told you; be relaxed and our thoughts will not be confused by humanity, and we will not hope for something that will not eventuate, or be impeded by the ancientness of Divine Sovereignty, so that our hearts feel constantly frustrated, for it is a big mistake to have conviction in something that does not belong to us. The *Divinity* is found in our triumphs, whereas *servitude* is found in our failures.

Do not rush after difficulties, but let yourself try things first with other people. I perish in defeat because of living beings, in my unwillingness I am defeated by those who are willing, in my inability I am defeated by those who are able, in my deafness I am defeated by those who hear, in my blindness I am defeated by those who can see, in my dumbness I am defeated by those who are speaking, in my forgetfulness I am defeated by those who remember, in my ignorance I am defeated by those who know, I am defeated in the frustration of my desires by those who are successful in theirs, in the failure of my endeavours I am defeated by those who succeed in theirs, in the failure of my words to come to fruition, I am defeated by those whose words do so. Do not forget these are gifts from the Lord, who does not choose those who receive it, even non-human life forms have their own triumphs granted to them by Divine Sovereignty. When feeling hot I am defeated by coldness, when feeling cold I am defeated by heat, when I am wet I am defeated by dryness, and my dryness is defeated by wetness. I always make my claims in failure, and I am always in fear of majesty. [279] This gives rise to the saying 'the price depends on the thing being sold'. The proof will be clear to you, Divine Sovereignty has a high price. Who would ever entrust a task to a corpse? Where is there a benefit from stupidity? Where is there a benefit from indolence? When is a deaf person given the job of listening? When does a blind person have the job of seeing? When does a dumb person have the task of speaking? When is a corpse better than a living person? When is a forgetful person better than one with a good memory? When is a lazy person better than a diligent one? When do the incapable exceed the capable? When do the deaf exceed the hearing? When do the blind exceed those who can see? When does a mute exceed one who can speak?

The place to appreciate poverty-ness [*kaiftiqoran*] is its opposite, sufficiency-ness [*kaistighnaan*], and these will not be separated because of an insistence that they be so, or that majesty is to be found in one or the other. And to insist this is to insist that there is a *Divinity* that has its own place, and that there is a *Divinity* that has its own time; and that there is a *Divinity* that forgets its surroundings, claiming the perfection of Divine Sovereignty, and has a sense of comfort because its own desires are met, and a sense of discomfort because its desires are not met. Finish off this allegorical musing, for it can go on too long! There is only one *essence*, there is only one *attribute*, its names are one, it is impossible for these to meet failure. We could say it failed if it was attacked by a tiger, but why would the *Divinity* wish to meet its own death? But we could also say that if the tiger was victorious, considering that the tiger always wins, this would also be a success for *Divinity*. So it is clear that, according to common belief, every failing can be put in harmony in accordance with the feeling we inherit from our parents. People say we must be able to go to the wilderness as well as the town,[8] to the wilderness in a state of hope, to the town in a state of fear; to the wilderness in a state of solitude, to the town in sociability; to the wilderness in a state of strength, to the town in a state of weakness; to the wilderness in a state of eternity, to the town in a state of ephemerality; to the wilderness in a state of descent, to the town in a state of ascent; to the wilderness in a state of *servitude*, to the town in a state of *Divinity*; to the wilderness in a state of duality, to the town in a state of singularity; to the wilderness in the daylight, to the town in night-time; to the wilderness in transgression, to the town in servitude; to the wilderness in a state of solitude, to the town as a group; to the wilderness

8 In the following passage, Mustapa works creatively with a poetic expression: *Bisa ka bala ka balé*, meaning literally '(One must be) able to go to the wilderness as well as the buildings (i.e. town)'. *Bala* refers to wild, unkempt spaces. A *balé* is a building, but refers more specifically to homes of the ruling elite and public/government buildings. The first six pairs of terms around which this passage are structured are from Arabic: hope/fear is *karoja'an/kakhaofan*; solitude/sociability is *kafarkian/kajam'ian*; strength/weakness is *kabasthohan/kakobdlohan*; eternity/ephemerality is *kabaqaan/kafanaan*; descent/ascent is *katanazulan/kataraqian*; servitude/Divinity is *kaabdian/kauluhiyahan*.

in our private capacity, to the town as public citizens; to the wilderness as a retired person, to the town as an active person; to the wilderness to be at a distance from our superiors, to the town to appear before them; to the wilderness in leisure, to the town for our duty; to the wilderness for our pleasure, to the town for discomfort; to the wilderness for worldly things, to the town for the hereafter; to the wilderness for the outer, to the town for the inner.

Because of this we should not confuse wilderness with town [*bala/balé*], or devotion with craving [*gagat/geugeut*], while holding fast to something because we love it. We yearn in separation, whether near or far; there is no place to search for alternatives. There is an expression: 'while walking along a corridor, we wonder where it will end'. We think that those who continually reflect will remember that they will do right, but in fact those who continually reflect simply forget about the wrong they will do. In the past it was not difficult to find medicine, if we had a headache we could be cured by herbs, our sore eyes were cured by drops of liquid, and our fever was cured by the oil of leaves, as if anything could be used as medicine. If we thought the medicine was appropriate for the ailment, our goal was simply to get better and nothing else. If it was not, and we were not cured, the end was simply death and nothing else. For those intent on making a living, the goal is simply to eat and nothing else. For those who suffer in seeking knowledge, the goal is to succeed and nothing else.

[280] In fact, a person who constantly desires a reward is like a tree that forgets to hold on to the leaves that fall from it. People say the same thing about a magic utterance and its object, meaning that a formula must be expressed with all our heart, in bright light we can hit the target we attack, so why do we hold fast to things other than *Divineness*? Its proofs are close but not to be seen, its manifestations are passed by if they are not felt, and this is the end of our efforts. We aim for prosperity, but this is to eat and nothing else; when sick, to be better and nothing else; whether noble or wretched, we all die and nothing else; whether ignorant or learned, we aim to remember and nothing else. Because of this, those who forget to reflect think they will find a cure for their forgetfulness. They think that their death can be avoided by a medicine, if not this one then another. But in fact it is already clear that the inner is impeded by the outer, so that a person is impeded by the outer. People think that we should take the shariah as our guidance, with the inner coming later, the outer must come first. If it were true that the inner should come before the outer, how is it that people still eat rice and drink water? Perhaps we forget the expression; we live to test each other's strength. As the Javanese say: *essence versus essence*. In Sundanese, we say this as 'truth versus truth'. In Sundanese, we say it as 'the authentic versus the authentic'; this is clear from the fact that we are never surprised by the result.

If it is true that our feeling is weighted to the inner, how can it be true that the outer impedes the inner? How could one be drawn to a big rice-barn if one knows that there is nothing inside? How could a person not want a package made of leaves if he knows there is a diamond inside? For this reason, the outer becomes the wrapping of the inner, for it is impossible for the cover to be the same as the contents. In the same way the outer is wrapped in the outer, and the world is wrapped in the world. Think it over by yourself: the afterlife is packaged by the world, the shariah is packaged by the essence [*hakékat*]. This is even more the case with afterlife, which is packaged in the afterlife. Is it not already clear that disbelief packages belief, and belief packages desire, and desire packages knowing, and knowing packages familiarity, and familiarity packages the yearning of separation, and yearning packages our togetherness? There are seven layers before the ultimate jewel is reached. The coconut's oil is packaged in its milk, the milk is packaged in its crushed flesh, the crushed flesh is packaged in its shell, the shell is packaged in its hair, the hair is packaged in the coconut's shell, and the shell is packaged in its blossom's sheath. The coconut's oil is enveloped in seven layers. Palm sugar is packaged by its sap, the sap is packaged in the juice, the juice is packaged in the stem, the stem is packaged in the trunk, the trunk is packaged in its clump, the clump is packaged in the roots. The nut of the sugar palm is also good: even when the fruit is just a new shoot, we remember the sweetness of its juice, we remember the sweetness of its sugar, the flavour of its ripened fruit, we remember its quill-like spine, which we can use as a pen to write with. This feeling can only be intentionally encountered if we hold steadily to its genuine value, which is pitting essence against essence, and from it we can make a table and chair.[9] If it is true that this is pitting one hard substance against another, it would be impossible to shape it as something decorative, for each would desire to be the dominant one, and as a result, we could not create a pillar out of it.[10] Not like the harmony between eating rice and drinking water, or the harmony of preserving what we receive from our parents; or the harmony in making use of the shariah, for otherwise we end up with oil without the coconut, or an *essence* naked of its coverings. Because of this, there is an essentialness within our feelings, and consequentially feeling is packaged in etiquette, and because of this feeling has no etiquette. Sugar is most likely sweet while it is still has the form of the plant's roots, and oil is perhaps fragrant while still in the form of the budding coconut, and perhaps the movement of inner feeling to etiquette happens because *ma'ani* is the essence of feeling, and vision cannot be veiled, and hearing cannot be insulated. If it is true that it is the essence of the feeling of the essence, it cannot be burdened by the feeling of our inheritance. [281] That would mean that the spices have not yet reached maturity, and we will miss the individual flavours of each. If there is too much saffron, we call that rancid, if there is too much salt, we call that briney, if there is too much water, we call

9 *Jati* means teakwood but also essence. Here Mustapa exploits the pun: the essence (*jati*) can be used to make a table and chair.

10 In the days when Sundanese lived in wooden houses, it was accepted that the best quality pillars for the house frame were those made of teak (*jati*).

that insipid. This is proof of blandness, mixing spices together without measuring them. People say that secret knowledge is revealed in whispered tones, thinking that secrecy requires this of itself, and are clearly in fear it will be inadvertently revealed to all. As a consequence they cover their faces with veils, as if in secret, like a bat during the daylight; the blind one thinks that others also cannot see. They stick their tongues out at people; all of you are not like me, for I already possess perfect knowledge! But in fact, this kind of perfection has no comparison simply because they do not behold any rivals to it, and they are wandering without any destination. To create this neatness, they deceive the people around them, thinking other people do not know they are crazy, falling from the essence that is the state of Muhammad. The state of Muhammad is for them the only essence, and the behaviour exemplified by the state of Muhammad is for themselves alone, whatever they wish, and is revealed now in their own selves, and the self does whatever it wants, the spirit of the holy spirit [*ruh idofi ruhulkudus*], revealed in all that appears in the world. So why should we disturb this comfort? The condition of this state is remembrance, but do not utter this remembrance, because it is forbidden.

In the realm of oneness [*alam ahadiyat*], if our remembrance causes the appearance of oneness, then the remembrance will pass right by our feeling, for it has not happened at the right time. They want us to not bring to light His *attributes* and acts [*af'al*], for that would place us under the authority of those who came before us, like the community of Allah's messenger. Be aware that we must be diligent in giving praise to the Prophet and giving alms to ensure that the status of each of us can rise. They say we should leave behind Allah and his messenger as things of the past, for now our own selves are manifest, a ladder for ascending colours. Some of them lie flat with open eyes, and when a shadow has appeared and passed over their entire body, that is held to be the manifestation of the connecting spirit [*roh idofi*], entering into their body. Some recite verses of praise, but do not invoke Allah's messenger, facing towards the sun, and when something descends into their body, that is the connecting spirit, entering into their body. There are those who press something hard on their bodies, and when a circular form appears, not red or black, not green, but something round and white, like a drop of dew, they consider that the unseen point of the connecting spirit [*nuthfah ghaibah roh idofi*], entering into their body. There are some who hold their breath to the point of nausea, and when a white form of the same size as their body appears in their vision, then that is the shape of the connecting spirit, entering into their bodies.

I have thought over all these things, and have even asked widely how these people should be treated, what they desire, what do they dislike, what they enjoin, and what they forbid. If they are right, what are the signs of this, and what should we do about that? What are the signs that they are wrong? And if they are wrong, what is the proof of that, and what should we do about it? If these are things spread by humans, who can we rely on other than the shari'ah scholars, basing it on the Qur'an brought by the messenger of Allah? If the spirit is entering them, and it is Allah's *essence* that does this, what are their special capabilities? Their knowledge? Where is their power that enables them to reconstruct the world? And to what kind of nobility do they aspire? If they wish to give us something, they should not give something people seek, nor should they seek something that people already have; and what do we have to fear about these people? If we need revelation, what is the use of getting it from humans? Such revelation has no greatness to cause shame, its nobility causes no fear; without feeling, if an order is given, who is it that will be ordered?

[282] As a consequence, this knowledge makes it very easy for people to fulfil the shari'ah, for people do whatever feels good according to their own choice, and with this shari'ah the self will not be troubled; it has already entered the self, everyone has angels, everyone has the Qur'an. But there are some conditions: First, utter remembrance, second, increase your mention of the name Muhammad, third, converse widely, fourthly, enjoy those dreams which we call divine intuition, fifth, do not distinguish right from wrong, for these distinctions do not exist in the hereafter, right and wrong are worldly frames. Because of this, don't feel burdened, for material things have no value if others desire them. No food is prohibited, and no food is permitted, if you like it, eat it, if you do not like it, don't. The state and heaven have the same meaning, the Qur'an is a reference for conduct, and hell is the same for transgression, for transgression is performed in the world, and heaven is all in the future, as well as things we detest. Everything emerges from *alif*, spreading the existence of everything. *Alif* fosters *ma'ani*, existence is not through feeling.[11]

Transfixed in silence, deeply sleeping,
sound cannot awaken you,
you stir but make no noise
just as you have done since childhood.
A swallow flies high over seven hills
forgetting from whence it set out.
Do not be taken by Iblis!
Do not be coerced by desire!
Do not be borne by Satan!
For after the bird has been trapped,
you are nauseous and sleep eludes you.
You are caught by changing names.
Majesty comes from imagination.
Nobility is in your dreams:
claiming the self to be Allah's essence,
though Allah is impervious.
That is the influence of Satan!
To be seduced by names.

What remains is for me to return to the *lordship* that appeared when I was still a child. I will speak without restraint of my servitude, truthfully feeling that my failures have been pushed aside by triumph, made weak by *Divine*ness. This is so that my heart will be calm, and will not accept incorrectly, for I give service to the proverb 'the young must be mature, having improved themselves since childhood'.

---

11 *Alif* is the first letter of the Arabic alphabet, and is also the first letter of the Arabic word Allah. Mustapa's statements in this paragraph are pitched in irony.

# CHAPTER 2

In Sundanese this means 'Have a long memory, don't forget your origin, and do not complain'. In the beginning, in my childhood, I would have been a total failure were it not for my parents, who acted as the threshold of *Divine*ness, *lordship* and mercifulness. I only managed to walk because my mother guided me by hand. The feeling of my mother was conveyed by her behaviour. I knew the heat of fire through my mother's warnings, and my mother's warnings were enough to prevent me from falling over. Her admonitions saved me from learning the hard way, warning me of the ghosts and ghouls. Her goal was to make me cautious. She washed and scrubbed my dirty body. She nursed me and distracted me when I was in tears. Mercifulness gave rise to *lordship*. When cold or hot, she proved her love. As time went by I went further out into the world to play, not disturbed by any caution. My father was quick to anger, when his love showed itself, it did so in ways that showed that his own comfort was the most important thing. When I came of age and parted from my parents, I always made a trade out of my weaknesses, the benefit being the protection of *Divine*ness. Free from my father, I sought refuge in teachers, comparing *ma'ani* amongst other people, always showing my shortcomings, brought together beneath the level of perfection. This revealed itself when my discoveries led me to other discoveries, and my capabilities gave me other capabilities. It could not be possible that if I bore myself with perfection, I would then go out and show my failings to all. If a person was possessed by *Divine*ness, I liked to catch its overflow. My life followed on from the lives of others, my learning followed on from my knowledge, my initiative followed on from my willingness, my capability followed on from my capability, my hearing followed on from hearing, my vision followed on from vision, my words followed on from fluency, these things increase and elevate, whereas ignorance is in everybody; the value is not in the container, for the perfection is in the thing contained. What is the purpose of the bees' labour if it is not so that their honey derives nobility from its *ma'ani*? They have a power within, and if emptied of it they have no value.

[283] In my case, when I was beset by misfortune, my parents wept because they could not help me. In my case, when I endured illness, my parents could not cure me. The thing that really set me apart from my origins was that I felt at ease in complaining, my *lordship* was taken away, and my sufficiency was concealed from my sight. Feel how painful it is to come back! It is our own fault that we feel at ease with something we borrowed. Feel the tears of a sudden turn of fortune! Good and bad times are based on our feelings, and complaining is caused by forgetting our origins. Eating was originally for the purpose of preventing weakness, but it expanded to all kinds of comforts; but we cannot stop these for it still saves us from weakness. A shirt and a dress save us from nakedness, but these have expanded to ornateness. They multiply, and their suitability is not derived from necessity, and in the beginning it was our fault that they became ornate, so

why are we shocked when deprived of the ornateness? We do not realise that we were originally naked, we do not realise that we had no *ma'ani* in the beginning. When we return we are aware of our nakedness. For too long we felt at ease with something borrowed, like a child who thinks that everything belongs to him, and when an adult takes these things from him, he weeps for them, and wants to play, even with the blade of a knife, or he wants to wear a watch in the river, not realising that is not good to do so. Because of this, the parental admonitions are never in vain, urging that we must patiently accept misfortune, for misfortune is something that comes from our origins. Those who return are not stricken by misfortune, they endure the good as well as the bad, so there is no longer any reason to be patient. *Lordship* is entrusted to us from above, while *Divinity* is our possession from the very beginning. The singular essence has its container and its contents. *Servitude* is the container of *Divine*ness, which causes both father and son to topple down. *Lordship* is a crown without a container. Make your own search for the perfection inside you, for one's parents do not contain it; it has been proven that even a person with no mother or father can still appear with his own perfection. We ride a horse to patch up our fatigue, and by riding it we share its strength. My teacher patches up my ignorance, by conveying to us his knowledge. The things people say are a patch for our observations, by our conversations we share what we see. I had arrived at perfect health and maturity, what remained was the search for a path to *lordship*, and only *ma'ani* sustained me, *ma'ani* was pitted with *ma'ani*. When I triumphed I searched for passengers, becoming the bearer of passengers; those without strength purchased my strength. Those who were unable would purchase my abilities, those who were ignorant would purchase my knowledge. The smallest thing I did was to share my love, and if others found success that was an extra. The *lordship* of others was something they purchased, and my *lordship* was from *ma'ani*. The *servitude* of others was realised by their needs, and my *servitude* was my profit. It makes no sense that those who hired me were intending to suffer a loss, even though if they wanted they could do it themselves. It would make no sense for *lordship* to be bestowed upon me if I did not pay service to His orders. In between feeding our heirlooms, we send gifts to each other, showing our obligation through feeling; make your own search for its *Divinity*. In order that the meaning of *All praise is Allah's* be correct; in order that the meaning of *We belong to Allah* be correct; in order that the meaning of *All salutation belongs to Allah* be correct; in order that the meaning of *There is no other power or strength* be correct; in order that the meaning of *Glory to Allah* be correct.[12] When a person arrives we say *All praise is Allah's*, and when they pass away we say *We belong to Allah*. We cannot control

12 The italicised phrases of this passage are written in Arabic in the source text, and are formulas and expressions that Sundanese Muslims commonly utter and hear in ritual and daily conversation. Similar clusters of phrases appear on pages 287 and 290.

the departed to make them return once more, for they arrive as they leave, and loss and benefit accompany each other. When we sell debasement for nobility, the profits are nobility and debasement, the nobility lies in selling the *ma'ani*, and the debasement lies in the lack of *ma'ani*, the nobility lies in buying *ma'ani* for others, the debasement lies in exchanging *ma'ani*. Make your own search for the location of its *Divinity*.

[284] It has greater realness than realness itself. When *Divinity* is spoken of, it has already passed by. One searches for it up to the station of Oneness, for to that point it has not yet been reached. From the beginning *Divinity* has been spoken of as the meeting of opposites, of success and failure in one thing. Mothers have success, and mothers have failings. Fathers have success, and fathers have failings. Teachers have success and teachers have failings; brilliance can't be created simply by carrying valuable knowledge. Horses have success, and they also have failings.

The *essence* of Allah is revealed in both. Allah's messenger emerges from both; the saints of Allah revolve through both. Their majesty or lowness depends on the manner in which they become manifest. Even prophets differ in their status: some are high and some are low, and their rank is their *Divine*ness; their servitude is making obeisance to its *ma'ani*, by using their feeling; their worship is not through words, in Sundanese we say; worship means humble acceptance, and acceptance is a sign of *Divine*ness. Lowness is a sign of *majesty*, *majesty* is a sign of *beauty*. You must feel these things lest people say you neglect them. Majesty is the product of thought, lowness is the product of feeling.

Do not be wrong in your acceptance and you will avoid embarrassment. The lowly accept their lowliness; its proof is the scope of what is accepted. The nobility are magnanimous in compassion, the proof is the scope of their worship, not worship in the form of ritual prayer, that is just giving form to our origins. Not worship by the pilgrimage, that is just making a journey. Not worshipping by fasting, that is just admonishing our origins. But worshipping through acceptance, something that is true by its own truth, and in error when it turns to others than Allah. Rather than worshipping with one's limbs in the right time and the right place, it is better to worship with the soul, something which has neither time nor place. Something with no proper time belongs with another thing with no proper time, and something with no proper place belongs with something else with no proper place. One cannot choose one's station, for each person will have their own station. One cannot choose its time, for each person will have their own time. A head of grain can be fulsome or paltry depending on the cultivation that produced it. The fulsomeness of the grain is not the product of the rainy season, for the rainy season sometimes brings pests. It is not the product of the dry season, for the dry season sometimes brings prosperity. One must think like a farmer, and grab both the seed and the fruit also, and care for them for the whole season, and grab both the mushrooms and the toadstools. Do not be inflexible in your behaviour, pulling weeds out of the paddy field to get the edible hyacinth, and to get the plants that usually grow there, continually grabbing at them in haste. Faith cannot be realised by words, for faith must be felt, which means it is never the same for all, for each person has his own faith according to his own feelings. Like the old people used to say: don't place your faith in rice, it's useless except for when it satisfies your hunger; don't place your faith in water, it's useless if one is not thirsty; don't place your faith in money, it's useless if it cannot be exchanged; do not have faith in people, for at some time you will part ways; do not put faith in status, for that is something that can be asked for; do not put your faith in material things, for these won't protect you from misfortunes; do not put your faith in your friends, for there is boredom in friendship; do not place your faith in comfort, for difficulties will come one after the other; do not put your faith in long life, for all lives come to an end; do not put your faith in knowledge, for knowledge is easily forgotten.

People think they know the causation of things, but in fact they invert the meanings of the language, when they say that the content derives from the covering, for the truth is that the covering depends on the content. The mortar is called that because chilli sauce is made on it, the pestle is known as such because it pounds the chilli. Body-hair exists only because of our skin; skin only exists as the package for our flesh; our flesh only exists as the container for our blood; [285] the blood only exists to keep liquid in our muscles, and these are covers for our bones, and the bones only exist as the container for their marrow; and the marrow only exists as the container for our life-spirits. But seeing that our life-spirit extends even into our body-hair, you say our body-hair is the cause of our skin; you say our skin is the cause of our flesh; you say the flesh is the cause of our blood; you say the blood is the cause of our muscles; you say the muscle is the cause of our bones; you say the bones are the cause of our marrow; you say the marrow is the cause of our life-spirits. But do we forget that much skin does not have body-hair, that much flesh has no skin, that much blood has no flesh, many muscles have no blood, many bones have no muscles, much marrow has no bones, many life-spirits have no marrow, many life-spirits have no body, and have you never met with a body with no life-spirit?

These things can be a cause of feeling incorrectly.

My goodness! One's body hair is nevertheless the body-hair of the universe, the skin is nevertheless the world, blood is nevertheless water, the vein is nevertheless of the *khourat*,[13] things understood by the experts in the laws of the field, which we call *natural science* [*natuurkunde*]. Our bones are nevertheless stone, the marrow is in fact substance, the soul is in fact life, which is in fact revealed by the soul, causing all these things to have their function, the revelation of Divine Sovereignty, which is to be felt by human beings who are sensitive to it, to the acceptance of *Divine*ness.

---

13 We have not found a meaning for *khourat*.

My goodness! Our blood is in fact the desiring self, giving rise to the expression, 'anger makes us red', but in a state of awareness blood becomes our life, the skin is in fact *incitement*, our flesh is in fact *rectitude*, our bones are in fact *self-criticism*.[14] This gives rise to the expression, 'a youth is strong in bone and flesh, destroying all in his path', meaning he acts fearlessly and randomly, having not arrived at the age of caution. The marrow is the abode of *peace*, giving rise to the expression: comfort can dominate the self, and discomfort also takes over the self. The external covers are chatting constantly, but the covers impede our vision, so who will try to find what is within? Because the senses cannot be compelled, the ugliness of something will be detected by the senses because the senses are the paramount thing. People will say that something is valuable, of the highest order, but no matter what its value according to the senses, it can be cheap according to one's feeling, and I have never encountered something so hidden from the eyes, so covered in secrecy, that it is not looked over by all like any visible thing; for if it is genuinely precious it cannot be possessed by everybody. The same is said of hearing, smell and taste. There is no one who can warn of this other than the Islamic teacher and the mid-wife, so don't look at just anything, don't listen to just anything.

Everybody can recognise something that is forbidden, and so it is covered and closed, in order that it not be seen by others, and to avoid beholding the ugliness of it, for even its name is offensive, as it marks the presence of all forbidden things; such things become valued according to the senses, which in turn become the cause for the revelation of the thing's nobility; even though it might be repulsive, something can become forbidden because of its hidden qualities no matter what the appearance of the thing is. For those who know the secret, there is nothing to be fought over, nothing to be disputed, nothing to be warned about, except for one's homeland, which is sensed by the feeling of Divine Sovereignty. Even the Prophet himself, forced to leave Mecca, went to Medina, taking the small road along the coastline. In the middle of the journey, he encountered a major road that wound its way to Medina, his heart was moved and his eyes filled with tears, lamenting as he remembered Mecca, the place of his birth. At this point he was consoled by Gabriel, who brought a verse of the Qur'an, assuring him that all his wishes would be fulfilled, that he would return to his birth place, to his final destination. [286] And even the Prophet David, who had ninety-nine wives, nevertheless felt tempted and distracted by the gorgeous wife of the Vizier Urian.

Feel it for yourself! Lest you miss its significance. *Divine*ness! The body's shadow is the universe, and the shadow of the soul is feeling. Singularity, *essence*, *attributes* and acts [*af'al*]; before these

14 The passage expresses a canonical Islamic distinction concerning the grades of self-cultivation, namely *al-nafs al-ammarah* (the inciting self), *al-nafs al-sawiyah* (the upright self), *al-nafs al-lawwamah* (the self-criticising self) and *al-nafs al-mutma'innah* (the self at peace).

were elaborated, there was nothing that granted attributes to them. Because of this, people forbid worshipping rice, lest it no longer satisfies us; they forbid worshipping water lest it does not quench; worshipping comfort lest discomfort arrives; worshipping heat lest cold arrives; worshipping cold lest heat arrives; worshipping something that has absorbed *ma'ani* lest it not reveal itself; worshipping the attributes that depend on *ma'ani* [*ma'nawiyah*], for it is clear that these are not things to be gained through planning. If you wish to worship, it should be to Almighty Allah, something attested to by all our feelings. Lying further on from Allah was existence [*wujud*], before the revelation of the names and *attributes*. The appearance of the names and *attributes* never occured for anything other than Allah, and it is left to us as to how we worship Him, and when we worship in the hope of gain, the names and *attributes* are for insuring our bodily wellbeing, and our feeling of worshipping will be shaped accordingly, despite the hopes of gain, whereas when we expect nothing by way of gain, then the awareness of Divine Majesty disappears (so say those who worship without hope of gain), but according to those who worship in hope of gain, the feeling of Divine Majesty is present, by virtue of the hope of gain, and even for those who worship other than Allah, it is still Allah, still Allah; the ego is still in desire, so to what shall it hope for gain? And this billows out as the elaboration of our feelings, which combine together to reveal as *ma'ani*. We emerge as babies, a small addition to our numbers, and have the ability to act, and our hope of gain is established, so we advance to the stage of eating, we advance to the stage of drinking, we become busy with all kinds of things, and then begin to inquire. 'I am the Lord' say those who hope for gain. 'I am a servant' say those who have no hope of gain. The truth is neither servant nor Lord, with or without a hope of gain. The absolute *essence* has no name.

At this position we are still under the influence of servant and lord, both drawing on the absolute, bound together in our feelings. Then explodes the feeling of realisation: I am water and you are water, I have no hope of gain, and I do not hope for gain from you. Feeling breaks out, the expectation of food and drink arise, a hope for eating, a hope for drinking, but I will only eat on your account, will only drink on your account, not on account of the providing of the drink. My origin is in the feeding of feeling and the drinking of feeling, we meet because I find you, I achieve through my experience, not as something I inherit from before the experience. Worship is the place of that flash of feeling, and so it is not derived from the inheritance we have received prior to that. Our father Ibrahim did not worship the sun and moon, for that would have been worship with hope for gain, towards something constantly changing. Idols are not objects of worship because they have no power. Although the essence is absolute, without any here or there, even the worship of Allah alone cannot be done just like that, let alone when it is done with a hope for gain. Even though Allah is an object of worship, who could worship Him if there were no other who could be a worshipper of something other than Allah? It should be that we give worship to Almighty Allah alone, but only if we are in awareness of our worship of Him. For it is only that which has no changeability, not only in its appearance, but in reality subsists still, subsists still. Those who worship idols are disparaged by those who worship with a hope of gain, but cause no concern to those who worship the absolute. Even humans are worshipped by those who have a passing hope for gain; but are disparaged by those who worship the eternal.

The Lord who is widely worshipped by people, even by those who are unaware, smiles in His singularity. Wow! I have warned you about squabbles over the correct object of worship. This is the fault of those who are busy in the world of observance, and as a result you wear your shoes on the wrong feet, each of you argues for their own correctness, I am right and you are wrong, not realising that your accusations are nonsense, and that you yourself can also be accused. [287] How could they wish to disparage each other, when those who disparage are consumed by their own feelings, and do not consider what others feel? They disparage those who dedicate themselves to working the land, but they themselves don't like to till the soil; they disparage people dedicated to trade, but they themselves do not like commerce; they disparage those dedicated to prostrating themselves, but they do not like servitude; they disparage those who dedicate themselves to the hereafter, but they manage their earthly business; they disparage those in fear, but they themselves are cautious; they disparage those who take enjoyment, while they themselves do not lack enjoyment. It's better to leave them alone, for do they realise whom they are worshipping? While they worship, they do not realise that they are in search of the answer to the question of who their Lord actually is. They think there are names other than Almighty Allah. We commonly call this 'taking everything on board', moving from one name to another, jumping ahead, and only then worshipping Almighty Allah. They think this name, which is the eternal one, is not the one. For this reason, they have two worships: one is the worship of Allah, the second is the worship of something else. But they are ignorant because they do not realise that worship must be prostration, not crawling along the floor in obeisance. They wish to be given something by those who could give something, to be forgiven by those who could forgive them, in fear of the omnipotent entity. They feel they are subject to omnipotent power. Let them be, for that is how they feel.

Worshipping without the feeling of worship is never called worship, even though worshipping in response to an order has no feeling. Worship under the influence of feeling, of feeling that had not previously been taught to the worshipper, of feeling that is not from compulsion, is also not usually called worship. When it takes place because of decrees and prior admonitions, worship by feeling gives the impression that worship and feeling are united within it, although they are not decreed to do so. Yet worship and decree are different things, even though this difference is not felt. Consequently, worshipping and feeling appear to be simultaneous. Because of this, the worship is not real, and the feeling does not worship. Both of them are Allah still, Allah still. The Almighty would say with a smile, there! That is the result: a feeling that does not worship, and a Lord that does not have lordship. If I remained silent, I would not speak so much, for worshipping by prostration does in fact give the impression of worship. Just let these things be, for these are just impressions, and nothing is real because of its impressions. Reality has no impression, and if something is an impression, who says so?

According to those who worship, worship gives an impression of something else; but according to those who give an account of their feeling, every discrete thing has one discrete name, comprehended by everybody, but only if it can provide a sustenance that satisfies a person's tastes; and if we fail in this, the resulting affliction is a severe one. Feeling should sustain other feeling, the body should sustain other bodies, decoration should sustain other decoration. Give sustenance, and human preference shall without doubt be satisfied; acceptance is an amulet of humanity, remembrance is the life of perfection. The body-hair of the cosmos originates in the elaborations of the world, feeding its decorations to its humanity. Sustain human character with other human character, and if this fails, it will do so along with those who have a preference for it. This will hurt, but only for those who are aware of their bodiliness. The body-hair of the cosmos is sustenance for our body-hair, the skin of the cosmos is sustenance for our skin. Everybody will clearly sense which will last longer, the sole of the foot or the sandals it wears. Which lasts longer, our skin or the clothes we wear? The task of the flower is to compete with its fragrance, and the task of the fruit is to compete with its sweetness, the chili competes with its hotness. There is never intimacy between things that are not the same. The body-hair of the cosmos is oiled when it is combed, firewood is for cooking, a fish accompanies the foods eaten with it, the vegetables are for giving shade to it. Originally, this world was naked.

In their original state, humans did not eat, so at this point we must realise our *humanness*, and respond with *All praise is Allah's!*, and at times of catastrophe we should say *Verily we belong to Allah.* [288] As the old saying goes: don't attract someone by wrenching their skin, and don't shake a tree so its fruit falls down. Let the shaking be shaking, let the skin be skin. Our pains are not shared by all, and our comforts are not shared by all. The earth's skin parallels skin, if we loosen the soil it will be loose, if the soil is arid it will be arid, because of their *human*ness; the loose soil can be tilled, the arid soil can be built on, the plan is to increase its value. The significance of my skin is in its acceptance of its humanness [*basariyah*na], when dirty it is scrubbed, its long hair is combed, for perhaps these may be seen by those who forget their humanness, but those who remember have humanity as their souls. The skin of the universe is well-managed and flattened, its loose soil is planted, its well-springs are maintained and cleaned, in order to sustain the skin of humanity, clear water is used for ablutions, for bathing, used as a place for building a mosque, as a place for studying religion. In case my skin be wrong in accepting this, my skin replies *All praise is Allah's* [*Alhamdulillah*]. A personal water-source, worship conducted in one's own place, in sufficiency, without needing any enhancing, ah! That is the soul of humanity. Body-hair is accepted by body-hair, skin is accepted by skin, and for that reason they will not seek any more than sufficiency, in fear it will not be able to receive it. The flesh of the universe sustains the flesh of humanity, which cannot fatten if it is not receptive to the flesh of the universe. The money I earn from my rice is the profit from roasting it.[15] The brick-maker will not become rich, the farmer will not prosper, but their blood gives quality to their flesh, the earth has value because of water, the sustenance of my own blood. This is why we never drink rainwater, it must first come from the earth, and only then do we drink it, and only then do we boil it. If one forgets their flesh, and their blood forgets to receive it, then that is human resignation, meaning something that fails to return an acknowledgement that his soul is in need of refreshment, and that its value is from its acceptance, and that the reply of the blood and flesh which accepts is *All praise is Allah's*. I would prefer to experience the collapse of my flesh and blood than the collapse of the soul of the earth and the soul of water, except that I would first make safe the feeling of humanity; elaboration is sustenance for elaboration, and if it collapses it is wrong for us to complain. It is impossible that a farmer could like pests, or that a tree could be fond of parasites. The forgetful ones never use the terms orange worm or the pomegranate worm, they call them parasitical worms, because they think the worm and the parasites exist for the same reason.

The bones of the cosmos provide sustenance for human bones. Everybody knows that the trade in stones and lime is very hard work, and that is why those products are expensive. If the stones are not given to those who would like them, the bones of the cosmos will not be accepting. The wellbeing of the bones depends on their acceptance, on possessing the feeling to acknowledge *All praise is Allah's*. The marrow of the cosmos is the crown of all forbidden things, for after all, rough diamonds, cut diamonds, opals, emeralds, rubies and other things of this kind are very difficult to obtain, and this is a sign of their high value. Those who remember are surely high in their acceptance, in responding with *All praise is Allah's*, for they know there is nobody who will show them the way, except for the one who has something stored away.

Living as husband and wife is an adornment of *lordship*, and is not the origin of our bodiliness, and if it collapses, it need not be mourned. Having many offspring is an adornment of worldliness, marking a trustworthy person. If one accepts with one's ability to accept, one feels trusted by the essence of Divine Sovereignty, and becomes a way to reveal nobility, if one believes in its substance. A cheap crown emerges in the way of degradation, its owner prefers

15 Sundanese commonly 're-use' rice that has already been cooked by roasting it.

the way of degradation. If a person is mistaken in his acceptance, he does not realise it. The feeling of true feeling, is a feeling that there is no other. But those whose remembrance is great, and even more those who feel this genuine feeling, accept *All praise is Allah's*. The work of the feeling of Divine Sovereignty, [289] entitled *lordship*, is to be attentive without comparison. This means not choosing in advance those things which will appear as reality without being packaged in their character, such as hot, cold, wet, dry, and things which obtain difficult names.

Do it! When will the feeling of Divine Sovereignty, which is constantly obscured, have the feeling of a human crown, for where do you think there will be a crown that is not covered? Where do you think gold lies? A crown, or a diamond? It turns out they are in the earth, like the pearl on the sea-bed; a diamond inside a stone, while gold is in gravel, and tin is found within clay. If a crown were to appear in just any place, of course it would have no value, as if there were an ocean of oil, or an ocean of butter. A crown is an expensive thing, and its cover is thick, and has multiple layers, even more so with the crown of genuine feeling, covered by the feeling that we could utter as *May Allah curse him!*, enclosed by wood, buried under earth, for humans are covered by humanness [*basariyah*], while the truth [*hakékat*] is covered by shari'ah, and the prophets and saints are covered by their orders, giving servitude to their shari'ah. The truth is not to be covered by dissolute behavior, for that is a sign of forgetfulness, the loss of selflessness, of disregard for prohibitions, although it might appear as liberty, this is how those under the devil's influence think; but as long as we possess our reason, we will never desire freedom from the conduct specified by the shari'ah. Transfixed by the words *May Allah curse him!*, we follow the pleasures of our own desires, for our own enjoyment, but we change the name, claiming it to be the wishes of Allah's *essence*, so we sleep soundly, unaware of the satanic path. People say a forgetful man is like an animal, whereas in fact animals of all places have nobility, for an animal stays at its own position, no more and no less. The character of perfection is found when we do not forget the *essence* of *Divinity*, mercifulness, *lordship*; the old saying is very correct: Teak is replaced by false teak, and the parasite takes over the fruit. This means that majesty is dominated by degradation, for it is clear that human perfection leads to the way of degradation, and if these things are not yet understood, language will lead us to the inversion of feeling, but if we persist with feeling, we will wish to verbalise it in language, and this is the meaning of *There is no deity other than Allah.*

What compels me to worship is the eternal mentor, for I realise this is the well-spring from the body of the Messenger of Allah, from his faith. The meaning of *Muhammad is Allah's messenger*, because it moves from body to body, and from soul to soul, is the pathway of *Allah's messenger*, which I myself follow. It is the Messenger's feeling of resolve that I feel. Do not follow the feeling of false feeling, nor the feeling that masquerades as feeling. Feeling is found here and there; feeling is found there and here; and so feeling is not visible. The feeling over there is sought by the feeling here, and the feeling here is sought by something real here. My awareness goes further than the Messenger of Allah, I am aware of being beyond him, but I borrow a name from Muhammad, I borrow the feeling of Oneness, wishing to be a follower of the Messenger of Allah, and without any doubt the shari'ah is dazzling. Just like when a peasant feels equal to a high-ranking official, and let him do so, except that if he disobeys the village-head, he will be beaten, handed over to the official, and tried for insulting his master. That feeling feels there is no hereafter, no Qur'an, paradise, hell, angels and all things that emanate from them, because it is a feeling of being beyond the prophets. A person who feels like that clears his throat to attract my attention, wanting to visit me and be my sibling. That is impossible, for we do not like the same sweetness or spiciness. He wants to fit in with the whole village, with those in forgetfulness, unaware that he is not of the same ancestry; I am a descendant of remembrance, he is a descendant of forgetfulness; I must remember for eternity, he must forget for eternity. [290] I utter 'Allah', he does what I do! I utter 'Muhammad', he does the same thing again, pretending to want to be called the same as me. I say that the desiring self is bad, he says the desiring self is bad. I always obey things other than desire, for the *will* has the same name but different feelings. Don't be forced into infirmity, quarelling about shari'ah, for the proofs of *will* can clearly be exchanged, and such struggling only occurs because it has the same name. I am not saying too much, for we differ according to our origins. Don't let it be claimed by others, for they are walking down the same corridor. Do not treat him cordially, lest he says he shares your essence, it is better to be questioning about why we fear the hereafter, and it is better to be questioning about why it is the Qur'an you recite; if I am in fear, why is this? If I feel shame, why is this so? Of whom am I afraid, of whom am I ashamed? For those things are human experience in this world. For there is no fear over there, and there is no shame over there. If you wished to be afraid, who would you fear? And if you want to feel shame, to whom? Who would you fear?

Dreaming the impossible, like sleeping in a drain, licking up the shit of the Prophet's followers, happening right before their wide-open eyes! Sharing their feelings while they sing in *mandalungan*, not going here or there.[16] They come here to be close to the messenger of Allah, they come from all places far from here, claiming to be on the same level as the Prophet, and to emerge from the light of Muhammad's essence. Muhammad for them is a name, but not the revered Messenger of Allah, the son of Abdullah. Even more with the shari'ah, it will not follow along, it will not take a different shape for them, for even the essence abides in its own source, and from it flow forth all faiths. Even our Lord Jesus, although possessing an excess of godliness, it did not descend to his followers, and he did not claim to be their master, but instead *Divinity* emanated to him, to the point where he was called Allah. The same with the prophet Moses, who had an abundance of Divine

16 *Mandalungan* is a Sundanese melody.

authority [*nasutiyah*], but had no follower who exceeded him, or felt himself to be within Allah's *speech*, or made a claim for himself, and the followers did not follow their prophet. The same with our Lord Hidir, who had an abundance of godliness, and claimed to be beneath the authority of Gusti Allah.

Feel it for yourself! Whom will you follow? If you wish to make a living, what will give testimony to that, other than the devil's dreams? Relaxed with lullabies, one will be forgetful unto death. Although all the prophets emanate from the condition of Muhammad, none of them claimed to go beyond him, they were still aware in tracing their genealogies, and aware of their bodiliness; they did not hold on to their dreams.

Oh omnipotent Allah! I beg You to protect my feeling, the feeling of true feeling, a feeling in tune with its reality, real through its power, the power of accepting coercion, coercion accepted through feeling, the feeling that cannot be resisted. Human perfection will only be realised when accepted through feeling, and all supreme power arrives with coercion, and everything that comes or goes, even as big as a nit in one's hair will only appear through the competition between feeling and feeling.

At this station, I speak my mind in arrogant self-confidence, and can say charcoal is caused by fire, whereas wetness is caused by water, that one person helps me, while another tortures me, and these things will not move from their proper places, and will not spread to people other than their rightful owners, and so in both humility and arrogance I am always right, and the proper response to both is *All praise is Allah's*, the proper response to both is *Verily we belong to Allah*, the proper response to both is *All things belong to Allah* , the proper utterance for both is *Allah is the most holy!* These responses are not made in language, but through feeling, that is through the feeling of acceptance, namely the following of guidance, the guidance from Gusti Allah, and following the straight path [*sirotolmustaqim*] instead of the path of forgetfulness.

## Sources cited


Chittick, William C.

1989 *The Sufi path of knowledge: Ibn al-'Arabi's metaphysics of imagination*. Albany, N.Y.: State University of New York Press.

Drewes, G.W.J.

1969 *The admonitions of Seh Bari: A 16th century Javanese Muslim text attributed to the saint of Bonań re-edited and translated with an introduction*. The Hague: KITLV/Martinus Nijhoff.

Al-Fudholi, Muhammad

2009 *Kifayatul 'Awam: Pembahasan ajaran tauhid ahlus Sunnah*. Surabaya: Mutiara Ilmu.

Kaptein, Nico

2014 *Islam, colonialism and the modern age in the Netherlands East Indies. A biography of Sayyid 'Uthman (1822–1914)*. Leiden/Boston: Brill.

Kartini, Tini, Ningrum Djulaéha, Saini K.M., Wahyu Wibisana

1985 *Biografi dan Karya Haji Hasan Mustafa*. Jakarta: Pusat Pembinaan dan Pengembangan Bahasa.

Montgomery Watt, W.

1962 *Islamic philosophy and theology*. Edinburgh: University Press.

Mustapa, Hasan

1937 *Gelaran sasaka di kaislaman*. Bandung: Comite Mendak.

Nicholson, Reynold Alleyne

1921 *Studies in Islamic Mysticism*. Cambridge: University Press.

Rosidi, Ajip

1989 *Haji Hasan Mustapa jeung karya-karyana*. Pustaka: Bandung.

Zoetmulder, P.J.

1995/1935 *Pantheism and monism in Javanese Suluk Literature*. Edited and translated by M.C. Ricklefs. Leiden: KITLV Press.

*Chapter 3*

# *THE TEACHINGS OF OUR ISLAMIC INHERITANCE*

## The drama of the human lifecourse

Ahmad Gibson Albustomi

*Editor's introduction*

Since Ajip Rosidi completed his majesterial work on Mustapa (Rosidi 1989), Ahmad Gibson Albustomi (b. 1965) has become the most prominent interpreter and advocate of Mustapa. He has carried out a lengthy research project on Mustapa's work, and has consistently mobilised Mustapa's ideas in contributions to newspapers and other media. Many of these pieces were collected in a volume published in 2012 under the title *Filsafat manusia Sunda* (Bandung, Skylart 2012).

Kang Gibson, as he is known in Bandung, is now a staff member at UIN Sunan Gunung Djati, where he teaches comparative religion and helps to maintain the university's computer network. In his years as a student at this institution, he was a core member of the *Pasamoan Sophia* (The Philosophy Gathering) foundation, which conducted regular discussions on Mustapa, Sundanese culture and everyday philosophy.

This chapter is an abridgement of Gibson's interpretation of the work translated in Chapter Two above (*The Teachings of Our Islamic Inheritance*). This research, completed in the post-graduate program of Bandung's Sunan Gunung Djati Islamic State Universty, is the most complete and detailed study of any single work by Mustapa.

Gibson wrote his research in Indonesian, and abridged it for inclusion here with the help of Mr Dédé Syarif. Stuart Robson translated Gibson's abridgement into English. A number of Arabic terms are left untranslated in the excerpts appearing in this chapter. These terms are defined above in the introduction to Millie and Setiawan's translation of *The Teachings* (Chapter Two). All non-English words are from Sundanese, except if indicated otherwise.

* * *

*The Teachings of Our Islamic Inheritance* (*Gelaran Sasaka di KaIslaman*) describes the course of a person's life as a series of choices made on the basis of various considerations and under certain conditions, both internal and external. Hasan Mustapa sets out and dramatises a process of interior dialogue through which a person chooses to adopt a position towards his or her life experiences, and also portrays the consequences of these choices. The work subjects social life to religious interpretations, understanding constraints as the basic conditions for the rise of freedom in a human being. Socially-imposed constraints, for example, provide the possibilities and conditions for a person to make choices regarding all potential situations. They form a stepping-off point for ontological understanding in making choices based on a knowledge of the ontological facts. On this basis, over the duration of one's lifecourse a person formulates a kind of epistemological system in determining the choices that he has to make. Hasan Mustapa uses this progression of decisions, constrained socially as well as from within, as the framework for his vision of the stages of the Islamic lifecourse.

Basing himself on a specific ontological viewpoint, namely that of *wujudiah* Sufism,[1] and taking as starting-point the mystical

1 Although such a brief definition necessarily does harm to the concept, I take *wujudiah* Sufism to mean those Islamic visions that equate Divinity with *wujud*, meaning existence or reality.

epistemology of the Seven Grades (*Martabat Tujuh*), Hasan Mustapa proposes a human lifecourse consisting of seven stations or stages (Sund: *lebah*, Arabic: *maqam*, station). These stations together form a process of rising (Arabic: *taraqqi*) that Mustapa also sets out in his work on the Seven Grades (Rosidi 1989: 293-309). The stations of *The Teachings* display similarities to the stations for achieving the state of the Perfect Man (*Insan Kamil*) taken from al-Jili (see Ali 1997: 144-145). In these seven phases, in particular the first five, Hasan Mustapa depicts the dialectic process that humans experience between their physical and spiritual tendencies. These phases are encountered as the subject endeavours to move upwards in order to find the synergy between these two tendencies. This synergy is achieved at the level of the Perfect Man, the person who has arrived at a universal and holistic awareness, a person who no longer views the differences and plurality of the world as something essential. Rather, he views this plurality and these differences as delusions that arise from the ensnarement of the human physical senses. This ensnarement produces a set of opinions and views that are dualistic in nature. These are plotted out by Mustapa in this work. An individual's position on one side or the other is revealed dialectically in the phases from Submission up to the phase of Unity.

In the process, he reveals the 'journey' of a person in search of their 'identity'. The term 'identity' (Ind.: *jati diri*; core of the self) has the same connotation as 'essence' in philosophical theory. In this work the 'achievement' of the essence or identity is discovered in accordance with the level or station which is being passed through, and the tendencies that accompany it. The achievement at each station does not represent the true essence, and the station itself does not represent the end-point of the journey of life, because in the end when one reaches the peak at each stage one goes back to enter upon further wanderings in order to reach a higher station. In this way Hasan Mustapa looks at life as an endless process. Mustapa expressed this in verse in his work The Seven Grades:

> Here are the Seven Grades explained:
> When broken down there are seven
> but like *rujak* [salad], their mixing is not felt.
> People talk of the individual contents,
> of one as opposed to the other,
> but they leave no trace separately.
> All seven are clearly topics,
> to be treated one by one,
> but together, like *rujak*, form a human
> of one authentic source
> the true feeling of feeling
> of neither excess nor shortage.
> Excess causes elation,
> shortage makes one languish,
> feeling searches for something to hold to
> and shows that one is not well,
> but repose has not yet vanished.
> A difficult heart has no character.
>
> From *Kinanti: The Seven Grades Explained* (Rosidi 1989: 307-308)

The seven stations are Submission (*Islam*, the initial stage in the journey of a religious life), Faith (*iman*), Virtuousness (*soléh*), Goodness (*ihsan*), Witnessing (*sahadah*), Truthfulness (*sidikiyah*), and

Oneness (*kurbah*). From the stage of Submission up to Witnessing, Mustapa divides his text into two tendencies or influences, that of the Devil (Iblis) on the left, and that of Divine Sovereignty (Sund.: *Kapangéranan*, Arabic: *Kauluhiyahan*) on the right. The human individual is depicted as a figure that is always subject to these two mutually opposed tendencies or influences. The two tendencies are by nature opposed but they also attract each other. They give rise to an internal dialectic within the individual, and this dialectic has the possibility of producing various different tendencies. These are set out by Mustapa in the first five stations.

The process of transition from one phase to the following one is in the nature of a continuum. The condition in the left-hand column is determined by the ontological achievement of the right-hand column in the preceding phase, but from the perspective of the subject's mentality, it represents a discrete continuation within the left-hand column. This is different from the right-hand column, where the previous phase is a continuation of the right-hand column in the preceding phase, with regard to both the level of subjective awareness and its epistemology.

**The station of Submission (Islam)**

The right and left-hand columns commence with the same sentence: 'When born into the feeling of Submission…' (*The Teachings* 249). But after that the distinctions between them become clear. The right-hand column specifies '… under the influence of Divine Sovereignty from the right' while the left-hand column says, '…under the influence of Iblis from the left'. There follows a choice, expressed in differing words in the two sides: the right-hand column runs: '… is it better to act upon it or not?', while the left-hand column says,

'What should we do? Is it a good thing to observe Islam, or not?' (*The Teachings* 249)

These questions are a key to the *Teachings*. As we follow the text we find that the rise of a 'feeling of being Muslim' brings with it the question of whether to follow or carry out Islam or not. At this initial level, this is a question about one's social conduct. This is religion as a 'socio-cultural' fact: 'Aaah! It's better to observe it because of the sayings of the old people and one's relatives ... and [in order to] be in harmonious accord with the people of one's own community' (*The Teachings* 249). At this level, 'performance' of Islam involves compliance with teachings which have 'culturally' become part of the system of cultural values of Sundanese society.

After this a dialogue takes place, presenting arguments on behalf of each tendency (Divine Sovereignty and the Devil). When the tendency of the Devil presents an argument that there is no use in following society and carrying out the laws of Islam, and that it might even be damaging to do so, the conscience prefers to follow the tendency of Divine Sovereignty. This choice is in accordance with the 'voice' or words of the heart (*rasa ati*). Hasan Mustapa explains the conscience as having, among other things, the character of criticalness and consistency. It underpins a process of dialogue (*pada nyarita pamanggih*) and deliberation (*timbang taraju*) (Moestapa 1955: 1–2).[2] It chooses, distinguishes and weighs up everything in a wise manner. Secondly, it is realistic, in the sense that it possesses a tendency to 'think positively' (Arabic: *husnu dzun*) in relation to the truth located outside itself ('... one will be in harmonious accord with the people of one's own community ...' *The Teachings* 249). The voice

2 These lines are quoted from stanzas 19 and 28 of *Kinanti Ngahurun Balung*.

of the heart is open, constantly engaging in relations with whatever is to be found outside it.

The dialogue that takes place between the power of Divine Sovereignty and the power of the Devil is opened with this contribution from Divine Sovereignty:

> But the result is the same either way, a person who practices it never obtains a benefit, a person who doesn't practice it doesn't suffer loss or misfortune. (*The Teachings* 249)

Compare this with the question on the column on the left:

> But the result is just the same, a person who practices it doesn't benefit from it, but rather he is at best under the command of other people, they suffer physically as they carry out something that doesn't bring any reward, but actually harms him: their physical welfare is damaged. (*The Teachings* 249)

At the outset the two tendencies, Divine Sovereignty and Iblis, put forward the same pragmatic argument to the effect that both observing and not observing the teachings of Islam and social norms do not give rise to loss or benefit. But the left tendency is expanded upon in a distinct way: 'One's property is expended without any benefit' (*The Teachings*, 249). This statement says explicitly that a person who is under the 'rule' of another (society, parents, and so on) is in fact suffering a loss from being in that position. The subject in the power of the Devil has a materialistic nature, requiring immediate and visible justifications: 'we are in ignorance, guided by proofs that appear at the time' (*The Teachings* 249).

With the individual who is under the influence of Divine Sovereignty, a similar dialectic takes place between the tendency to obtain happiness or personal gain and social pressures. But this dialectic is settled by following the promptings of the heart (*ceuk ati*), which produces a realistic attitude in confronting the social realities within which one lives. By following the conscience, one forms a strategy to postpone the drive to channel and satisfy one's instinctual needs directly, by means of 'sharing feeling with feeling' (*The Teachings* 249). That is, by reconciling one's own feelings with the feelings of society. This can be achieved in three ways, namely: (1) preserving harmony with one's fellow members of society, or being 'in harmonious accord with the people of one's own community' (*The Teachings* 249); (2) listening to and concurring with the words of parents and colleagues through 'paying proper attention to the old sayings', (*The Teachings*, 249); and (3) the tendency to give way, or 'follow obediently' (*The Teachings*, 249). In this way, one obtains peace of mind and 'social security', and feels satisfied because one receives approval as a 'good person' (*jalma hadé*). The consequence of sharing feeling with feeling is a submissive nature, achieved by following 'social norms' in the guise of conforming to the teachings of religion or the customs and traditions that the community subscribes to. Hasan Mustapa calls this situation 'Islam with the body, and faith with the heart' (*The Teachings*, 250).

Meanwhile, with the individual who is under the power of the Devil, the opposition between the need to satisfy instinctual desires and the pressures of society is reconciled by deferring to hedonistic criteria: 'But what we humans seek is profit and comfort' (*The Teachings*, 249). The individual subject draws back from relationships and has a defensive nature. It has difficulty in accepting anything that comes from outside and tends to be suspicious: 'This station is not progress, but is in fact a reversal to unbelief, from giving service with one's body, from giving service with one's heart' (*The Teachings*, 250). This is different from the individual who adopts the strategy of sublimation and finds opportunities for himself in other people. At that moment the wanderings of his 'intellect' are more and more challenged to answer and provide 'arguments' regarding what he is doing. This is developed in future stations. But when the individual retreats from the possibilities of Islam as sociability, even though he is restrained within the confines of the crowd, his own identity and integrity experience a process of being made uniform. The individual loses his subjectivity and autonomous 'sense of self'.

**The station of Faith (*Iman*)**

The station of Faith represents a continuation of the station of Submission, at the point when the tendency to seek physical fulfillment directly (the influence of the Devil) can be overcome; 'At this point, one has arrived at the stage called Submission with the body, Faith with the heart; a person soon rises from here to the stage called Faith' (*The Teachings*, 250). The individual under the influence of Divine Sovereignty is, whether willingly or by force, already in a state of 'union with society'.

The tendency of the individual under the influence of the Devil to be 'guided by proofs that appear at the time' is still strong. It offers a way of looking at reality that produces a hedonistic mentality:

> What is the benefit for those who make observance? For those who believe? As for me, I have not yet met a person who resisted observance and suffered for it, who didn't believe and was placed under pressure. Their hardships did not increase, their status did not worsen, nor did they suffer greater loss to their material wealth. (*The Teachings*, 251)

This mentality encourages a defensive position that makes one static and closed:

> Do not exhaust yourself by making the sacrifices that are necessary to follow the path recommended by the old people, but make them now and then only, for there are many other things that must be done, and one's lot in life is to search for happiness: perhaps the old people and relatives will forgive this, and won't force us to the point of fatigue in body not to mention heart. As for me, I am exhausted either way, out of breath from seeking approval... (*The Teachings*, 251)

The cause of this closed attitude (toward human relations) is the tendency to always feel that what one already has is enough. The resulting stagnation means the subject under the influence of the Devil is struggling at the stage of submission under the influence of Divine Sovereignty. When we look at the statement, 'As for me, I have not yet met a person who resisted observance and suffered for it, who didn't believe and was placed under pressure (*The Teachings*, 251)', we glimpse the same subject that thought at the stage of Submission: 'But the result is the same either way, a person who practices it never obtains a benefit, a person who doesn't practice it doesn't suffer loss or misfortune' (*The Teachings*, 249). The difference is to be found in the tendency to embark on relations with other individuals in society or not. As was mentioned above, an individual under the influence of the Devil has a very defensive nature, is closed and static. Even if he does embark on relations with society, this is carried out merely to obtain physical satisfaction and appreciation from society as a good person: 'The old people say: Gusti Allah created me. Because of this, I give observance, both to Gusti Allah and to the old people, so that they will say I am of good character' (*The Teachings*, 251). Once again, this statement is almost the same as the experience of the subject at the station of Submission under the influence of the power of Divine Sovereignty:

> It's better to observe it because of the sayings of the old people and one's relatives, and when one is willing to practice Islam, one will be in harmonious accord with the people of one's own community, and in this way earn praise as a 'good person', who pays proper attention to the old sayings. (*The Teachings*, 249)

In this way, the Muslim enters into a subject-object relation with her environment, in which society is made the object of one's happiness:

> The hadith and Qur'an are shown to them
> but they merely grin
> because they have no feeling for it.
> The only things that move them are the old sayings.
> When they rub against their feelings,
> the lips go north, the heart to the south,
> their attention is not deep
> for their hearts are tangled in thought
> like a cat pondering a fish steamed in leaves
>
> (*Sinom: The return of Acceptance*, Moestapa 1955: 20)

By contrast, at the station of Faith under the power of Divine Sovereignty, we find that the prospect of social relations brings with it a number of hopes, that is, hopes for achieving proof of one's conviction by interacting with society, and of believing in what society believes in:

> I just perform my duty, hoping that proof will appear in the long term. As good as it would be to meet such proof while not believing, to receive the command while not practicing it, it is better that I first believe in what the old people say before I come across proof of it, to carry out the command before I understand

> it, rather than being in a state of anxiety. The things the old people say may be very lengthy but they are not all lies, for as long as I have been practicing Islam with the body, my power and efforts have not been exhausted, so there will be no loss to myself or to other people. (*The Teachings*, 251)

The attitude of 'trial and error' is an expression of an open attitude, even though it is still hesitant. Hesitation represents an attitude between acceptance and refusal which gives rise to anxious hope. At this station, and in this condition, the development of an epistemological understanding takes place, from an individual truth to the truth of the group. In other words, this is a truth which is measured by a number of people, who embrace and hold to it, and which is based on a common manner of thinking:

> The old people say: There will be a final day, just believe it, for it is certain that after tomorrow comes the day after, but it is impossible that there be no end to it. (*The Teachings*, 252)

On this basis, an epistemological change takes place in the disposition one adopts towards the metaphysical aspects of one's religiosity, from 'practicing Islam with the body, and practicing faith through the heart' (*The Teachings*, 250) to 'practicing Islam through the body of Allah's messenger, practicing faith through the heart of Allah's Prophet' (*The Teachings*, 252). This takes place because the 'news' about the presence of the Prophet, whom one has never known directly, is believed and accepted implicitly via stories that develop and are believed in by society or parents, and have become a system of cultural values and beliefs in society. The term 'Prophet' in this connection is a symbol of a social compact. Truth is based on a social compact. On the other hand, the term 'body' in the phrase 'practicing Islam with the body' suggests that what is carried out is merely bodily expressions, to achieve a physical happiness and only to the extent that it does not interfere with that physical happiness. In this way there is a paradigm change in how relations are conducted, from the paradigm of one's own happiness as starting-point for truth and goodness to a collective truth, although at base still founded on the principle of private happiness:

> But I have already sensed that rather than being harmed, my friends and relatives do not hate me for practicing Islam, and many of them love me for it [...] I make observance, but only now and then, merely because I believe what people say in order to be noticed by the people saying those things. (*The Teachings*, 252).

The ascent to the next station is made possible by a desire to continue carrying out the pillars of Islam and articulating a belief that is based on the reports from parents, with the hope that there is a linkage between acts performed with the *hati* (heart) in carrying out the rules of Islam and the *nyawa* (soul) in enacting faith:

> It is better that I now make a habit of practicing all those Islamic things that are obligatory for individuals, and of avoiding the things that are forbidden. I do not think about the afterlife, but just wish to be praised in this earthly world, and am consistent in my belief in the things people say, so that I can keep observing with my heart and body for practicing Submission, and with my soul for practicing Faith. (*The Teachings*, 252)

**The station of Virtuousness (*Soléh*)**

The station of Virtuousness begins with the rise of an awareness of the bases for making one's choices. This awareness is a need to know that one is consistently basing oneself on rational arguments that represent the exercise of one's own choice. At the very least, the station of Virtuosness is characterised by three things. First, there is the feeling that one has reached the condition of being truly adult (*sawawa umur, geus balég*) and must therefore take responsibility for all one's actions. Secondly, there is an awareness that one's own ideas are emerging as important resources. This is a sign that one is beginning to enter the stage of intentionality, and is beginning to set aside considerations that are of a temporal nature. Thirdly, one has broken the ties with parents, and they no longer watch over one's good or bad conduct.

> ...the old people are no longer here, and the ones who still are cannot give orders to me [...] My father, my mother, and all the old people no longer exist, only my friends remain. It will bring nothing if I practice my Islam, and it will bring nothing if I just abandon it. Believing in the stories of the old people will bring nothing, and so will not believing in them. (*The Teachings*, 253)

The rupture of the link with parents, as those who are closest and have the most influence in one's life, has enabled one to make optimal use of all one's opportunities and potential as an autonomous individual. The individual begins to become aware of a greater opportunity to make use of his own thoughts, choices and arguments in making decisions without pressure from parents. Mustapa writes elsewhere:

> Now is the time to think
> about the substance of what people say
> as a desiring human person
> following the promptings of the heart
> wherever it may face,
> rather than arbitrary feelings.
>
> (*The Quail laments in its cage* Rosidi 1989: 91)

The individual has begun to liberate himself from the tendency to tag along with the 'perceptions' of society or to perform something merely because of social pressures. Even so, this does not imply that the individual is sterile or distant from the system of socio-cultural values held by his society. At the very least he still has a system of cultural values from his society that he adheres to, including its system of belief. The station of Virtuosness signals a transformation. Earlier in the progression, the subject did not subscribe to the beliefs that exist in society, but felt helpless in the face of the society that encircled him, feeling it to form a cage that robbed him of his own authenticity. Deep bonds with parents and others were experienced and faced as a form of pressure, a cage that confined his freedom:

> It will bring nothing if I practice my Islam, and it will bring nothing if I just abandon it. Believing in the stories of the old people will bring nothing, and so will not believing in them. (*The Teachings*, 253)

The loss of these bonds does not cause him to abandon the injunctions and instructions of his parents. But seeing that the decision to hold this system of belief is based upon his own deliberations, it has become 'his own authentic property'. He declares his determination to carry out whatever had previously been regarded as an obstacle to his freedom. The attitude of an individual such as this, in the context of psychoanalysis, would be termed 'subsequent repentance'.

Before this transformation, Islam as a system of belief to which society subscribes had become something external to himself. It had become a set of values that confined him and obscured his own authenticity. But now, the decision to continue to carry out Islam as his religious conviction is no longer due to the pressures of society, but is a product of his own choice. Commencing from rejection of the meaninglessness of the values that society adheres to, as explained above, he decides to keep on using them in his life, even though he is not yet convinced enough to entertain speculation about how it will work out:

> But ah! I have come so far that it is better to simply continue, so I do not lose out. Perhaps the things I didn't understand in the past will be understood in the present. In the past I observed Islam, but only to be praised by the old people; but now my Islam might be accepted by Gusti Allah... if I continue to believe, my desire to know what will happen after that will grow. (*The Teachings*, 253)

With the above attitude the pressures on one also shift, that is, from social pressures to those emanating from the values that one believes in:

> If I stop and abandon the old people's admonitions just because they are no longer around, I will be very afraid of being tortured by Gusti Allah, for my parents said: If you abandon Islam or if you violate its prohibitions or if you cease believing, you will be tortured by Gusti Allah, if not in this world then in the hereafter. So, what I fear is His anger. (*The Teachings*, 253)

It is apparent that the decision to place one's conviction in what society takes as its belief system entails consequences arising from that system. On the other hand, it can be seen that a very basic shift has taken place: one's authenticity, previously shrouded in fear from the pressure of society, has emerged and has engineered a crucial shift. One now holds fears for the consequences of a failure to act in accordance with one's conviction.

And what of the individual under the influence of the Devil at the station of Virtuousness? This individual holds a viewpoint which does not yet display any progress, but is still within the confines of society:

> I wish to practice Islam, but just to the extent where it doesn't interfere in my life, in my status, and in my work. I will go on practicing, for perhaps it will give help just when I am being strangled by difficulties, and perhaps I should keep holding on to the words used for asking the Most Holy Gusti Allah for wellbeing, because the old people say that Allah is the one who gives help, who provides for His servants. (*The Teachings*, 53)

### The station of Goodness (*Ihsan*)

> [...] at this point the feeling is not one of increasing heaviness, but of increasing weightlessness, and the impediments do not multiply, but apprehensions become fewer. Free from the old people, free from father, knowledge increases, conviction increases. (*The Teachings*, 255)

At this point, arguments in support of one's conviction are articulated. These are founded on cosmological considerations relating to causality. These signal progress from the early stations, when belief was based on the names one encountered in one's environment: 'In the beginning, at the stage of Islam, I knew the names of Allah, which I uttered so I would not forget them' (*The Teachings*, 266). Mustapa presents a variation on a classic argument for the existence of God: It is impossible for there to be a Creator if He does not have a creation, and as soon as there is a creation, it is not possible for the Creator not to possess the power to create it. This means that the existence of the creation proves two things consequentially, namely the existence of God and His power. Furthermore, it is not possible to create something without paying attention to it (*The Teachings*, 265). And hence the impossibility of 'seeing' God is no longer a basis for refusing or doubting the existence of God. The above arguments produce a rational consequence that is also a moral one arising out of one's conviction, namely a total 'surrender', in the shape of *nyembah* (worship) and *kumawula* (devotion).

Earlier in the journey, Submission signified a helplessness that possessed an element of rejection. This has now become an acceptance based on understanding. Understanding fundamentally and inherently contains within it the meaning of acting with full awareness.

The lifecourse started as Submission without knowledge in relation to what was being done, because the Submission was not to the subject (God), but to society, through its social values, so that the individual was nothing more than a 'passive player' in what is being done. The individual is an object of the social dynamics in which one lives. At the station of Goodness a radical shift takes place, namely the shift to becoming a subject that is aware of its existence, and 'resigns' toward the factuality or destiny that it finds, a factuality that is a gift of God. In this resignation one adopts a certain position and participates actively in one's life and social dynamics. This acceptance of destiny resembles what Nietzsche meant when he said "Saying 'yes' to life". In his submission the human being discovers a certainty in his life, and at that moment he finds a freedom based on knowledge of his own limitations. This awareness of factuality (destiny) gives birth to a pattern of mutual relations, mutual understanding and confirmation of one another's existence. One has endeavoured not to carry out an objectification toward anything that one faces, experiences and finds out. And the most important thing is that one's own authenticity and integrity have been achieved, and at that point one's existence as a human being is already within one's grasp.

Obstructions to the formation of an attitude of Goodness at this station arise in the form of a static and apathetic attitude. This attitude arises from a tendency to withdraw from or reject relations with something outside one:

> Why should I take on further inconvenience and difficulty? [...] I will never be shaken as long as I feel happy, or for as long as I am in faith. Even if my belief comes under attack and I should lose touch with the divine injunctions, or if from time to time I should fall into doubt, these things will be weighed up by Gusti Allah Himself. Even if I become unsteady when visited by something that causes me to lose touch with the divine orders or to break a prohibition, these things are in Allah's power. (*The Teachings*, 255)

This attitude arises because everything outside one tends to be turned into an object and a mere source of pleasure, and the relation that is subsequently formed is suspected as something that will damage and diminish, or even steal, one's freedom. An attitude of this kind has appeared from the outset, that is, since the station of Submission.

This relation is a fetter on one's freedom, to the extent that the attitude of resignation that is formed at this phase makes the subject helpless when it comes face to face with pressures from outside itself, namely pressures that do not form a source of strength for producing its own existence. In this case the individual is completely caught in the illusion of another strength coming from outside it:

> As for resignation, it is absolutely obligatory, but not as long as I must suffer the common human condition that we are sometimes in comfort and sometimes not. As for believing in Allah, that is absolutely obligatory, but only if all my options are exhausted. As for accepting our fate, that is absolutely obligatory, but only when I am no longer curious. As for being pure-hearted, that is obligatory,

> but only if I have forgotten how I came into the world, ashamed of human eyes, afraid of human criticism. As for loving the Loving One, this is obligatory, but only while I am not yet convinced that all bounties and hardships are granted by Allah. (*The Teachings*, 256)

**The station of Witnessing (*Sahadah*)**

In broad terms Hasan Mustapa defines the Confession of Faith (*Sahadah*) as: 'The attentiveness of the heart to the Lord who possesses the actions of the heart' (*The Seven Grades*, Rosidi 1989: 294). The resignation which has been achieved at the station of Goodness as a product of understanding and awareness toward the assurance and certainty of the existence of God as well as a number of consequences of these becomes all the firmer at the station of Witnessing. This is because one's certainty and submission to God have become an inseparable part of oneself, and have become united in one's heart: 'No matter the pain and fatigue, providing I keep in accord with my heart' (*The Teachings*, 259). And so there arises a longing to know Allah more closely:

> How could I have the nerve to testify for so long that there is no deity other than Gusti Allah! What if someone asks me: How do you know? Maybe I will only be able to answer with: Because the old people said so! Because my father said so! How could this be believed? How can testimony rely on talk alone? So! Because of this I will persist in warning that I will not fail in my wish to get real proof. For instance I have been asked: How do you know what a chilli tastes like? I replied: Of course I know, for I have tasted that it is spicy! Do you know sugar? I replied: Of course I know, because I have tasted that it is sweet! Do you know salt? I replied: Of course I know because I have tasted that it is salty! I do not answer: My father told me! (*The Teachings*, 259-260)

When the longing has reached its climax, then the manifestations of God's generosity in a physical form no longer attract our attention. What we direct ourselves towards is the Giver, God:

> Earlier, I longed for Him, hoping my love would be returned in love, but now, it really doesn't matter, I still long for Him but not because I want to receive a gift, I still love him but not for the rice. It doesn't matter, even though I am clapping with one hand without any response, for it's my own doing that as time goes by it becomes clearer that I am sending without any expectation, having concern without any return.(*The Teachings*, 258)

In this way, a change has taken place in one's viewpoint with regard to the aim of life. Initially the aim of life took a material form, and this shifted to become something abstract, oriented toward values. It has gone from physical pleasure to spiritual pleasure. The desire to arrive at the true reality has begun to shift one's viewpoint from a materialistic one to a more substantial one, from form to significance:

> In the past, I was happy to receive rice, but now I am happy when I get rice and the feeling of satisfaction.(*The Teachings*, 258)

> I do not want the cananga plant, I only want its flower; I do not want its flower, I just want its perfume. I do not want the cananga's perfume, I only want its nectar. I do not want a gift, I just want the giver. (*The Teachings*, 259)

These examples reveal the most important feature of the station of Witnessing: the rise of a very strong longing and desire to become acquainted with God in a more substantial way: '[I] wish to get real proof' (*The Teachings*, 260). This is marked by the loss of a desire for physical aspects, even though one is aware that all of them represent part of the substance of God's love. Even if one has to undergo fatigue and difficulties, one does not feel oppressed in any way. This is because one is so convinced that God is, after all, all-merciful, although mankind does not know him, and all the more when mankind does know him.

The shift in orientation from material considerations to ideas or values arises as a process of self-criticism within oneself. The shift arises from a rational potential of a dialectical nature. It is a negative dialectic, commencing with what is in one's thoughts, and then proceeding to its inverse or oposite. This, dialectically, produces a reflexive self-criticism, or a unique kind of self-awareness, that characterises this station. The appearance of this dialectic thinking illustrates the rise of a more systematic kind of ontological and epistemological way of understanding. The stage marks the movement from a rational and empirical outlook to a process of dialectic thinking which engenders self-criticism.

Yet Hasan Mustapa states that this attitude of separating and splitting forms an obstacle to arriving at true knowledge, the truth of conviction (Arabic: *hakkul yakin*) or the authentic feeling (*rasa saenyana*) (*The Seven Grades*, Rosidi 1989: 294). The individual who is in such a condition is aware that while there has been a shift from the physical pole to the spiritual pole he is still in fact in the same condition as before, thinking in a material and physical way:

> If you do not force yourself, you will have a vested interest, longing for the green and fertile, only liking the prosperous things, approving of bounties only, enjoying the profits alone, comfortable with good health, desiring only the sweetness. That would mean worshipping pleasure and comfort, without the unpleasantness, but then who makes the unpleasantness? Who has this attitude? Without doubt this is what is known as a love of *jamaliyah* [beauty] and an aversion for *jalaliyah* [majesty]. It is precisely this that forms the constraining wall, a curtain that obscures the message.

> We will not comprehend while failing to discern, worshipping *beauty* and shrinking from *majesty*, even if we can recognise it, the recognition will come and go throughout the night and day; we discern in the daylight, but this disappears in the evening. (*The Teachings*, 260-261)

In this way, the Witnessing at this station is still unclear, as it is still trapped in polarisation, even though there has been a shift, namely a shift from the concrete level to a spiritual one at the abstract level of significance. Nevertheless, an awareness of the existence of a duality of truth has become a primary input for comprehending the reality that one faces. That is, the existence of a consciousness of substance and shape, symbol and what is symbolised:

> At this point we begin to lament:
> I thought it was a black butterfly
> it turned out to be a colourful one.
> Water retreats and flows back.
> Water flows to a grave.
> Tomorrow's dusk may be in darkness
> and may be glimpsed for but a moment.
>
> (*The Teachings*, 261)

Within the obscurity and confusion mentioned above, one is provided with knowledge and awareness of the duality of the truth and the reality of symbolism. A number of symbols for the truth are laid out within one's awareness. And so, no matter what one faces, in an indistinct way it is evident that there are always two sides, including what can be seen and what lies behind that:

> At this point appears an obscure image of the gate at the margins of [the station of] Truthfulness, the outposts of the divine abode, an abundance of Divine Mercy [*Rahmaniyah*]. We gaze in amazement: Oh my! What is that? We look but cannot see, scared to blink lest it vanishes. We pace back and forth to the nearby square, avoiding the heat under the shade of a flowering tree. I approach it again, it became clearer, and I stand and watch the gate. The approach has five steps, the sixth is the threshold. The gatehouse has seven pillars, and seven windows. Its chandelier has ninety-nine levels, to which innumerable bright lights have been added. Even the grains of its sands are lovely, the rocks are gleaming. There is not enough ink to describe it in words, not enough pens to write it. Its name is the Perfection of Divine Sovereignty [*Kamalatul Uluhiyah*], its shade is called the Perfection of Humanity [*Kamalatul Insaniyah*]. (*The Teachings*, 261)

The above brings forth the strength to address, penetrate and formulate this dualism of truth. Mustapa proceeds by quoting the text uttered in ritual worship (*salat*) (the italicised text is in Arabic in Mustapa's text):

> I pause at the threshold, look above and look below. I feel it with my hands. It opens up as I recite: *May the peace of Allah be upon you.* Three times. No one answers. I then recite: *May the peace of Allah be upon you, Oh Prophet, and His mercy and blessings. May the peace of Allah be upon us and upon all His pious servants; then I praise His greatness: Allah is great! I turn my face to the One who rules the heavens and earth, and I am not one of the polytheists.* (*The Teachings*, 260-261)

At this moment there arises a consciousness of the duality of reality and a strong desire to open the veil of this duality of truth. The tendencies of the Devil leave one, but not for good. In Hasan Mustapa's scheme, the Devil is never completely out of the believer's life:

> At this point, the Devil complains: 'Aargh! We've been together for a long time, but now we are parting. Alright, if you resist my

> affections, that's okay! If you don't receive me here, perhaps you will do so there. He thinks I will not squeeze my way through. He thinks he will not pass through here again. That's okay, he thinks it will not affect him, for we are old friends, the wood might be rotten but it is still teak. No matter how vicious the tiger, she will not eat her offspring. I will certainly persist. Goodness, the time! Excuse me! Allow me to end this audience with Divine Mercy'. (*The Teachings*, 261)

**The station of Truthfulness (*Sidikiyah*)**

The station of Truthfulness is the stage after a subject has entered an integrated form of existence, where a distinction is no longer made between the spiritual and the physical. This is because the self is experienced as a complete whole. It is the state where the individual has used the dimension of his feelings – spiritual feelings, not physical ones. In *The Teachings*, this dimension of spiritual feelings is called the *rasa rahmaniyah* (feeling of compassion), which occurs simultaneous with the dimunition of physical perception. Symbolic perceptions gain significance in one's outlook: 'It turns out the gate is actually an allegory' (*The Teachings*, 263). Reality is made up of symbols, and emerges as a layered progression.

The station of Truthfulness constitutes the highest one before the final station, Oneness. It is the stage at which an individual is no longer under the pressure of the influence or power of the Devil. At this stage the various entrapments that appeared as the subject endeavoured to comprehend and move toward ultimate truth begin to be swept aside. Or at least he obtains clarity on why humans tend to be trapped within the poles he has himself made.

The station of Truthfulness commences with the awareness of being entrapped by text or symbols. The greetings and calls, made as a means of exposing the ultimate truth sought for up to this station, turn out to be made at the surface level, so that these calls do not get an answer, falling short of what is hoped for. 'Aeeh! Why does no one reply to my greeting?' This is followed by: 'It turns out the gate is actually an allegory' (*The Teachings*, 264). In other words, up till now it has only expressed the symbol of a symbol. And so the relation (the attempted greeting) is nothing more than a mere imaginary relation, a relation between oneself and a shadow or image within oneself regarding the shadow of something, rather than that 'something' itself. The knowledge or truth that is found is still centred on a recognition of the essence of characteristics and names, which are located behind the phenomena of the world. Names constitute a materialisation of characteristics, and characteristics are a materialisation of substance, and so on, 'The names are manifested by the attributes; the attribute is manifested by the essence' (*The Teachings*, 266).

At the station of Truthfulness, the diversification or distinction between the nature of *beauty* and *majesty* is problematised. This can be depicted in symbols:

> The ninety-nine levels of the chandeliers are actually the beautiful names [*asma ul-husna*], some of which are *beauty*, some of which are *majesty*, and some are *perfection* [*kamaliyah*], along with innumerable names of perfections. (*The Teachings*, 263)

One's identity (Arabic: *nafsiyah*, sense of self) is discovered in the relation or connectedness and confrontation with *Rahmaniyah* (God's Love) which 'we feel with our feeling, we sense with our senses' (*The Teachings*, 263). This happens in one's deepest feelings, feelings which are capable of touching the hidden (Arabic: *sirr*) secrets behind what can be seen, the essence.

This identity forms a basis upon which one's existence is established. Freedom, as the root for the formation of one's existence, finds space in the harmony between majesty and beauty. With this, borders have been done away with, because they have become an inseparable part of oneself. Discovering the truth within oneself means discovering the relation with others within oneself. And so one always finds one's own existence while being in a relationship within oneself via one's deepest feelings, and finds freedom in this relationship. The freedom and existence that are built on relationships are without borders of any empirical shape, but are built on an understanding that the whole of empirical appearances are an actualisation of the name and character of God.

The equivalence between beauty and majesty which is present in man's consciousness still signals the existence of a basic separation between the two. Hence there arise a number of expressions and unanswerable questions at this station, such as:

> In ignorance of what happened because of *ma'ani*, the nature of Divinity, I wanted to know this happening, but when it actually happened, I disregarded it. It is good to meet with its *essence*, but what is its *nature*? It is quite good to meet with its nature, but what are its names? It is quite good to meet a man, but what are his deeds? It is quite good to meet his deeds, but what is his name? But this is knowing the name before the actions, and then, after meeting the actions, asking where the person who did them is! When these are mixed, it is a long process. When we have learnt about the owner of the actions, we are going round in circles. When we will come across the traces of the Lord's *ma'ani*? (*The Teachings*, 265)

> Oh! I used to think that *beauty* was singular, and *majesty* was singular. But in fact, they operate in the same way on the same level. The moon shines in the night because of *beauty*; it does not shine

> at night because of *majesty* [...] How could I go so astray? How could I still be spending time distinguishing *beauty* and *majesty*? Allahness is beyond time and place; and don't the two things go together, not one before the other? Allah's names are manifested by the *attributes*; *attributes* are manifested by *essence*. If *attributes* are fixed in time; *ma'ani* has its beginning. If the *attributes* have an end, that means it is wandering aimlessly. Perfection cannot be given an end or beginning, or else we turn to something other than Allah. (*The Teachings*, 266)

In this way the equivalence and unity of *beauty* and *majesty* have not yet found their exact 'formulation'. This is because we find there is still an opposition within ourselves in relation to our comprehension of the significance of the facts, including ourselves. Hasan Mustapa uses a Sundanese idiom to describe this situation: 'a battle in captivity is a war with no end' (*The Teachings*, 267). There is still a dispute that is hard to settle, between what is in our understanding and the facts that we experience.

**The station of Oneness (*Kurbah*)**

The station of Oneness is the final stage on the path toward the level of the Perfect Man. Hasan Mustapa states that the station of Oneness is where: 'Words come to an end, because of such closeness, we possess things as one, I with God am one skin and one flesh, for ever and ever' (*The Seven Grades*, Rosidi 1989: 294). In the context of Islamic mysticism, specifically *Wujudiyah* (existential) mysticism, the words 'of one skin, of one flesh' have frequently caused great sensitivity. This is because these terms are often understood to point to pantheism. By using these words, Hasan Mustapa's pantheist orientation is revealed. This is because with the words 'of one skin, of one flesh' there arises the thought or conclusion that man and God share one body, one essence and one substance.

Such an assumption becomes all the firmer when we look at the first page of this final stage:

> Where did your *ma'ani* go? Because these are mine. Where are your *attributes*? Because these are mine. Where are your *af'al*? Because this is mine [...] I vanish, pushed aside by *Divinity*, He disappears, pushed aside by *servitude*; He cannot be called I because He is He, I cannot be called He because I am myself, He cannot properly be called I because he cannot be pushed aside by *ma'ani*, and I cannot be called Him because I am experiencing *majesty*. (*The Teachings*, 269)

This state produces a disturbing confusion within one's human (Arabic: *Insaniyah, Ubudiyah*) consciousness, putting the subject into a state of ambiguity: 'I stand in silent relection, it does not feel like day, it does not feel like night, neither hot nor cold, neither sunny nor shady, neither bright nor dark, neither low nor high, neither I nor Him' (*The Teachings,* 269). Once again, mankind has a tendency to experience an 'in-between condition', which is expressed in the form of confusion.

In this way, the station of Oneness is introduced with the experience of an ambiguity of positioning between human nature and the divine. More than that, there is a lack of clarity in the ontological position between the servant and the Divine.

Hasan Mustapa offers a preliminary solution: 'Do not forget our beginnings. *Divinity* is the origin of *lordship*, *servitude* was my name since childhood' (*The Teachings*, 269). Hasan Mustapa says that truth and ultimate reality will only be found in two scenarios. The first emerges when man has arrived at an awareness of himself as a servant and has discovered his epistemological position and his own ontological position as a servant. This awareness and position are described with the degree of *Servitude*. Hasan Mustapa states:

> The only sign that we can take as proof of the perfection of our status in *servitude* is our wholeness beside our original creation, these can't be mixed up but must stay firm, and then we will know our status is not wrong [...] solid and stable in perfect balance. (*The Teachings*, 270).

The second occurs when a human has become capable of setting up communication that makes it possible for one to receive the truth on one's own. The truth is not sought but is received. Man's readiness to receive it is brought about by two factors, 1) feeling oneself, ontologically, to be an integral part of that very truth, because within man there is found the nature (*wawatek*) of knowledge; and 2) man has become aware of his shortcomings (Arabic: *iftiqor*), to the extent that he longs to find and receive the truth, the truth which is radiated from the knowledge of the Love of God (*Rahmaniyah*), by means of opening himself (his heart).

In his description of the station of Oneness, Mustapa locates the subject once more in the human lifecycle that has been his dominant reference point throughout the entire work:

> Before we were not sharing together, but now we share together, in the past we did not share our ups and downs, but now we do so. Nowadays, I do not wait to be told by the old people first, for what will be favourable to God will be favourable to me, and what is unwelcome to God will be so to me also, even though I will not have made a complaint beforehand [...] In the past, I turned from my mother to my father, or turned from my father to my mother, but as time passed I consulted at their graves, as further time passed I asked for something from their Allah, and as further time passed I simply arrived at their Allah. (*The Teachings*, 269)

Translated by Stuart Robson

## Sources cited

Ali, Yunasril

1997 *Manusia Citra Ilahi: Pengembangan Konsep Insan Kamil Ibn al-'Arabi oleh al-Jili*. Jakarta: Paramadina.

Moestapa, Hasan

1955 *Gendingan dangding Sunda: Parasaan birahi djeung wirahmana, Djilid ka 1, tjitakan ka-II*. Bandung: Panitya Jajasan Galih Pakuan.

Rosidi, Ajip

1989 *Haji Hasan Mustapa jeung karya-karyana*. Bandung: Pustaka.

*Chapter 4*

# THE DOCTRINE OF THE SEVEN GRADES IN HASAN MUSTAPA'S VERSE

Jajang A. Rohmana

This essay discusses Mustapa's literary treatments of an Islamic concept that is central to his sufi vision, namely the doctrine of the Seven Grades. This has been a popular theme in the scholarly tradition of Nusantara Islam, and is encountered in Islamic manuscripts produced in diverse locations including Aceh, Palembang, Buton, Java, West Java, and Banjar. The doctrine is a pivotal theme in almost the entirety of Mustapa's verse, and without having some familiarity with it, one would most likely face difficulty in interpreting the range of metaphors and figures through which he expresses his spiritual vision. Mustapa's poetic constructions frequently draw on a scholarly and technical vocabulary not known to non-specialists, and this explains in part why his works are not well known to many Sundanese. It also explains why Millie confessed to inadequacy in his understanding of Mustapa's world, and to 'scratching his head' when confronting his verses (Millie 2014: 110-11).

The doctrine is encountered in many works belonging to Mustapa's corpus, and he produced a longish work that dealt solely with it entitled *The Original Teaching of the Seven Grades*. This work is not a detailed and comprehensive treatise on the subject. It is a compilation of brief, highly creative commentaries by Mustapa about the doctrine, and was probably put into writing by Wangsaatmadja, Mustapa's secretary, based on Mustapa's notes or sermons. The work is preserved in one of the copies of Mustapa's work made by Wangsaatmadja (Moestapa no date), and is reproduced in part in Rosidi's compilation (Rosidi 1989: 291-309), under the shorter title of *The Seven Grades*.

One of the notable aspects of Mustapa's poetry was the way he expressed the Seven Grades in specifically Sundanese forms. Most of Mustapa's verse is an expression of his inner feeling, and the combination of this Islamic doctrine with Sundanese language and culture provided the tools for this expression. This is not strange in the traditions of Archipelagic sufism: symbolic language and sufistic concepts are the natural vehicles for the human expression of closeness to God, and like Hamzah Fansuri (d. 1527) in the Malay language, and Ranggawarsita (d. 1873) in Javanese, Mustapa gave material form to his feelings through Sundanese genres.

In what follows, I read Mustapa's adaptation of the Seven Grades as confirmation of a hypothesis first presented in detail by Johns (1965) and later confirmed more generally by Azra (2004) about the role of scholarly sufi networks in the Islamisation of Southeast Asia. The hypothesis, in its detailed form, concerned the influence on the Islamic traditions of the Archipelago of a short work written originally in Arabic around 1590 entitled *The Gift Addressed to the Spirit of the Prophet*, hereafter referred to as *The Gift* (Johns 1965). The author was the Gujerati scholar Muhammad ibn Fadhlillah Al-Burhanpuri (1545-1620).

Johns argued that this work is a 'doctrinal watershed to which virtually everything subsequent [in the Sufi thought of the Indonesian archipelago] can be referred' (Johns 1965: 8). I am not the first to study the influence of this work in West Java: Christomy has already demonstrated Al-Burhanpuri's influence on sufi tradition in West Java by exploring the metaphysical doctrine of the *Syattariyah* order in Pamijahan, where Sheikh Abdul Muhyi (1640-1715) developed and taught the doctrine (Christomy 2008). Jahroni has briefly discussed *The Original Teaching of the Seven Grades* (Jahroni 1999). In this chapter, I wish to locate Mustapa in a chain of Archipelagic interpreters of the Seven Grades Doctrine, focussing on a number of his works in verse and prose.

**The Seven Grades in the Archipelago**

The Seven Grades is an attempt to resolve the philosophical problem of the relations between the Absolute and the relative, between Singularity and multiplicity. It has its roots in the denial of the doctrine of 'creation from nothingness' (Latin: *creatio ex nihilo,* Arabic: *al-khalq min al-'adam*) (Nasution 1973: 22-23). The followers of philosophical sufism challenged this by proposing the theory of God's 'manifestations' (*tajalli*). This theory saw creation as emanating from the essence of the Creator. God creates beings as objects of His love. These creations do not come from nothingness, but emerge through the determinations of His attributes concerning His own essence, with the result that creation is a manifestation of the Creator. The creations appear in a hierarchy of realities consisting of seven levels, which are named the Seven Grades.

Al-Burhanpuri was the pioneer of this teaching, and *The Gift* found an appreciative audience in the Archipelago. As I explain below, it was prominently circulated within the circles of the *Syattariyah tariqah* (sufi order) (Kraus 2010). According to Yunasril Ali (1997: 129), the work was an abbreviated explanation of the voluminous metaphysical teachings of Ibn 'Arabi (1165-1240) and Al-Jili (born 1365/6) about the emanations, and was an attempt to reign in the extremist inclinations of a number of Indian mystical groups, and to formalise the teachings as practically valuable texts about the basic teachings of Islam. In other words, *The Gift* can be regarded as a representation of orthodox sufi teachings (Suryaningsih 2013). This is demonstrated in Al-Burhanpuri's description of his own treatise as 'mystical reality brought into harmony with the shariah'. In this characterisation, he clarifies his position as a scholar making a reconciliation between sufism and Shariah (Johns 1965: 14).

The table below presents a brief scheme of the Seven Grades doctrine. The left column gives the Arabic terms for the seven grades. Nusantara scholars have in most cases continued to use these Arabic terms in their writings on the doctrine. The definitions in the right column are extracted from Voorhoeve's translation of *The Gift*, published in Johns (1965):

**Table 1: The doctrine of the Seven Grades**

| The Seven Grades | Definitions from Voorhoeve's translation of Al-Burhanpuri's *The Gift* (Johns 1965: 140-141). |
|---|---|
| 1 Ahadiyah | Innermost essence of Almighty God. |
| 2 Wahdah | The first determination, which signifies God's knowledge of His essence, attributes and existents as a generality. This grade is also the Reality that is Muhammad. |
| 3 Wahidiyah | The second determination signifies God's knowledge of His essence, attributes and all existents in their particularity. This is the grade of the reality that is Man. |

| | |
|---|---|
| 4 Alam Arwah | World of spirits. |
| 5 Alam Mithal | World of ideas. |
| 6 Alam Ajsam | World of bodies. |
| 7 Insan Kamil | The manifestation of all the above as the Perfect Man. |

The popularity of *The Gift* and the Seven Grades in the Archipelago has its origins in the Jawi community. This term was used in the Arab Peninsula to describe the students from the Archipelago seeking Islamic knowledge in the holy cities of Mecca and Medina. Long after Al-Burhanpuri, in the 1870s, Mustapa would become a member of this community. *The Gift* arrived in the Archipelago after Acehnese members of the Jawi community made contact with Gujarati followers of the *Syattariyah* sufi order in Medina in the 17th century (Kraus 2010: 212). The first nameable scholar of the Archipelago to adapt the Seven Grades doctrine was Shamsuddin Al-Sumatra'i (1550-1630), who studied the doctrine after receiving a copy of *The Gift* that was sent to Aceh from India (see Kraus 2010, Johns 1975, 2009).

The Seven Grades doctrine was the subject of communications between authoritative teachers in the Holy Land and Sumatra. Two names have special importance in this regard, namely Ibrahim Al-Kurani (1616-1690) and Abdurrauf bin Ali Al-Jawi, also known as Al-Sinkili (1615-1693). Both are associated with the *Syattariyah* sufi order (Kraus 2010).

Al-Kurani was born in Shahrazur, a town in present Iraqi Kurdistan, near the border with Iran, and became a noted teacher in Medina. Although he never went to Southeast Asia, he taught many students from the Archipelago. He has special meaning for this discussion because around 1665 he wrote an important commentary in Arabic on *The Gift* entitled *The Bestowal dedicated to one of discriminating intelligence in explanation of the 'Gift addressed to the spirit of the prophet'*. This was written in response to a request from the Jawi community in the Hijaz, who were concerned about a controversy surrounding the Unity of Being and Seven Grades doctrines that had broken out in Aceh (Fathurahman 2011). His interpretation of the doctrines reconciled heterodox sufi interpretations that had been considered as deviations from the shariah.

The second name, Abdurrauf Al-Sinkili, is significant because this Acehnese scholar was a conduit for the later movement of the Seven Grades doctrine into West Java. This occurred through the network of the *Syattariyah* sufi order. His name features in almost all *Syattariyah* genealogies in the Archipelago (Fathurahman 2016). Students of his are recorded in Sumatra, Java, Sulawesi and even in the Malay Peninusla (Trengganu). Amongst his students was Sheikh Abdul Muhyi (1640-1715) of Pamijahan, West Java. This man has been the most influential *Syattariyah* figure on the island of Java, and brought the Seven Grades doctrine into the environment in which Mustapa was active.

It is important to note that the milieu of the sufi orders was not the only space in which the Seven Grades doctrine was cultivated in Java. The teaching spread into other genres, such as the Javanese palace literature of the 18th and 19th centuries (Zoetmulder 1991). The famous *Book of Centini* reveals harmonious blends of traditional Javanese mysticism with more textually canonical Islamic forms (Soebardi 1971). These are examples of what Ricklefs called 'the mystic synthesis'. In representing the Seven Grades doctrine, the writer of the *Book of Centini* adopted the Hindu-Javanese metaphor of the relationship of Wisnu and Kresna, thereby representing an identity that was at once Muslim and Javanese (Ricklefs 2013: 36-7). This tendency to mystical synthesis is apparent also in the *Book of Cebolek* and *The Book of Dewa Ruci* (Soebardi 1975). The *Wirid Hidayat Jati* (Prayer for True Guidance) of Ronggowarsito also displays the influence of the Seven Grades, blending the doctrine with Javanese tradition such as the narrative of *Dewa Ruci* (Simuh 1988, 1992). A verse associated with the Javanese saint Sunan Bonang, named the *Suluk Wujil* (Mystical Path of Wujil), adapts the Seven Grades doctrine alongside a number of other mystical concepts (Drewes 1968).

The Sundanese also appropriated the Seven Grades, expressing it in didactic forms. In the Priangan of the 20th century, the doctrine of the Seven Grades circulated in the form of the *wawacan*, the verse narrative made up of *dangding* verses [ed.: For definitions of these literary terms, see the Chapter by Setiawan]. Its imprint may be found in a number of Sundanese verse works, an example being the didactic *Poem for Muslims, male and female* (*Wawacan Muslimin-Muslimat*) (Sudibjo and Sudjana 1985).

**Mustapa and the Sufi Tradition**

In his journey of acquiring Islamic knowledge in Java and Arabia, Mustapa studied with teachers who were influential within a range of sufi orders. One was the *Qadiriyah* and its variant, the *Naqsyabandiyah*/Qadiriyyah. In his hometown of Garut, he studied with Muhammad of Cibunut, whom he later identified as a Qadiriyyah teacher (Wangsaatmadja 1932: 57). The *Naqsyabandiyah* order was another: in Mecca Mustapa studied with central figures in Archipelagic *Naqsyabandiyah* genealogies, Abdullah Al-Zawawi and Abdulhamid Daghastani (Bruinessen 1992: 72-73; Laffan 2011: 186). Mustapa also studied with the Madurese scholar Halil Bangkalan, known as a *Naqsyabandiyah* guru.

The sufi order with which he seemed to have the closest association was the *Syattariyah*. Amongst the manuscripts sent by Mustapa to his patron Snouck Hurgronje, *Syattariyah* tracts were very prominent (Laffan 2008; Ekadjati 1988: 231-2), and some of the Dutchman's writings show very clear knowledge of *Syattariyah* practice, which he must have obtained from Mustapa (Laffan 2011: 155-156). This order is mentioned a number of times in Snouck's writings, such as the reference he makes to '*Syattariyah* secrets' in his Qur'anic commentary (Rosidi 1989: 428). Most importantly, Mustapa appears as a link in a number of *Syattariyah* genealogies. One example is contained in a manuscript from Pamijahan, in which the *Penghulu* (government-appointed Islamic official) of Bandung is mentioned as the successor of Abdul Muhyi through Haji Abdullah (Christomy 2001: 74, 82; 2008: 105). In another version, Mustapa is connected with Raden Kartinagara or Abdullah Saleh (died around 1911/1919), the editor of the *History of Sukapura*. This man was a fifth-generation *tariqah* teacher after Abdul Muhyi and the Bupati of Sukapura, Anggadipa III (also known as Dalem Sawidak) (Hermansoemantri 1979: 93-96, 823).

**The Seven Grades in Mustapa's verse**

The sufi literature of the Sundanese developed with the spread of Islam commencing after the defeat of the Sundanese Kingdom in 1579. The process of Islamisation occurred through the port cities of Banten and Cirebon, both of which were outposts of the Javanese Mataram Kingdom, and Sundanese Islamic writing was influenced heavily by Javanese models. The early works encountered in the Sundanese verse forms were originally Javanese. The language of *dangding* (versification) became the sign of a well-educated Sundanese person who had absorbed the influence of Javanese culture. The themes covered in *dangding* verses were wide and varied, including narratives (especially romances) and religious expositions (Danasasmita 2001: 171-2). Like the Javanese genres on which they were modelled, the Sundanese forms were commonly performed in melody (Rosidi 2010: 30-1, 194).

Mustapa created a vast body of sufi verse in the Sundanese language. Much of this dealt explicitly with the Seven Grades. He presented a concise definition of the doctrine in one of his verses, *Pucung: The unlucky monkey climbs onto the bishop-wood fence*:[1]

| | | |
|---|---|---|
| 34. | *Alam tudjuh nu tilu bagian itu*<br>*Ahadiat wahdat wahidiat kabéh*<br>*Lamun nelah di aing ngan bobodoan* | The seven worlds include these three:<br>*Ahadiyah, wahdah, wahidiyah.*<br>If they appear in me, I am lying. |
| 35. | *Anu opat bagian aja di mahluk*<br>*Njawa misal djasmani insanan kabéh*<br>*Lebah dieu lahir njembah kabatinan* | The four others are found in creation:<br>*Nyawa, mithal, jasmani, insan.*<br>Here one's inner worship becomes manifest. |

From: *Pucung: The unlucky monkey climbs onto the bishop-wood fence* (Mustapa 1976: 183)

The names of the Seven Grades[2] are the same as those used by Al-Burhanpuri, reflecting Mustapa's location in the scholarly genealogy commencing from the famous Gujerati (see Johns 1965). The first

1 Mustapa's verses are conventionally given titles that consist of two components, the first being the poetic pattern of the stanzas (Sund. *Pupuh*, such as *pucung*, *sinom* and *kinanti*), and the second being the first line of the opening stanza.

2 The word *nyawa* in verse 35 means soul, spirit, and is a synonym for the Arabic term *arwah* (spirits) that Mustapa elsewhere uses to name the fouth grade.

three grades are in God, the remaining four are in creation. The three first manifestations of God have the character of *qadim* (Arabic: not created, pre-existing), while the reality of the servant is *muhdath* (Arabic: created, an occurrence) (Santrie 1992: 114). The doctrine commences from the assumption that God is an Absolute Reality. He manifests in the world of appearances through seven levels of 'emanation'. *Ahadiyah*, *wahdah*, and *wahidiyah* are three states without external reality, while the remaining four (*arwah/nyawa, mithal, ajsam/jasmani, insan kamil*) appear in external forms (Johns 1965: 7).

Mustapa adapted this teaching as a basis for developing gradations of spirituality. He interpreted the seven grades, often calling them 'worlds' (Arabic: *'alam*), as grades of sufistic spirituality. As is characteristic of Mustapa's work, the human subject is involved in this scheme through feeling. He concisely defined the feelings of the Muslim when they are present at each of the grades, and for Mustapa, those feelings convey the character or nature of each grade:

> The nature of *Ahadiyah* is: to feel oneness, although in essence it is many forms, the feeling is of oneness;
> The nature of *Wahdah* is: feeling upon feeling, the result is a feeling of floating, two are counted as one, two bodies are felt as one;
> The nature of *Wahidiyah* is: multiplicity is felt, but the feeling is one of singularity, as a result we count spirits, though many they are felt as one;
> The nature of *Arwah* is: it has many bodies but one feeling, and is affirmed by its body, it has many bodies but only one feeling;
> The nature of *Mithal* is: many bodies but one form, for they originate in the same world;

> The nature of *Ajsam* is: it is felt as if one, the influence of
> Ahadiyat, five natures reside in one body;
> The nature of *Insan* is: there is neither high nor low, it belongs to
> all, but the difference is how one receives it.
>
> (From *The Seven Grades*, Rosidi 1989: 308)

Mustapa extends the doctrine of the Seven Grades, adding to it the figure of the searcher. He represents metaphysical being as something that descends from God to creations, and identifies this process as the same one in which the sufi searches for authentic spiritual grades in a process of ascending (*taraqqi*). The comparison with his *Teachings of Our Islamic Inheritance* is important here, for in that work he develops the seven grades as stages in a spiritual trajectory that he adapted from Al-Jili. Mustapa describes the phases as Submission, Belief, Virtue, Goodness, Witnessing, Truthfulness, Oneness (see the translation in this volume and analysis by Ahmad Gibson al-Bustomi). In fact, these stages are developments of the Seven Grades. If the Seven Grades are emanations from God, descending through the trajectory of the perfect man as the image of God, then the stages in *The Teachings* form the human journey, ascending towards the achievement of the perfect man (Ali 1997: 144-5). Mustapa seems to creatively play with the Seven Grades as a process of descending and ascending, as befits the pattern of a cyclical spiritual journey. It becomes a journey of the created being – the self – striving to return to its authentic origin by manifesting the image of God on the earth:

> *Ahadiyah* is unification, having neither past nor future, without form, with no substance that can be inferred from the unseen, one meditates on it to find its external form, as a resource when one is

in need, helped by the knowledge of people more diligent, and as a result seeks to dominate, and will never have sufficiency.

*Wahdah* unites the servant and Master, the servants in fact belong to the Master, while their Master is *Ahadiyah*, an unseen force they seek benefit from, and the servant never emerges from servitude to those who have received the majesty of the Master, which he can only feel with His help.

*Wahidiyah* is the unification of bodies, I am a servant and my friend is a servant, this is the essence of Muhammad, whoever has received the spirit of Muhammad, then that person is our better, and so humans enter the Seven Grades, Allah's oneness, the singularity of Muhammad, the oneness of servitude, of serving the oneness of Allah.

*Arwah* is unification of the spirit world and the body that serves it, every perfection has sufficiency in its worldly form, and as a result we praise the perfect One, and praise the idea of Oneness, and perhaps we will find perfection in spirit, and leave a legacy of nobleness.

*Mithal* is the unification of the excellent one with the Master, when the physical body worships the physical body, the spirit worships the spirit.

*Ajsam* is the unification of the body, with the essence of Muhammad, giving service to *mithal*, as a result there is never sufficiency, its mastery is like service to one's feelings, and dissolves into desire, and cannot be aware of its own existence.

*Insan Kamil* is perfection without flaw, for it searches by itself with the help of *Ahadiyah*, and finds majesty in its suffering.

(From *The Seven Grades*, Rosidi 1989: 309).

Like Al-Burhanpuri, Mustapa was an orthodox interpreter of concepts about the metaphysics of being. In His view, the Seven Grades meant an inner spiritual search carried out through a framework of metaphors and symbols. Mustapa never denied the existence of this outer reality, but considers that it could not be separated from God and as very dependent on Him. For this reason, Mustapa cannot be considered amongst the extreme followers of the Unity of Being doctrine. Like many scholars writing in the field of mysticism, however, he had critics who took issue with misunderstandings of his ideas. He responded to them in the book *The fulfilment of the promise dealing with the extinction of the thunder* (Cod. Or. 7205), which was written in response to a critical letter addressed to him by Sayyid 'Uthman in 1902. This Batavia-based scholar called Mustapa the 'Devil of Bandung' (Rosidi 1989: 434, 494; Kaptein 2014: 191-2). Mustapa was accused of deviating from the Shariah. Mustapa discussed this experience in his verse entitled *Sinom: The teachings of Runcangkundang*, denying the accusation that he was a disbeliever and heretic by expressing his affection for the Shariah – and specifically the ritual worship (*salat*) – for as long as he could remember (Mustapa 1960: 53):

| | |
|---|---|
| *Bédja madjarkeun kaula* | There was talk that I |
| *geus leungit élmuning santri* | had lost my scholarly knowledge |
| *geus ngaruksakkeun agama* | and had harmed the religion, |
| *djadi kapir djadi djindik* | becoming a disbeliever and freethinker, |
| *djindikna djadi mungkir* | a freethinker and denier |
| *kana tutur lampah rasul* | of the Messenger's traditions |
| *kana salat puasa* | of worship and fasting. |
| *ana malik kula njeri* | But in fact I was upset |
| *kahuruan ngadjawab djeung handaruan* | and was moved to respond with ardour. |
| *Handaruan djeung susumbar* | My ardour was defiant: |
| *aéh naha kitu teuing* | How did it get to this? |
| *kitu kutan kitu kutan* | Why is this happening? |
| *nu palid tinggaleun palid* | Let bygones be bygones! |

| | |
|---|---|
| *palidna nja pribadi* | But it was my self that was carried away, |
| *geus ngalun ka alun-alun* | flowing down to the town square. |
| *alunan nu sampurna* | The perfect flow |
| *malik ka bagdjaning diri* | is the return of the self to happiness, |
| *aduh biang kasampurnaning sambéang* | Oh Mother! to the perfection of worship |
| *Sambéang mustika urang* | Worship is our jewel |
| *kabeuki ti barang éling* | and has been since I can remember. |
| *baheula djadi kalangkang* | At first it was just a shadow, |
| *geusan mihajang miéling* | a place of desire and memory. |
| *éling-éling geus éling* | But now that remembering is over |
| *singhoréng tungguling tangtung* | it has become the trunk of existence, |
| *tangtung geusan rumingkang* | a place to exist and pass through, |
| *djadi kabeuki aing* | and has become something I love. |
| *aing sirna bagdja teu tjara saria.* | Unlike in the past, I now vanish in joy. |

From *Sinom: The teachings of Runcangkundang* (Mustapa 1960: 53)

Like other Sunni Sufis, Mustapa emphasised a reconciliatory sufism focussed on the mysteries of a God who can only be known through His creations. The same can be seen in the work of Hamzah Fansuri (Al-Attas 1970; Steenbrink 1995: 84). For this reason, in many of his verses, Mustapa uses a cluster of symbols and metaphors that enable him to distinguish between the self and God, even though they cannot be separated. He distinguishes the areca palm's sugar from its fruit, the bamboo shoot from the bamboo, bamboo from its multiplicity of varieties, the bamboo from the bamboo musical instrument known as *angklung*, the young coconut from the shoot that grows out of the ripe coconut, the husked rice from the unhusked, the sprout from the seed, the jackfruit from its bud, the chicken from the egg, the frog from the tadpole and so on (Rohmana 2013: 325-75). This distinction of the Creator from the created is a general characteristic of the Nusantara Sufis of the 17th and 18th centuries, who also tended towards reconciliatory sufism.

This separation of Creator from created also characterises Mustapa's symbolic representation of the Unity of Being doctrine.

This emerged in his portrayal of the meeting between humanity (*nasut*) and Divinity (*lahut*) in the human self. The mystical path (*suluk*) is a journey of unknowable distance between these two points. Mustapa portrayed this quest as one from bamboo to *angklung*, from existence to the ego, from south to north, from east to west, and from non-existence to existence. This is a return to the place from whence one originally set out. One feels one is returning to a place one has already visited. It is a cycle, from *ahadiyah* to the Perfect Man, from the Perfect Man to *ahadiyah*.

The process of becoming human originates from God, and necessitates a return to God. The subject must experience unification of existence (Unity of Being) so that it can radiate the gem of His being, revealing His greatness, and bearing forth the Divine attributes. This is the search for humanity and Divinity. Its paradoxical logic is between form and essence: aspects of humanity are found in the Divinity, and vice versa (Jahroni 1999: 62-3).

**Arriving at the point of departure**

Like Ibn 'Arabi, Al-Jili, Al-Burhanpuri and the Nusantara scholars of the 17th century in general, Mustapa tended to interpret the Seven Grades not merely as a synthesis of the Divine emanations, but also as the human quest to improve their spiritual level in the direction of an authentic spiritual essence. The gradations of metaphysical being reflect the process through which the secrets of His love and His existence are revealed. The perfect man represents the final level of this search, arrival at the inner secret of God (Arabic: *al-insan al-sirri*). For this reason, the perfect man of humanity can achieve perfection when through his own knowledge of himself he is able to achieve the Divine knowledge and understand from where he originates and to where he will return. He is at the point of return at which thinking about God has passed over a number of levels towards material form, and has now returned to His Absoluteness (Johns 1965: 7). Mustapa revealed this process of returning in a short verse entitled *Kinanti: The Seven Grades of the Essence of Muhammad*:

| | |
|---|---|
| *Asal gé balung sabalung* | From the very beginning I was of one bone. |
| *asal gé daging sadaging* | From the very beginning I was of one flesh. |
| *asal sungsuam sungsuam* | From the very beginning I was of one marrow. |
| *asal gé getih sagetih* | From the very beginning I was of one blood. |
| *kuma kasonoanana* | It depends on one's yearning |
| *ka nu hiji ti sasari.* | for oneness, something that is common. |
| *Asal gé hayun sahayun* | From the very beginning I was of one life. |
| *asal gé hurip sahurip* | From the very beginning I was of one happiness. |
| *asal gé hayat sahayat* | From the very beginning I was of one existence. |
| *asal gé jati sajati* | From the very beginning I was of one realness. |
| *kuma kasonoanana* | It depends on one's yearning. |
| *asal lautan sahiji* | In the beginning I was of one nature. |

From *Kinanti: The Seven Grades of the Essence of Muhammad* (Rosidi 1989: 307-8)

In these verses, Mustapa attempts to express his feelings upon returning to an originating authenticity in the world of inner spirituality. He uses metaphors for the body to recall this awareness. He is aware that he originated in the Absolute, of one bone, one flesh, one marrow and one blood. This is a metaphor for a unity which cannot be separated. He moves to a feeling of disappearing in domination by God, and expresses this situation as 'one life', which also expresses his original state of being in one breath and one spirit with the Absolute. The closing metaphor – in the beginning I was of one nature – conveys his awareness that his origins have their source in the Supreme One.

Mustapa describes the feeling of 'returning to the origin of one's authentic self' in the world of *Ahadiyah* frequently in his verse and prose. Mustapa interpreted 'returning to the point of departure' as the highest point of the cycle by which a human becomes aware of their authentic self. This is the feeling of the perfect man when he returns to the world of *Ahadiyah*. Millie called it 'arriving at the point of departing' (Millie 2014: 110-111):

*Ngalantung méméh ngalantung*
*ngalinjing méméh ngalinjing*
*néangan méméh néangan*
*nepi ka méméhna indit*
*datang saméméhna iang*
*indit saméméh mimiti.*

Strolling before going for a stroll.
Nervously pacing before nervously pacing.
Searching before going on a search.
Arriving at the point of departure.
Getting there before leaving.
Departing before setting out.

From: *The quail laments in its cage*, (Rosidi 1989: 98)

This stanza is one of Mustapa's most striking expressions of his Islamic outlook. As noted, the cycle of the Seven Grades is something that descends upon the seeker (Arabic: *tanazul*). Through the feeling that results from this, the Muslim experiences this descent as an upwards quest (Arabic: *taraqqi*). On arriving, Mustapa expresses the realisation that his quest had already started, in Divinity, even before he was aware of setting out on the journey of feeling. The following prose excerpt is the reflection of the Muslim arriving at their authentic self, which is found at a point he has already inhabited before setting out:

> We have reversed this qiblat so that the followers of Allah's messenger be known: the heart returns to its origin and can be said to return to the place from which it departed. Hence the expression: From here it emerges, over there it recedes.
>
> From *The Noble Qur'an* (Rosidi 1989:398-399)

This excerpt is interesting because it shows Mustapa overlaying his concept of returning onto canonical Islamic historical materials. It comes from the compilation of Mustapa's brief Qur'anic commentaries. This one specifically focusses on verse 144 of the second chapter (*The Cow*), which describes the change of the location of the qiblat for ritual prayer.[3] The verse states Allah's intention to move the qiblat from its site at Jerusalem to Mecca, regarded as the original site of the Abrahamic revelation. Mustapa overlays the return of the qiblat to its place of origin with the spiritual return of Muhammad to his authentic prophecy. Historically, the verse concerned was revealed when Muhammad was more than forty years old, an age that reflects a certain spiritual maturity through which a human is aware of his origin.

In the verse entitled *Sinom: Jump to the entrance-hall of homecoming!* Mustapa gave a further twist to the concept of 'returning to one's point of departure', suggesting a continuation to an eighth stage beyond the Seven Grades:

| | |
|---|---|
| *Pakandangan sasampalan* | Enclosed in the pasture |
| *munding mareuting di munding* | the buffalo spend their night. |
| *sirna pangawulan rasa* | What disappears is our servitude |
| *rasaning pirbadi aing* | to the feeling of individuality. |
| *aing kari nunggeling* | The self is left alone, |
| *geus ripuh di alam tujuh* | fatigued in the seven worlds, |
| *kadalapan ayeuna* | and is now in the eighth, |
| *indit mawa geusan balik* | setting out to the place of return, |
| *kadalapan ngalayang di pamulangan* | the eighth floats over the homecoming. |

From *Sinom: Jump to the entrance-hall of homecoming!* (Cod. Or. 7876b: 6)

In this stanza, Mustapa's reflection on returning to one's origins after a period of wandering is brought together with the Sundanese expression 'The buffalo returns to its enclosure', meaning that it is human nature to return to the place where one belongs. After passing through the seven worlds, the eighth is the place of return. The buffalo

3 The first qiblat towards which Muslims prayed was in Jerusalem. The key part of the verse reads: We have seen the turning of thy face to heaven (for guidance, O Muhammad). And now verily We shall make thee turn (in prayer) toward a *qiblah* which is dear to thee. So turn thy face to the Inviolable Place of Worship [the Sacred Mosque in Mecca], and ye (O Muslims) wheresoever ye may be, turn your faces (when ye pray) toward it.' (Al-Baqarah 2: 144)

has its place of origin in its pasture, and spends its nights there with its fellow buffalos. In the external world, the return of a human is made to its place of birth. In the dimension of authentic feeling, the human returns to God. At this point it experiences the *disappearance of the mastery of feeling* within its own self. God melts with feeling, and feeling with its object (God). God's self remains alone. Mustapa expresses fatigue at having passed through the seven gradations, and returns to home in the eighth, feeling as if he is floating in the world of returning.

**Metaphors for the Seven Grades**

I have already mentioned a number of metaphors Mustapa employs in his exploration of the Seven Grades, but in fact these are only an initial glimpse of the creativity involved in his linguistic treatments of the doctrine. In the verse below from *Kinanti of the one standing resolute in authenticity*, Mustapa asserts that the Seven Grades of the spiritual world cannot be separated one from the other. He borrows the metaphor of the Sundanese food known as *rujak* to express the mixing and blending of the seven grades within the self. Enjoyment of the Seven Grades is like enjoyment of the *rujak*, according to Mustapa. The *rujak* consists of a blend of various tropical fruits with chili and spices added according to taste. Sundanese people enjoy it most around midday after eating a midday meal. Mustapa likens this to the Seven Grades, which are enjoyed by those of good moral character:

| | |
|---|---|
| *Tepi ka martabat tujuh* | On arriving at the Seven Grades |
| *Diracik dirucak-racik* | they are thoroughly mixed together, |
| *Rujak lada sambarana* | like a *rujak* enhanced by its spices. |
| *Dahareun geus sisip budi* | Food for those who lack insight, |
| *Gahar di tengah poena* | fresh when eaten at midday |
| *Walagri tepi ka burit.* | it sustains until twilight. |

From the *Kinanti of the one standing resolute in authenticity* (Iskandarwassid et.al 1987: 38)

*The Original Teaching of the Seven Grades* contains a short verse work entitled *Kinanti: The Seven Grades Explained* (Moestapa no date: 66-7; Rosidi 1989: 307-308) in which Mustapa further explains the mixing and gathering of the Seven Grades. Being inter-related, they all inhere in the Perfect Man, a process which involves no loss of any of the Grades. It is up to the seeker whether he is capable of blending them together in order to achieve the level of the Perfect Man. The process of searching is not an easy one:

| | |
|---|---|
| *Kacatur martabat tujuh*<br>*tujuhna dipiriwinci*<br>*teu karasa ngarujakna*<br>*marukan di hiji-hiji*<br>*hiji misah ti kadua*<br>*unggal hiji taya bukti.* | Here are the Seven Grades explained:<br>When broken down there are seven<br>but like *rujak*, their mixing is not felt.<br>People talk of them individually,<br>of one as opposed to another,<br>but they leave no trace separately. |
| *Puguh katujuhna bukur*<br>*bukur hiji kuma hiji*<br>*dirujak jadi manusa*<br>*sahiji asaling jati*<br>*jati di rasa pangrasa*<br>*mukti teu kurang teu leuwih.* | All seven are clearly topics,<br>to be treated one by one,<br>but together, like *rujak*, form a human<br>from one authentic source,<br>the true feeling of feeling<br>of neither excess nor shortage. |
| *Leuwih matak langguk tangtung*<br>*kurang matak kurunyinyi*<br>*rasa nyiar pamuntangan*<br>*tandaning henteu walagri*<br>*tacan sirna lalugina*<br>*sulit ati taya budi.* | Excess causes elation,<br>shortage makes one languish,<br>feeling searches for something to hold to<br>and shows that one is not well,<br>but repose has not yet vanished.<br>A difficult heart has no character. |

From *Kinanti: The Seven Grades Explained*
(Rosidi 1989: 307-308)

Mustapa's vision of the search includes the difficulty experienced by the seeker in achieving oneness through the blending of the Seven Grades. In *Kinanti: Seeking mystical knowledge at dawn*, Mustapa expresses the process as a nausea akin to a feeling of spinning. Mustapa experienced this after singing a verse (*kinanti*), in which he had 'packaged' a feeling of repose:

| | |
|---|---|
| *Hiji di martabat tujuh*<br>*diracik jelema hiji*<br>*jelema nu sahayuna* | The units of the Seven Grades<br>are blended by humans into one,<br>by humans whose desire |

| | |
|---|---|
| *daék indit daék cicing*<br>*daék susah daék betah*<br>*saméméh kalandi hiji.* | is to roam and stay still also,<br>to be in difficulty but also in ease,<br>before they can be said to have united them. |
| *Nalutur martabat tujuh*<br>*jumpalik tilu jumpalik*<br>*geus lanjung lalaganjungan*<br>*bari nembangkeun kinanti*<br>*tembang rasa papaésan*<br>*rujuk mutmainnah ati* | To traverse the Seven Grades<br>is to fall over three times<br>to be dizzy and then become dizzy<br>while singing *kinanti*,<br>a verse that expresses frivolity<br>and the oneness of a heart in repose. |

From *Kinanti: Seeking mystical knowledge at dawn*
(Iskandarwassid et.al. 1987: 410)

*Sinom: Jump to the entrance-hall of homecoming!* is particularly rich in metaphors conveying the quest of the seeker. I have already discussed the image of the buffalo returning to its cage above. Apart from that example, the work is rich in figurative language recognisable to rice-farmers: 'the place of homecoming has one headwater, [the journey to it] covers seven hillsides'. Referring to the Sundanese custom of ritual bathing, he further described the destination as something one reaches after 'after bathing in seven waters, ritual cleansing in seven rivers', until eventually 'in the eighth one bathes in the sun, and hums a melody, Oh mother! I have vanished, what happiness!' (Cod. Or. 7876b: 6-7). The Seven Grades are stages of purification for the seeker. Mustapa adds the eighth, a place of vanishing, Sundanese melody, and full contentment.

## Concluding words

This analysis has discussed Mustapa's creative adaptations of the Seven Grades doctrine. These adaptations are localised articulations, manifest in the genres and conventions of Sundnese literary verse, of the doctrine traceable to *The Gift* of Al-Burhanpuri. I argue that Mustapa's corpus is a confirmation of a hypothesis already stated most eloquently by Anthony Johns: that the teaching of the Seven Grades, a significant element of the greater Islamisation process of the Netherlands Indies, succeeded in circulating through the Indies through localised traditions of sufism. For this reason, the verse forms of the literature of the Sundanese, and of other cultural groups in the region, are critical knowledge for the student seeking to understand the successful indigenisation of Islamic teachings.

Translated by Julian Millie

**Bibliography**

Ali, Yunasril

1997 *Manusia Citra Ilahi: Pengembangan Konsep Insan Kamil Ibn 'Arabi oleh al-Jili.* Jakarta: Paramadina.

Al-Attas, Syed Muhammad Naguib

1970 *The Mysticism of Hamzah Fansuri.* Kuala Lumpur: University of Malaya Press.

Azra, Azyumardi

2004 *The Origins of Islamic Reformism in Southeast Asia: Networks of Malay-Indonesian and Middle Eastern 'Ulama' in the seventeenth and eighteenth centuries.* Honolulu: ASAA-Allen & Unwin and University of Hawai'i Press.

Bruinessen, Martin Van

1992 *Tarekat Naqsabandiyah di Indonesia: Survey Historis, Geografis dan Sosiologis.* Bandung: Mizan.

Christomy, Tommy

2001 '*Shattariyah* Tradition in West Java: the Case of Pamijahan', *Studia Islamika* 8:2, 55-82.

2008 *Signs of the Wali: Narratives at the Sacred Sites in Pamijahan, West Java.* Canberra: ANU E Press.

Danasasmita, Ma'mur

2001 *Wacana Bahasa dan Sastra Sunda Lama.* Bandung: STSI Press.

Drewes, G.W.J.

1968 'Javanese Poems dealing with or attributed to the Saint of Bonan', *Bijdragen tot de Taal-, Land- en Volkenkunde* 124: 2, 209-240.

Ekadjati, Edi S.

1988 *Naskah Sunda: Inventarisasi dan Pencatatan.* Bandung: Lembaga Penelitian Unpad-The Toyota Foundation.

Fathurahman, Oman

2011 '*Ithaf al-Dhaki* by Ibrahim Al-Kurani: A Commentary of Wahdat al-Wujud for Jawi Audiences', *Archipel* 81, 177-198.

2016 *Shaṭṭārīyah Silsilah in Aceh, Java, and the Lanao area of Mindanao.* Tokyo: Research Institute for Languages and Cultures of Asia and Africa/Tokyo University of Foreign Studies.

Hermansoemantri, Emuch

1979 *Sajarah Sukapura: Sebuah Telaah Filologis.* Disertasi Universitas Indonesia Jakarta.

Iskandarwassid et.al.
1987 *Naskah Karya Haji Hasan Mustapa.* Bandung: Proyek Sundanologi.
Jahroni, Jajang
1999 *The Life and Mystical Thought of Haji Hasan Mustafa (1852-1930).* Unpublished thesis submitted to INIS, Leiden University.
Johns, A.H.
1965 *The Gift Adressed to the Spirit of the Prophet.* Canberra: Center of Oriental Studies A.N.U.
1975 'Islam in Southeast Asia: Reflections and New Directions', *Indonesia* 19.
2009 'Reflections on the Mysticism of Shams al-Din al-Samatra'i (1550?-1630)', in Jan van der Putten and Mary Kilcline Cody (eds.), *Lost Times and Untold Tales from the Malay World.* Singapore: NUS Press, 148-163.
Kaptein, Nico J.G.
2014 *Islam, Colonialism and the Modern Age in the Netherlands East Indies: A Biography of Sayyid 'Uthman (1822-1914).* Leiden: Brill.
Kraus, Werner
2010 'The Shattariya Sufi Brotherhood in Aceh', in Arndt Graf, Susanne Schröter, Edwin Wieringa (eds), *Aceh History, Politics and Culture.* Singapore: ISEAS, 201-226.
Laffan, Michael Francis
2008 'New Turn to Mecca: Snapshots of Arabic Printing and Sufi Networks in Late 19th Century Java', *Revue des mondes musulmans et de la Mediterranee* 124 (2), 113-131.
2011 *The Makings of Indonesian Islam: Orientalism and the Narration of a Sufi Past.* Princeton: Princeton University Press.
Millie, Julian
2014 'Arriving at the Point of Departing, Recent Additions to the Hasan Mustapa Legacy', *Bijdragen tot de Taal-, Land- en Volkenkunde* 170:1, 107-112.
Moestapa, Hasan
No date *Aji Wiwitan Martabat Tujuh. Kenging ngumpulkeun sarta ngatur Wangsaatmadja sareng para panitiana.* Handwritten manuscript.
Mustapa, Hasan
1960 *Dangding Djilid Anu Kaopat.* Stensil copy prepared by Ajip Rosidi. Tjihideung.
1976 *Gendingan Dangding Sunda Birahi Katut Wirahmana Djilid A.* Bandung: Jajasan Kudjang.
Nasution, Harun
1973 *Falsafah dan Mistisisme dalam Islam.* Jakarta: Bulan Bintang.
Ricklefs, M. C.
2013 *Mengislamkan Jawa.* Jakarta: Serambi.
Rohmana, Jajang A.
2013 'Makhtutat *Kinanti [Tutur teu Kacatur Batur]*: Tasawwuf al-'Alam al-Sundawi 'ind al-Hajj Hasan Mustafa (1852-1930)', *Studia Islamika* 20:2, 245-276.
Rosidi, Ajip
1989 *Haji Hasan Mustapa jeung Karya-karyana.* Bandung: Pustaka.
2010 *Mencari Sosok Manusia Sunda.* Bandung: Pustaka Jaya.

Santrie, Aliefya M.
1992 'Martabat Alam Tujuh, Suatu Naskah Mistik Islam dari Desa Karang Pamijahan', in Ahmad Rifa'i Hasan (ed.), *Warisan Intelektual Islam Indonesia.* Bandung: Mizan, 104-129.
Simuh
1988 *Mistik Islam Kejawen Raden Ngabehi Ranggawarsita.* Jakarta: UI-Press.
1992 'Aspek Mistik Islam Kejawen dalam 'Wirid Hidayat Jati", in Ahmad Rifa'i Hasan (ed.), *Warisan Intelektual Islam Indonesia Telaah atas Karya-Karya Klasik.* Bandung: Mizan, 57-75.
Soebardi, S.
1971 'Santri-Religious Elements as Reflected in the Book of Centini', *Bijdragen tot de Taal-, Land-en Volkenkunde* 127:3, 331-349.
1975 *The Book of Cebolek.* Leiden: KITLV-The Hague-Martinus Nijhoof.
Steenbrink, Karel
1995 'Qur'an Interpretations of Hamzah Fansuri (CA. 1600) and Hamka (1908-1982): A Comparison', *Studia Islamika* 2:2, 73-95.
Sudibjo, Z.H. and T.D. Sudjana
1985 *Muslimin jeung Muslimat.* Jakarta: PNRI dan Balai Pustaka.
Suryaningsih, Iin
2013 'Al-Haqīqah al-muwāfaqah li al-šarī'ah: al-tasāluḥ bayn al-Taṣawwuf wa al-šarī'ah bi Nusantara fī al-Qarn al-Sādis 'Ašr al-Mīlādī', *Studia Islamika* 20:1, 97-128.
Wangsaatmadja
1932 *Boekoe Tjarita Djeung Sadjarah Djoeragan Hadji Hasan Moestapa Hoofd Panghoeloe Pansioen, Marhoem Bandoeng.* Bandoeng: Dachlan Bekti.
Zoetmulder, P.J.
1991 *Manunggaling Kawula Gusti: Pantheisme dan Monisme dalam Sastra Suluk Jawa.* Jakarta: Gramedia Pustaka Utama.

## Manuscripts stored in Universiteits Bibliotheek, Leiden University

Cod. Or. 7876b, *Sinom: Jump to the entrance-hall of homecoming!*
Cod. Or. 7205, *Injaz al-wa'd fi itfa' al-ra'd (The fulfilment of the promise dealing with the extinction of the thunder).*

*Chapter 5*

# 'IT IS INCUMBENT UPON INDONESIAN MUSLIMS TO BE LOYAL TO THE DUTCH EAST INDIES GOVERNMENT'

## A study of a fatwa by Hasan Mustapa

Mufti Ali

[An earlier version of this chapter was published in volume XXVII/2 of *Hamdard Islamicus: The Quarterly Journal of Studies and Research in Islam* (2004), published by the Hamdard Foundation, Pakistan.]

The Muslim scholars appointed to exercise Islamic legal authority under the Dutch colonial government, known as *penghulu* (lit. head person), were confronted with a dilemma. On the one hand, the *penghulu* had to act in accordance with the letter and spirit of his vocation, but on the other he was urged to satisfy the political interests of his 'employer'. Professionally speaking, the duty of a *penghulu* was that of a *qadi*, an authority responsible for determining facts and passing judgement, as well as that of a *mufti*, the giver of 'legal' advice in accordance with the interests of the people, corresponding to the sense of justice prevailing in the Muslim community.[1] Yet the *penghulu* may sometimes have been compelled to give legal advice against the interests of the people. When he became the Chief *penghulu* in Aceh, Hasan Mustapa compiled a series of questions and answers in which he dealt with, among other things, the question of whether Acehnese who were waging war against the Dutch East Indies soldiers had a duty to be loyal to the Dutch East Indies Government. That compilation, which takes the form of a manuscript stored in Leiden University's Universiteits Bibliotheek (UB) and bears the title *Kashf al-Sara'ir fi Haqiqat Atjeh wa Fidr* (Revelation of the Secrets about the Reality of Aceh and Pidir), is the subject of this chapter.[2]

This paper clarifies the context that would lead Mustapa to take the position expressed in his *fatwa*. I find that context in Mustapa's loyalty to the Dutch Islamicist and government-adviser Christiaan Snouck Hurgronje (1857-1936). The relationship between these two men, as well as Snouck Hurgronje's deep involvement in Dutch efforts to end the Aceh War, provide the relevant background to understanding Mustapa's fatwaa.

I commence with an examination of Mustapa's relationship with Snouck Hurgronje, which involves consideration also of the latter's involvement in the Aceh War. There follows a discussion of *The Revelation* and its key features. I extrapolate two answers from the book, which constitute a *fatwa* about the obligation of Acehnese Muslims to support the colonial government. I extend this discussion of the *fatwa* by comparing it with a number of other *fatwa* on the same topic that were circulating at around the same time.

1 For a discussion of the role of the *Penghulu*, see Ismail (1997), and Pijper (1977).

2 The MS bears the identifying number Cod. Or. 7636.

**Haji Hasan Mustapa and Snouck Hurgronje**

Christiaan Snouck Hurgronje was a Dutch orientalist who had studied theology and semitic languages in the Netherlands. In 1884-1885, the young Snouck Hurgronje had visited Mecca, where he had studied Meccan society, with special emphasis on the Indies subjects living and studying there. He revealed his intentions in going to Mecca in a letter to Theodor Noldeke dated August 1, 1885, informing his friend that the main goals of his activities in Mecca were to study the daily activity of the pilgrims, as well as the behaviour of the 'ulama' and their political activity concerning the pan-Islamism which was being disseminated in the Muslim world by the pilgrims, especially among Muslims in the East Indies (Koningsveld 1989: 56). During this visit, he most probably met with Hasan Mustapa. Snouck Hurgronje became a Muslim and took on an Islamic name while in Mecca. The two volumes published out of that experience made him instantly famous. After that, he travelled to the Netherlands East Indies and commenced his career as civil servant there, initially as Adviser for Eastern Languages and Islamic Law, and later as Adviser for Indigenous and Arab Affairs. On leaving the Indies in 1906, he returned to the Netherlands and took up a position as Professor of Arabic at Leiden University. His collected writings about Islamic life in the Indies are a valuable source of information about Indies life and Islam in the nineteenth and early twentieth centuries.

Mustapa returned from his last period of study in Mecca in 1885, and began to teach various Islamic subjects in the Mosque of Garut. In 1889, he met once more with Snouck Hurgronje, and became his research assistant in his travels through Java. After completing that journey he went back to Garut and resumed his teaching. In 1892 Mustapa was appointed Chief-*penghulu* of Kota Radja (Aceh), a cultural environment greatly different from his home in the Sundanese lands, on the recommendation of Snouck Hurgronje. His new status as a *penghulu* involved him directly in the affairs of the Dutch colonial government. He was now the official responsible for Islamic religious matters, but was simultaneously performing an unofficial role as informant to Snouck Hurgronje. I will say more about the political background to this appointment below.

Mustapa arrived in Aceh to take up his new position as the Chief *Penghulu* of Kota Radja on February 22, 1893. He held this position for three years. The appointment did not end well. The Governor of Aceh Besar wrote in 1894 that Mustapa was 'biased' and 'not to be trusted', and that he had not been able to derive benefit from Mustapa's talents (Koningsveld 1990: L-LIV). Snouck Hurgronje wrote in defence of Mustapa, pointing out that he had not been well-treated by some of the Europeans in Aceh, and that Mustapa, by virtue of his outsider status, might have posed a threat to the 'deceits and intrigues' being practised by the indigenous officials of Kota Radja. Snouck Hurgronje ended his defence of Mustapa by recommending a similar appointment somewhere else, 'for example in the Priangan' (Koningsveld 1990: LV). Mustapa was appointed as head *penghulu* of Bandung in September of 1895. The appointment in Kota Radja has an important context: the political background of the Aceh War and Snouck Hurgronje's role in that conflict.

**Snouck Hurgronje and the Aceh War**

Aceh, located on the northern tip of Sumatra, was a sultanate with a long history and proud tradition. In the nineteenth century its exports of pepper and other products were high. Devotion to Islam was high in the Sultanate, and Islamic officials were significant players in political matters. In the London Treaty of 1824, the Dutch and English, fierce trade rivals, undertook to respect Acehnese sovereignty, but the Dutch subsequently perceived that an independent Aceh, located geographically within the sphere of Dutch influence, was vulnerable to outside powers.[3] As the nineteenth century progressed, English resolve to maintain a free Aceh diminished, and after the Sumatra Treaty of 1871 the Dutch were no longer restrained in making advances on Aceh.

The Dutch sent a number of envoys urging the Acehnese government to acknowledge the sovereignty of the Dutch Colonial government. The Acehnese rejected the requests and conversely urged the Dutch Colonial government to give back lands that had previously formed parts of Aceh, such as Sibolga, Nias and Langkat. Perceiving their interests in Sumatra to be threatened, the Dutch government declared war on March 26, 1873. On 8 April 1873 the Dutch army landed in Pante Ceureumen, in the eastern region of Ulee Cheue under the command of J.H.R. Kohler. After having waged war for several days, the Dutch were able to hold only the Great Mosque of Kota Radja. Due to the pressure of the Acehnese army, however, they later abandoned it. Kohler was shot and the Dutch army left Aceh on April 29, 1873. The first attack had failed (Alfian 1987: 87).

This was the start of the Aceh War. In the decades to follow, the Dutch were to establish civil rule in Aceh, but at the same time expended great human and material resources in an attempt to subdue a population who generally did not support the colonial power and who valued their independence. Religion had much to do with this. The Islamic scholars of the Sultanate saw the war in religious terms: for many Acehnese, the war was a 'War against Unbelievers'

3 Sources on the Aceh War include Reid (1969), Veer (1969) and Alfian (1987).

(Acehnese: *perang kaphe*) or a Holy War (Malay/Acehnese: *perang sabil*, lit. war for the way [of Allah]).

The Aceh War attracted a measure of Muslim support from around the world. It is known that under the cover of the pilgrimage weapons were secretly being dispatched to Aceh from Istanbul (Koningsveld 1989: 182). The leaders of the Acehnese rebellion who escaped from Aceh and were sought by the colonial authorities were known to reside in the Holy City of Islam. Mecca became the central city of agitation. Aware of this, Kruyt, the Dutch consul in Jeddah, proposed to the Ministry of Colonies in The Hague the training of local secret Muslim agents who could enter Mecca freely. Since this initiative was rejected by the Ministry of Colonies, he suggested another proposal, namely the dispatching of two envoys among the pilgrims entering Mecca. This proposal was also rejected by the Ministry of Colonies. Finally, Snouck Hurgronje was recommended for dealing with this 'secret duty'.

His experience with the Acehnese community in Mecca helped his subsequent career in the East Indies. From July 1891 to 1892, he resided in Kota Radja, the capital of Aceh Besar district, fulfilling a commission from the Indies government to report on the role of religion in the conflict and to advise on ways to resolve it. He developed relationships with Islamic elites to the point where he could collect valuable information that would enable him to design a colonial policy concerning the centres of religious learning in the East Indies. Snouck Hurgronje's influence on Dutch policy in Aceh was to increase over the following years (Reid 1969: 270-278).

Snouck Hurgronje's involvement in the Dutch struggle in Aceh provides the necessary context for understanding the appointment of Mustapa as *penghulu* in Kotaraja. Mustapa held sufficient qualifications in the Islamic sciences, but more than that, his appointment offered political advantages for the Dutch. Snouck Hurgronje wrote that Mustapa was reliable and was not a 'radical', and that his status as an outsider – Mustapa was ethnically Sundanese rather than Acehnese – could enable a perspective free of the internal interests of the Acehnese officials (Koningsveld 1990: LI). Furthermore, Mustapa's credibility was bolstered by the fact that he had not initially been interested in the position, due to the negative implications it might have held for his social status. After some encouragement by Snouck, he finally decided to accept it.

Snouck Hurgronje's mode of work sheds further light on the appointment. As already noted, the Dutchman was highly successful in establishing close relationships with capable Indies Muslims who kept him well-informed about issues connected with Islamic life in the Indies. This was an element of his success as a government adviser. Mustapa appears as one of a number of indigenous Indies subjects who assisted Snouck Hurgronje in his work for the colonial government, both in Arabia and the East Indies. Haji Aboe Bakar Djajadiningrat is often considered Snouck's most loyal assistant, as he supplied most of the information for a large part of Snouck's book *Mecca in the latter part of the nineteenth century* (Koningsveld 1989: 19, 100). He supplied information to the Dutch Consulate in Jeddah about the rebellious leaders from West Java who had escaped and resided in Mecca. Furthermore, he oversaw the activity of Indonesian pilgrims, collecting information about them and secretly tracking the activities of the rebels from the East Indies. In a letter sent to Euting, the Strasbourg Orientalist, on December 11, 1888, Snouck wrote about his next journey to the East Indies: 'In Suez, I might meet a companion for the journey. He is a well-educated Javanese [Djajadiningrat], who has been in Mecca for 12 years. He has been my most loyal informant for years, and also helped me loyally when I was in Mecca' (Koningsveld 1989: 38).

Hasan Mustapa was another Indies Muslim who attracted high praise from Snouck Hurgronje. As noted, he accompanied Snouck Hurgronje during his journey to study the Islamic schools of West and Central Java in 1889 and 1890. He collected information about these schools in an effort to design a colonial policy dealing with these centres of Islamic learning. In 1896 Snouck acknowledged that 'Hasan Mustapa accompanied me in 1889-1891 on a number of my journeys in Java. Due to his indispensable assistance, a great number of indigenous people gathered around me from whom I could gather valuable information' (Koningsveld 1989: 199).

Hasan Mustapa contributed to the Dutch cause in Aceh in a number of ways. While serving as *penghulu* between 1893 and 1896 he sent weekly letters to Snouck Hurgronje in Batavia, informing him of developments there. Of these letters, Snouck Hurgronje wrote '...these were an important way for me to form an image of changes occurring subsequent to my departure from Kota Radja' (Koningsveld 1990: L).[4] Hasan Mustapa also advocated for the Dutch cause. He wrote at least one letter to an Acehnese leader, Teungku Moehammad Zen Bantara Paloe, in which he requested him to be loyal to the East Indies Government and to command his own people not to wage war against it.[5] Yet another contribution was his collection of questions and answers on social, political, cultural and religious matters entitled *The Revelation of Secrets About the Reality of Aceh and Pidir.*

4 Hasan Mustapa's letters to Snouck Hurgronje are stored as Cod. Or 18097, s. 16 (Arabic Letters form Kotaraja, Correspondence with Snouck Hurgronje, 1893-1895); Cod. Or. 18097 s.9 (letters sent to Snouck Hurgronje in Weltevreden, 1893-1894); and in Cod. Or. 8952 (Arabic Letters sent by Hasan Mustafa, Hoofd-Pendhulu in Bandung to Snouck Hurgronje, 1911-1923).

5 Cod. Or. 18097 s. 9, letter dated November 13, 1894.

*The Revelation*

According to its introduction, he finished writing *The Revelation* on Wednesday July 25, 1894 (Muharram 21, 1312 H). Although bearing an Arabic title, the book is in fact written in Mustapa's hand in Malay (the language that is now the national language of the Republic of Indonesia). Interestingly, I have found no further information about the publication or circulation of the book. It seems it was never printed. In all of the letters Hasan Mustapa sent to Snouck Hurgronje which are kept in the Leiden University Library, no discussion can be found concerning the publication of this book.[6]

This book is presented in a sequence of questions and answers in inelegant Malay. In all, the book's 190 pages contain 154 questions. It is difficult to read. The punctuation is not clear, and the syntax does not give much help to the reader. Some paragraphs contain only one sentence which in some cases extend for more than one page. The numbering of the questions is carelessly written, especially in the last one third of the book. The book contains scribal errors, which are marked by efforts to cross them out. Furthermore, the author does not use any systematic method in explaining the subject matter. He describes, for instance, the Acehnese people in a number of questions distributed throughout the book. So if one wants to know his reflections on the Acehnese people, one has to read questions 11, 12, 13, 7, 37, 52, 51, 53, 43 and 78. Mustapa was aware of this,

6 It is rather surprising that Hasan Mustapa did not discuss this book with Snouck Hurgronje. In his letters, which were generally sent twice a month, Hasan Mustapa informed Snouck Hurgronje about his own activities, events of Kota Radja, and his own personal experiences. Mustapa included important documents such as examples of poetry on the Acehnese war, maps, his letter attempting to persuade certain figures to be loyal to the Dutch, and other important information concerning the Acehnese war.

stating that in writing this book he merely followed his mind haphazardly. Any effort to understand the book, therefore, requires multiple readings.

Mustapa presents his motive for writing this book in questions number 69 and 82. In those two questions he explains that he wrote this book to prove that he had been in Aceh, and to help the *kompeni* 'cure' the 'disease' of the Acehnese. (The Acehnese continued to use the word *kompeni* to refer to the Dutch government even after the Netherlands East India Company had ceded its authority in the Indies to the Dutch crown). Since the book contains a description of the disease of the Acehnese, he assumes that the book will be read by the 'Great People' (the Dutch East Indies Government), as the 'doctors' who were treating the disease. According to Mustapa, the doctors could not cure the disease if they did not know the disease well.

Generally speaking, Hasan Mustapa had a bad impression of the Acehnese people.[7] Aceh is described as a country whose people always deceive each other. According to him, one can see many examples of deceit, such as between the members of the nobility, brothers, and even between sons or daughters-in-law and their parents. Mustapa maintains that it is difficult for them to refrain from their inclination to deceit. The Acehnese share a stubborn and firm character, easily forget the goodness and the favour of others, and always refuse good advice. Once they are annoyed by others, Mustapa claims, they will be angry forever. He attributes this bad character to a low level of education and literacy. In Mustapa's vision, the reflection of the poor character of the Acehnese can be seen in the *Kompeni*, the rivals of the Acehnese people in war.

7 Mutapa expressed these opinions in questions 31, 32, 48, 51 and 53.

Mustapa represents the *Kompeni* as people who want to establish justice, as a powerful people who rule the country cleverly, despite their status as non-believers.[8]

In a number of passages, Hasan Mustapa puts forward his opinions concerning ways to handle and manage the Acehnese. According to him, two difficulties are encountered in dealing with Aceh: (1) the stubbornness of its nobility, and (2) the stupidity of its people. Nevertheless Mustapa regretted the continuation of the war: it was causing 'a great number of diseases, such as murder, deceit, slander and so on'. The cause was worth the application of 'a great quantity of medicines to cure those diseases' (Question 80). But the solution was not to be found easily: 'One may destroy the Acehnese people, but they will emerge again' (Question 33).

Mustapa also stressed the significance of religion in dealing with the Acehnese. He regrets the fact that in Aceh political and trade matters are often mixed with religion (Question 53). If one wanted to gain popularity and the sympathy of the Acehnese, one should first speak about the excellence of those killed in the Way of God (*mati sahid*), and one should obey the rule of the religious teachers, which had become the customary law for the Acehnese (*hukum adat*).

His account of the Sultan is noteworthy.[9] According to Mustapa, the Sultan resides in Greater Aceh and speaks Malay and sometimes Arabic. The people trust the Sultan very much due to his spiritual loftiness and dignity. The Acehnese people take the water which the Sultan uses for washing his feet, and use it for curing the sick. The populace's love and appreciation for him is reflected in their

8 The relevant questions are 25, 53, 81.

9 The relevant questions are 11, 111, 118 and 133.

reference to him as a 'jewel' (*intan*). The loyalty of the people to the Sultan is incomparable.

He paints a less impressive picture of the other elites (*raja*). Some of the *raja* are given a salary by the *Kompeni*, and are therefore loyal to the *Kompeni* and will extinguish any rebellion against it in the area of their jurisdiction.[10] Some of them are not loyal to the *Kompeni*, because the latter has not been able to restore them to their earlier glory. He attributes the *raja* with stubbornness, one of the two characteristics which make it difficult for the *Kompeni* to handle Achenese. They constantly feud with each other and most of them are violent to the people. *Raja*s make use of 'coarse' language in their daily communication.

To describe another class of elites, the *uleebalang*, Hasan Mustapa refers to the words of a minor noble who said that the heart of an *uleebalang* is like a *buah mancang* (a sort of fruit). The fruit smells good and is yellow in colour. But its interior is rotten.[11] Mustapa describes political conflict between the sultan and the *uleebalang*. The sultan considered the *uleebalang*'s submission and loyalty to the Dutch East Indies as a menace threatening their control of the Acehnese people, as well as an insult to their sovereignty. From the *uleebalang*s' perspective, the Acehnese kings were concerned with their own dignity, power, wealth and self-interest. In their perception, the Acehnese kings were indifferent to the people's interest.

Mustapa's advice concerning Sultan Muhammad Daud (reigned 1874-1903) reveals his strategic orientation. Hasan Mustapa suggests

10 Answers to questions concerning the raja are found in 21, 67, 21, 86, 88, 111.

11 Concerning the *uleebalang*, see 37 and 110.

that the *Kompeni* should accept the idea of the 'goodness' of Muhammad Daud, because Acehnese loyalty to him was quite strong. Mustapa mentions a learned relative of Muhammad Daud named Tuanku Hashim (Question 121). According to Mustapa, Tuanku Hashim was a prudent and wise man who held great influence among the Acehnese. If the *Kompeni* wanted to gain control over the whole of the Acehnese people, it should make peace with Tuanku Hashim, who could speak Malay, Arabic and Hindustani (Urdu), and who was well versed in the history of ancient kings and the history of some European countries, Bombay and Sumatra (Question 145).

In another passage, Hasan Mustapa maintains that for the Acehnese, cooperation with the Dutch East Indies soldiers was a matter of shame that could cause their dignity and self-esteem to decline. According to Mustapa, the collaboration of Teuku Umar as well as Tuanku Hashim with the Dutch East Indies' soldiers was merely a strategy to gain financial aid from the *Kompeni*. In fact, they used the financial aid to support the Acehnese war.[12] Their indifference to the Dutch East Indies' soldiers sprang from their belief that the Dutch East Indies government was causing the Acehnese kingdom to decline and become disintegrated.

In Mustapa's view, the Acehnese should maintain a good relationship with the Dutch East Indies soldiers, because the *Kompeni* was their 'sultan', and was striving on behalf of the interests of the Acehnese people (Question 19). The Aceh war was the embodiment of Acehnese stubbornness, and was preventing the people from being loyal to the colonial government.

---

12 See answers 20, 37, 44 74 and 150

## The Fatwa

### *Questions*

64. On being asked about whether or not I see goodness amongst the *raja* (indigenous elites) in Greater Aceh.

[...]
72. What are the signs of the stupidity of the religious scholars [*'ulama*] of this country?

### *Answers*

64. One must see that the cleverest among the *raja* are those who are closest to the Dutch East (Indies) government.

[...]
72. I write here that the religious books are of course in harmony with the prevailing government. In order that readers can read my view easily, I write my answer here in Malay. First, the hadith [traditions of the Prophet] state that religion is an easy matter. Secondly, the Holy Qur'an states that it is incumbent upon Muslims to be loyal to the ruling government. Thirdly, it is stated in the *Nasa'ih al-Muluk* [Advices for the Kings] that the ruler must use a thousand methods in ruling his people. But all those ways serve two aims: the advancement of the country and the happiness of the people. Fourthly, Ibn Qayyim said that the proof of justice is embodied in the religion of God. He [God] does not establish justice in one exclusive form, and because of that, most religious people think that religious law always changes. In fact, it will not change unless people have learnt this, for then they will understand that this saying is true. Ibn Hajar in 700 H. stated that we are not allowed at all to say that the religious law changes. But we say that change in law is caused by the change in legal cases.

I have selected these questions out of the 154 in *The Revelation* because they clearly convey Mustapa's ideas about the relationship between the Acehnese and the Dutch East Indies government, and furthermore, answer 72 does so in an exercise of religio-legal reasoning. In other words, Mustapa was wearing his *penghulu* hat when giving these answers. None of the other questions in the book are answered in this way, and considering Mustapa was an Islamic expert writing in an environment where Islamic opinions mattered greatly, this answer deserves special attention. Basing himself on traditional texts — a passage of the hadith, a verse of the Qur'an and an opinion of the author of *Nasa'ih al-Muluk* as well as the opinions of lbn al-Qayyim and lbn Hajar – Mustapa gives Islamic legitimacy to the authority of the Dutch East Indies Government in Aceh, and states that it is obligatory for Muslims of Aceh to be loyal to it. He believes that as long as the *Kompeni* is concerned with the two goals recommended above, it deserves the loyalty of the Acehnese. Importantly, Mustapa's opinion would mean that those Acehnese opposing the Dutch would be committing rebellion rather than supporting a Holy War against a tyrannous oppressor.

The essence of the fatwa is that Muslims should provide prima facie support to the prevailing government, and that the proper relationship between Islam and the state may manifest and be preserved in many forms, and these forms change over time. Implicitly, a colonial government is one such acceptable form. Mustapa's fatwa needs to be read not only against the political situation outlined above, but also against the consensus of Islamic legal opinion directed to the same issues. His fatwa is a contribution to a heavily-politicised dialogue. It speaks against other texts circulating at the time which argued contrasting positions. Mustapa's contribution overlooks, for example, a number of widely known passages of the Qur'an that can be interpreted as prohibiting Muslims from acknowledging non-believers as rulers, some of which are mentioned in the Acehnese poetry concerning the war against the *Kompeni*.[13]

Furthermore, Mustapa's fatwa is at odds with similar statements from other Muslim scholars. Shaykh Muhammad Nawawi al-Bantani (1813-1897) was a scholar from the West Javanese region of Banten who lived in Mecca beside Mustapa (Snouck Hurgronje 1931: 268-273). He published his opinion concerning Holy War in his book *Nihayat al-Zayn* (Nawawi 1881). He expressed the position that the necessity of Holy War depended on two conditions. First, if a Muslim country has been occupied by infidels the obligation to wage a Holy War becomes a firm societal obligation (Arabic: *fard kifayah*). The Holy War should be declared once a year by Muslims. Second, if an enemy, an infidel for instance, invades a Muslim country, the obligation to wage a Holy War would become an individual obligation. At the time of invasion, there is an obligation on every Muslim to defend the country.

Van Koningsveld (1990a) has analysed another fatwa issued specifically for Acehnese conditions by Muhammad ibn Hasab Allah al-Makki al-Shafi'i (1828-1917). This man was the Mufti of Mecca for the Shafi'i legal school during the time of the Aceh War. His fatwa addressed a number of difficult questions arising out of the Dutch occupation of Kotaraja, including the issue of the religious status of those Acehnese who had surrendered to the Dutch. Did they retain any rights as Acehnese Muslims? The mufti's answers included a statement that it was a grave sin to surrender one's dwelling place

13 The verses include: Al 'Imran: 28, Let not the Believers take for friends or helpers unbelievers rather than believers; Al 'Imran: 118, O ye who believe! Take not into your intimacy those outside your ranks: They do not fail to corrupt you; Al-Mumtahanah: 1, O ye who believe! Take not My enemies and yours as friends (or protectors …).

to unbelievers, but nevertheless, those who did so were not to be considered as unbelievers and did not lose their property and other rights in the process. They were obliged, however, to emigrate to a place where they could perform their religion in safety and protect the honour of their women (Koningsveld 1990a: 93).

These issues were of great importance for Acehnese of the time, for Acehnese society was being divided brutally. Some had no choice but to surrender, others chose martyrdom, others still chose to collaborate with the Dutch. It was natural that such an esteemed Mufti's opinion would be sought on these issues. Van Koningsveld (1990a: 94) pointed out that Ibn Hasab Allah's fatwa probably played a role in the discussions of the various Acehnese resistance-leaders. It did have flow-on effects. Teungku Kutakarang, for example, in his pamphlet entitled *Tadhkirat Al-Rakidin* (Reminder to the Inactive Ones), seems to have relied on Hasab Allah's fatwa in his approach to his fellow-Acehnese who had surrendered to the Dutch. He (Teungku Kutakarang) urged the Acehnese people to participate in waging war, but he did not consider them as kafirs, non-believers, if they did not.[14]

**Concluding words**

These opinions, or at least the ideas underpinning them, would almost certainly have been known to Mustapa. He associated with Acehnese nationalists during his time in Mecca and (probably) also during his appointment in Kota Radja. The consensus of Islamic opinion does not support Mustapa's position. *The Revelation* does not reveal its author as a diligent and impartial source of guidance for the Muslims of Aceh. Rather, it validates Snouck Hurgronje's judgement

14 Snouck Hurgronje's summary of Kutakarang's writings may be read in Gobée and Adriaanse (1990, vol 1, pp. 109-114).

of Mustapa as a man who was free of radicalism and could be relied upon in his exercise of his *penghulu* duties. It reveals Mustapa as a person whose loyalty to his brilliant Dutch colleague outweighed his commitment to Islamic legal thinking.

This loyalty had political effects. Mustapa's book stands as an attempt to induce the Acehnese people to quit their rebellion against the Dutch East Indies government, and to assure them that the colonial government was their legitimate ruler which deserved their loyalty and obedience. It may have been intended to have the same propaganda effect for Muslims in other parts of the Indies. The Dutch knew that the successful establishment of civil government in Aceh after 1881, which consequently changed the status of Acehnese resistance from waging war to a rebellion, required legitimacy in the eyes of the people. Mustapa's intervention argues that religious duty required the Acehnese to quit their rebellion against Dutch rule and to be loyal to it. One might argue that this fatwa was written as propaganda rather than legal advice. And this was not the only help Mustapa gave to the Dutch in relation to the Aceh War. In effect, due to this friendship itself, one may suggest that Hasan Mustapa occupied his position as *penghulu* as an 'informant' of his friend, Snouck Hurgronje, rather than as a professional legal official. This loyalty yielded a political benefit for the Dutch colonial government.

## Bibliography

Alfian, Teuku lbrahim

1987 *Perang di Jalan Allah, Aceh 1873-1912.* Jakarta: Pustaka Sinar Harapan

Gobée, E. and C. Adriaanse

1990 *Nasihat-Nasihat C. Snouck Hurgronje Semasa Kapegawaiannya Kepada Pemerintah Hindia Belanda 1889-1936.* Volume 1. Jakarta: Seri Khusus INIS.

Ismail, Ibnu Qayyim

1997 *Kiai Penghulu Jawa: Peranannya di Masa Kolonial.* Jakarta: Gema Insani Press.

Koningsveld, P Sj. van

1989 *Snouck Hurgronje dan Islam.* Jakarta: Girimukti Pusaka.

1990 'Pengantar: Nasihat-Nasihat Snouck sebagai sumber sejarah zaman Penjajahan', in E. Gobée and C. Adriaanse, (eds), *Nasihat-Nasihat C. Snouck Hurgronje semasa kepegawaiannya kepada pemerintah Hindia Belanda 1889-1936.* Jakarta: Seri Khusus INIS, XI-LXXIII.

1990a 'Bererapa aspek keagamaan Perang Aceh sebagai tercermin dalam tiga naskah berbahasa Arab yang tak diterbitkan', in W.A.L. Stokhof and N.J.G. Kaptein (eds), *Beberapa Kajian Indonesia dan Islam.* Jakarta: INIS, 77-105.

Nawawi, Muhammad b. 'Umar

1881 *Nihayat al-zayn fi irshad al-mubtadi'in bi-sharh Qurrat al-'ayn bi-muhimmat al-Din.* Al-Qahira.

Pijper, G.E.

1977 *Studien Over de Geschiedenis van de Islam in Indonesia 1900-1950.* Leiden: Brill.

Reid, Anthony

1969 *The Contest for North Sumatra: Atjeh, the Netherlands and Britain 1858-1898.* Kuala Lumpur: University of Malaysia Press.

Snouck Hurgronje, Ch.

1931 *Mecca in the Latter Part of the Nineteenth Century*, J.H. Monahan (transl). Leiden: Brill.

Veer, Paul van 't

1969 *De Atjeh Oorlog.* Amsterdam: N.V. Uitgeverij de Arbeiderspers.

### *Manuscripts stored in Universiteitsbibliotheek, Leiden University*

Cod. Or. 18097 s. 16, (Arabic Letters from Kota Radja, Correspondence with Snouck Hurgronje, 1893-1995).

Cod. Or. 18097 s. 9, (Letters sent by Hasan Mustapa to Snouck Hurgronje in Weltevreden, 1893-1894).

Cod. Or. 7636, (*Kashf al-Sara'ir fi Haqiqati Atjeh wa al-Fidr*).

Cod. Or 8952, (Arabic Letters sent by Hasan Mustapa to Snouck Hurgronje, 1911-1923).

# *Chapter 6*

# HAJI HASAN MUSTAPA

## Floating downstream

Ajip Rosidi

Editor's note: This is a translation of Ajip Rosidi's essay 'Haji Hasan Mustapa: Silanglang Lalayaran', originally written in 1960. The source text is found in the collection of Rosidi's writings entitled *Ngalanglang Kasusastran Sunda* (1969). The essay was translated by Rabin Hardjibrata, Hawé Setiawan and Julian Millie. All footnotes are additions by the editor.

All Sundanese are familiar with the name Haji Hasan Mustapa, the chief *penghulu* of Bandung whom people liked to call 'eccentric' [Sund: *mahiwal*]. Even though not many people have read his writings, he is generally regarded by the Sundanese as the most prominent member of their literati.

But strangely, if we were to open one of the books on Sundanese literature that are available today [in 1960, ed.], and are used in schools, compiled by well-known scholars of Sundanese language and literature, we might find the occasional picture of Haji Hasan Mustapa, but discussions of his literary works would be non-existent. The books give a simple description: Sundanese man of letters. No convincing reason is ever given for why he is called 'man of letters'. In fact, some scholars of Sundanese language and literature without any hesitation give Hasan Mustapa the title of 'The Great One', and without batting an eyelid confess that in truth they themselves do not really understand this 'man of letters' (e.g. M.A. Salmoen in the newspaper *Sipatahoenan*). It is quite possible that even those who call themselves experts on literature and include photos of Hasan Mustapa in their books have no knowledge whatsoever about Mustapa's literary works, which in fact provide the very reason for including his photograph in their books. In most cases, the only book they refer to as an example of Mustapa's literary work is the *Treatise on the Customs of the Priangan People and other Sundanese*, which in fact is more accurately categorised as an ethnographic work than a literary one.

The reason for this lack of knowledge is that Hasan Mustapa's writings circulated among a very limited community. Although some of them were printed and published as books, the majority of them are still found only in manuscripts or typed form, or at best, as stencils. In actual fact his corpus is massive. His poems alone, according to those who have counted them, consist of more than 10,000 verses. Apart from these Mustapa produced other writings in prose about all kinds of things, but mainly about philosophy and religion.

We occasionally might hear about a Sundanese person who, having encountered his poems and reading them once over, feels it sufficient to just give a comment such as, 'deeply insightful,' or 'the average person will not get it; it needs interpretation by experts', or 'not for general reading', and so on, thereby revealing the gaps in his own knowledge while at the same time protecting himself, likening men of letters to magicians capable of all kinds of tricks, and saying that the writer is not writing for him anyway. This reveals the cowardly mentality of a cock who has given up before he has even entered the arena. He is a product of that tendency to see literature as a crossword puzzle, and to regard symbolism as its distinguishing characteristic. This attitude is perhaps an extension of the outlook on life that says 'Whatever the *kiai* [Islamic teacher] says is correct, for he has a monopoly on the holy books'.

Yet the reality is that no matter how profound a literary work might be, it can nonetheless be accessed and understood by anyone who is willing, providing they really desire to do so. The poet's feelings are those of a human, and the language he uses is human language, so how could it be impossible for ordinary humans to read it? Isn't the Qur'an the word of the Lord revealed in the language of the Prophet Muhammad SAW, and originally passed down by him in that language? Humans have studied it, interpreted it, and understood it. And here I am discussing a Sundanese writing in Sundanese! How could it be that a Sundanese would have to ask someone else to read Mustapa's works for him?

Surely a writer expresses the inspiration of his feelings because he wants to communicate it to others, in other words, to his fellow human beings? A Sundanese bard once put it like this in one of the Sundanese epics:[1]

| | |
|---|---|
| *diteundeun di jalan gedé* | Left on a main road, |
| *bukaeun nu ngaliwat* | to be opened by those passing by, |
| *anu weruh di semuna* | by those who know its appearance, |
| *anu terang di jaksana* | those who recognise its content, |
| *anu rancagé di haté* | those who are creative in feeling. |

This means: the essence of the epic is meant for everyone, and does not distinguish noble from commoner, and anyone who is genuinely interested will certainly be able to open it, delve into it, and understand. Of course, those of us who pass by only for a

1 Rosidi is here referring to the oral epic genre known in Sundanese as *pantun*. Rosidi headed a massive project to record these bards in the 1970s (see Rosidi 1973).

moment will miss out, not having time to pay attention to things they encounter along the side of the road, and will not arrive at the state of 'knowing the appearance, recognising the content', even more so if they are not 'creative of feeling'. There is no value in a fleeting engagement.

In their analyses of literature, Sundanese men of letters have generally felt satisfied in praising the alliterations, or counting the number of syllables of every line. This was the general procedure before the (Pacific) war, for at that time the value of the poem was determined by the number of syllables and the sonorities of its alliteration. Literature was evaluated according to its beautiful words and the difficult *kawi* words that were added to it.[2] Literature consisted of rhetorics made up of clichéd formulas filled with the ringing sounds of alliteration and with *kawi* words not understood by ordinary people. But what was being revealed? What was the content? What was being expressed? These things were never inquired into, never analysed. The literature scholars were so used to the beautiful appearance that they forgot about the spirit that was in fact its content. That was its soul. Eventually, what they studied and examined was only the shell which, they thought, could be separated from its content. This is like dressing up a corpse, something which has no life, in fancy new clothes.

Even today there are many people who consider themselves to be literary experts who follow that way of thinking about literature. But in contemporary times, after the war, we find many broader reflections, opinions and comparative frameworks. Sundanese people have mixed more widely in comparison with earlier times. One can

2 *Kawi* is an archaic literary lexicon that is used in literature and other contexts such as performances of the rod-puppet theatre (*wayang golék*).

imagine how absolute that attitude and perspective on literature was in the pre-war world, when the Sundanese were still isolated.

In those times, the Sundanese held tightly to the view that beauty in versification was the one and only method for composing poetry. The number of lines of each stanza, the number of syllables of each line (the rules of scansion), as well as the vocalisation of the final syllable of each line (the rules of rhyming) were considered unequivocal requirements of beautiful literature. If a poem deviated from those well-established requirements, it was considered of lesser value. At times it was even considered to have no value.

According to this view, 'beautiful' language is language intermixed with clichéd words and similes. Full of alliterations and sprinkled with *kawi* words. What had previously been considered merely as one *element* of beauty, was then held to be the *aim* of poetry. Aesthetic constraints which had earlier constituted an element of poetic beauty then became the absolute aim and goal. Apart from that, these unequivocal rules of beauty resulted in many poems without spontaneity. Spontaneity is a characteristic of art which is never felt in its presence, but which is keenly felt in its absence.

That was the literary environment in which Hasan Mustapa wrote his poems. But although he employed the standard forms of versification, which were wholly subservient to their formulas and constraints, Hasan Mustapa's verses maintained their colour and spontaneity.

His words were well-selected and were highly suggestive, resounding with alliterations that were very rich but not at all clichéd, and with infrequent use of the *kawi* language that was considered the 'language of literature'. Instead, we frequently encounter Arabic words (sometimes entire phrases), used not for the sake of chasing after 'the beauty of literature', but because they were irreplaceable content. The language Mustapa uses is authentic Sundanese that would later cause the Sundanese themselves to feel inadequate, so rich is his lexical repertoire, and so artfully was it employed. The same applies for his metaphors and poetic imagination, which are original and plastic, for example:

| | |
|---|---|
| *Ngebul curug Cikapundung,* | Mist rises as the Cikapundung falls, |
| *cai tiguling teu éling,* | its water tumbling down unaware, |
| *séahna ayeuh-ayeuhan,* | swishing without stopping, |
| *cai mulang cai malik,* | flowing back and forth, |
| *leumpang laun reureundeukan,* | slowly walking in absorption, |
| *taya kalali kaéling.* | neither forgetting nor remembering. |

From: *An audience with the Lord (Kinanti)*

In this poem, a description of the physical world blends together with a spiritual impression, executed without any explicit markers of figurative language such as 'like', 'as if', 'in the manner of', 'resembling', 'for example' and so on. Spontaneity and movement emerge even in the first line: Hasan Mustapa depicts the rising mist of the waterfall on the Cikapundung. But in the second and the following lines, the description of the waterfall is not merely a description of the Cikapundung falls, but is also an impression of human life that 'swishes without stopping, slowly walking in absorption, neither forgetting nor remembering'.

The *kinanti* poetic pattern is mobilised without forcing or doing violence to the words, without compressing or changing sentences to conform with the model, as we find in so many other poems.[3] The comparisons are not artificial, but are spontaneous and plastic,

3 In the 19th and 20th centuries, most Sundanese verse was written according to the versification system known as *tembang* or *dangding*. The system, which originates from Javanese models, consists of stanza forms which differ from each other according to the number of lines in the stanza, the pattern of end rhyme, the mood or character of the verse, and the melody in which the verse was sung. In this essay, Rosidi quotes verses written in the forms of *kinanti*, *pangkur*, *sinom* and *asmarandana*. Sundanese

bubbling up out of an attentive feeling. In describing the Cikapundung falls, Hasan Mustapa has elevated his description of nature to a universal level, and at that level, not only do we witness the beauty of the seething water of the falls. He goes beyond that to ask us to examine humanity in totality.

Hasan Mustapa considers the verse patterns as an element of poetic aesthetics, not as the all-embracing poetic method that the majority of Sundanese writers at the time considered it to be; they thought that method to be structure, foundation as well as goal. The same applies with the 'nature' or 'character' of each verse pattern, which at the time were held to be 'set in stone' (for example *asmarandana* was to be used for describing romance or advice, *sinom* is for depicting anxiety, *maskumambang* for sadness, *pangkur* for anger or going off to war, and so on). Hasan Mustapa did not hold firmly to these conceptions. For him, every verse pattern was the same, as long as it properly expresses the feeling.

A verse of whatever pattern must be in harmony with its feeling. The feeling and the content are mutually determining. If the verse projects a feeling that is inadequate or lacking, even though it might fit the verse pattern, it is impossible for that to be refined – as it is clear in the following verse:

| | |
|---|---|
| *Pangkurangna nya hidayat*<br>*lamun taya sarina dina Kinanti*<br>*masih jujur dina Pangkur*<br>*da rasa mah rasa*<br>*pangabetah teu beunang dikudu-kudu*<br>*teu beunang digeura-geura*<br>*lamun lain pangabeuki.* | Above all, humans lack divine guidance<br>when the *kinanti* lacks its essence,<br>even if be truthful in its *pangkur*,<br>for feelings are feelings;<br>a source of pleasure cannot be forced,<br>and cannot be compelled,<br>if one lacks a fondness for it. |

From *Humans lack guidance above all: Pangkur*

poets used these stanza forms to produce works in a number of genres including *wawacan* (long narrative) and *guguritan* (shorter lyrical sequences of verse). See the chapter by Setiawan in this volume and Rosidi (2011a, 2011b).

In the same way, Mustapa acknowledged that the verse pattern called *dangdanggula* conventionally represented the flavour of sweetness, but only, according to Mustapa, if our feelings communicate this. It will only convey this flavour if the verse is 'in harmony with our feelings' (see his poem *The flavour of sweetness: dangdanggula*). For him, writing poems was nothing more than tracing the essence of feeling, regardless of whether the verse pattern was *mijil*, *sinom* or *pangkur*. For Mustapa, all *Kinanti* are not the same, neither are all *mijil*, nor *sinom*, nor *pangkur*. Each depends on its own true feeling, and any change in our condition leads to changes in our feelings. This is made very clear in *Moving forward to Kinanti: Asmarandana*, which goes like this:

| | |
|---|---|
| *Gilisir jadi kinanti* | Moving forward to *kinanti* |
| *lar liwat asmarandana* | and passing by *asmarandana*, |
| *raos dangdanggula sinom* | sweet *dangdanggula* and *sinom*, |
| *mimijilan papangkuran* | doing *mijil* and *pangkur*, |
| *mapay sarining rasa* | tracing the essence of feelings, |
| *jucungna nepi ka pucung* | terminating in *pucung*, |
| *pindah alam pindah mangsa.* | changing worlds, changing times. |

In short, for Hasan Mustapa the verse patterns are nothing other than receptacles for feelings. And feelings are changeable, for he once wrote 'what gives pleasure cannot be forced, cannot be urged on, if one has no feeling for it'.

Hasan Mustapa was aware that the verse forms common in Sundanese literature at the time were actually not the authentic verse forms of the ancestors, but had been adopted by us from [the Javanese Kingdom] Mataram. So these forms were borrowed ones. In *Humans lack feeling above all: Pangkur*, he made this clear:

| | |
|---|---|
| *Lain asal ti Pasundan,* | These did not come from Sunda, |
| *gendang-gending tembang harurang-hariring,* | singing, poetry, humming, |

'The original resolve of the Sundanese' he wrote in the same poem, 'was found in the mystical verse of (King) Siliwangi, and for that reason, the bardic texts have not disappeared.' It is the mysticism of Siliwangi that Hasan Mustapa traced, investigated, studied, explored and revealed in his poems. It is this that makes Hasan Mustapa outstanding or 'idiosyncratic' in comparison with other writers in the world of Islamic mysticism. When he explored the canonical Islamic sources, he consciously tried to connect them with the beliefs that existed in his homeland. He exchanged the stories and histories adapted from the Muslim chronicles with stories known to the Sundanese, such as [figures of Sundanese epic and myth] *Harian Bangga*, *Ciung Wanara*, *Sunan Ambu*, *Prabu Siliwangi*, *Ratu Galuh*, *Dayang Sumbi* etc.

This explains why he selected only 105 verses in his interpretation of the Qur'an.[4] He felt this number to be sufficient for the needs of the Sundanese, because the themes of these verses were closer to the life conditions of the Sundanese. He wrote:

> The common people have difficulty in using most of the [Qur'an's] verses, for they are not equipped to understand what its allusions, etymologies, metaphors and idioms could mean for their own feelings and souls, and for overcoming the deceptions of this world, such as those found in the stories of the Occupants of the Cave, Pharoah and Moses, Abraham and Namrud, Adam and the devil, the story of Ujer (Ezzra) and Nasaro, Moses and Khidir, Yunus and his nation, Moses and his nation, Noah and his people, Jesus and the Jews, Alexander and the story of Allah's Prophet in Mecca, of Abu Jahal, and other ones also. I have not included these, because

4 Rosidi is referring to Mustapa's work entitled *Quotes from the Qur'an, their Decorum and Method* (*Petikan Qur'an katut Adab Padikana*). Rosidi included the book in his 1989 compilation (see Rosidi 1989: 389-434).

> they are too remote from the symbolic resources, knowledge, works, genealogies and capabilities in Arabic of my own people. In their wisdom, worldview, and etymologies, my people only extend as far as the [Sundanese genres of] allusion [*sisindiran*], folk etymologies [*kirata*], and pantun [*wawangsalan*]...[5]

Hasan Mustapa's poems and other writings generally remind us of forms such as the bardic epics, mantra and mystical poems that appear in the ancient literature of the Sundanese. This is extraordinary in the context of Sundanese literature of his time, and contrasts strikingly with the general content of Sundanese poetry of that period. Although some Sundanese writers of the time made adaptions of the bardic epics (for example, some adapted *Prince Mundinglaya*, *The Starling and the Monkey*, and *The Lost Ape* into verse narratives), significant traces of the contents of those works can be found only in the verses of Hasan Mustapa and Kalipah Apo. In the numerous verses that were mass-produced in the period before the war, it is difficult to find 'continuity' with the spirit that in any deliberate way could connect them to the bardic epic and mantra, that is to say, to the Sundanese spirit of old mentioned by Pa Sursa as the 'spirit of the Almighty' this (see Pa Sursa, *Adeg-adeg Sunda*, in the magazine *Manglé*, no. 1, 1975).

But he knew that the verse forms he used were borrowed [from Javanese]. For that reason, Hasan Mustapa was aware that even though it was the Sundanese ancestral legacy that he was putting into verse, the mysticism of Siliwangi, his readers or listeners might include some who would recoil out of a sense of strangeness, and consequently be repulsed because they sense it was clothed in something that was not their genuine ancestral inheritance:

5 The excerpt translated here can be read on page 433 of Rosidi (1989).

| | |
|---|---|
| *Temahna dipicawérang* | The result is a flavourless taste, |
| *sada Sunda tapi lain* | it sounds Sundanese but it is not; |
| *bongan saha bongan tembang* | whose fault is it? The verse's, |
| *lain ku jamak nu urang* | for this is not what we are used to. |
| *da ieu mah ngan hening* | But my verses are mere reflections, |
| *répéh kitu gandéng kitu* | and whether silent or loud, |
| *taya béda rarasaan* | their taste does not differ, |
| *mun iklas tina rohani* | as long as they come from sincere feeling, |
| *moal béda dipisari dipicamplang.* | flavour and blandness are not different. |

From *The melody of sensing: Sinom*

This poem reveals Hasan Mustapa's opinions concerning form and its relevance to literary production. If some people vaguely recognise the sounds of Sundanese (contents, feelings, mystical poetics), but at the same time feel strange because they are expressed in a form that is not Sundanese, then that is because the *tembang* form is indeed a borrowed form. It is not truly Sundanese.

But it was not important for Hasan Mustapa whether the form was original or not, and the praiseworthiness of the melody was even less important. It made no difference to Mustapa if other people made the poem pleasant or bland [in their performance of it]. This poem gives a clearer expression of his attitude and position about form in poetry specifically and literature in general. Form does not matter, for the poem depends on its content. If the content has value, it will certainly materialise in a form that will also have value.

This attitude of 'rapt contemplation', of not caring whether a poem is pleasant or bland, is notable. It is extraordinary when we consider the youth of today, most of whom write literature or poems with no intention other than to 'blow their own trumpets'. Mustapa's attitude differs from the opinions of those writers who consider that they write literary work for no other purpose than to make communication with others.

Hasan Mustapa was the reverse. He considered himself to be a person in the middle of singing, rapt in contemplation, strolling towards the setting sun, humming as he goes, in search of the essence of his feeling. The topic of his singing is his 'ego' (very individualistic!) and is certainly heard 'by nobody except those who are distracted by my verses'. Because of this, his poems or his legacy are nothing other than the remnants of the feelings of an individualistic human who is rapt in contemplation, humming to his own self:

*Ieu patilasanna*
*keur ngahariring nunggeling*
*basana tembang midangdam*
*ngan muni kadua kuping*
*meujeuhna hunang-hening*
*ngalantung bari ngalayung*
*haleuang humaleuang*
*nu matak miaing-aing*
*lain geusan rungueun nu teu kagembang.*

These are the remnants,
for someone to hum to himself,
verses of melancholy,
heard by my ears only,
rapt in contemplation,
strolling at twilight,
singing aloud,
engrossed in myself
unheard except by those distracted
[by my verses].

From *The melody of sensing: Sinom*

In his Sundanese language, Hasan Mustapa often used phrases or affixations not commonly used by others, but which were nevertheless correct and easily understood, and which in fact opened up space for using the vitality of the Sundanese language in more suggestive and intensive ways. He tried all possibilities, and the results have opened possibilities for broader possibilities. In the poem just quoted we find the word '*miaing-aing*' [to be self-engrossed]. At a glance, I felt the word did not exist in Sundanese, but in fact I was wrong. After thinking it over and giving it some scrutiny, I realised that the word '*miaing-aing*' originates in '*aing*'. This word is affixed with '*mi-*', which has a similar meaning to the prefix '*nga-*', meaning 'consider' or 'name as'. An example is '*miindung*', which means '*nga-indung*', in the sense of 'considering as mother' or 'naming as mother'.

Hasan Mustapa used the language of daily conversation, not the poetic language with its well-established formulas that determined phrases and lines. In the first of my excerpts above from *The melody of sensing: Sinom* for example, the third line is daily conversation, 'whose fault is it? The verse's'. And if one recites it aloud, one must stop a moment and take a breath between *saha* and the second *bongan*. If we read it by using the verse patterns conventionally used in reading verse narratives [*wawacan*], that is line by line, one would lose the point, and miss the meaning of the poem. Because if we read the line just mentioned '*bongan saha bongan tembang*' in the conventional, verse-narrative style, it is difficult to understand. And if we were able to understand it, it would be a very different understanding from the one intended.

Mustapa's habit of using phrases from everyday conversation can be found in all of the stanza forms he used. Because of that, when studying the meanings of Hasan Mustapa's verses, one must not be enticed into softly humming [the melody associated with the pattern], for this would make us want to hear more, and we would them hum along, swept away in the waves of the melody. This doesn't mean that Hasan Mustapa's verses cannot or should not be sung. On the contrary! Hasan Mustapa's verses are truly affective when sung. But this affect relies not so much on the contents, nor on their profundity, but on the richness of the sound, on the poetic language, on the variety of language as well as reality of the vocal performance.

For me personally, when someone says 'Hasan Mustapa's verses cannot be understood, but are enjoyable when hummed, and are pleasurable to the feelings', this means that the speaker has been swept away by their external beauty, and this has happened because it he or she hummed along. Hasan Mustapa's verses are much easier understood when read in the style of daily conversation, that is, in the style and tone of ordinary [not poetic] language. For example:

| | |
|---|---|
| *Na saha nu ngebon sintung,*<br>*ngan aya nu melak kitri,*<br>*duwegan gé saliwatan,*<br>*geuwat bisi kolot teuing,*<br>*kaporotan ganti ngaran,*<br>*duwegan santri teu amis.* | Who would plant a coconut sheath?<br>People only plant the budding fruit.<br>The young coconut is fleeting;<br>hurry lest it be too old,<br>too late and it changes name.<br>A mature coconut is not sweet. |

From *To end up sitting in melancholy: Kinanti*

or:

| | |
|---|---|
| *Kudu lawung pada lawung,*<br>*sajajaran pancakaki,*<br>*gumelar lebah usumna,*<br>*maju teuing mundur teuing,*<br>*matak sarosopan rasa,*<br>*pinggan paéntép jeung piring.* | We must all come together<br>in the same line of descent,<br>presenting ourselves at the proper time,<br>if one moves too far forward or back,<br>a mismatch of feelings is caused,<br>like bowls wrongly stacked with plates. |

From *To end up sitting in melancholy: Kinanti*

If we were to hum these verses with one of the *kinanti* melodies, while weaving, for example, or just humming to ourselves, we would become lost, attracted only by the beauty of the metaphors and the humming. By contrast, if we read them in the tones of day to day conversation, they are quickly and more easily understood.

I would now like to make some notes concerning the metaphors used by Hasan Mustapa in this verse and in his verses in general. In order to express the reality that all things are named according to their individual contexts, he makes metaphors with the names given to the coconut plant. No one ever plants the *sintung* [the sheath of the coconut flower]. People plant the *kitri* [the coconut that has sprouted] – even though the *sintung* comes from the *kitri*, or in actual fact, the *kitri* originates from the *sintung*. But these cannot be mixed up. And apart from that, the *duwegan* is just a temporary name before thc fruit becomes the mature coconut [*duwegan santri*], the juice of which is not sweet.

Similarly, in describing the assortment of feelings caused by the merging of different contexts, Hasan Mustapa uses the metaphor of stacking bowls with plates. Like the others just mentioned, these metaphors are plastic. But it is not the plasticity that fascinates, for when it comes to plasticity in poetry, our Sundanese ancestors have already shown amazing creativity. The bardic stories contain many examples: to the point where people who like to exaggerate are said to be 'like a bard'. The bards exaggerate because they strive for plasticity. When they describe the court clown/messenger, who can run as fast as a rifle bullet or a galloping horse, they enhance this with humorous statements about the noise of his knees, and the comical movements of his bottom and as he falls over and gets up again. Or when expressing the beauty of a princess, even the sands are elegantly curved, rocks sparkle, and the grasses smile because of the princess's aura, and so on.

But there is a difference between plasticity of the bardic stories and the plasticity of the metaphors Hasan Mustapa creates in his lyrical poems. If the comparisons in legendary stories are on the whole hyperbolic, it is because the bard wishes to bring humour to the audience, whereas Hasan Mustapa's metaphors are generally simple but clever.

In the bardic stories, the metaphors are generally applied to extraordinary phenomena. In Mustapa's verses, they are in fact taken from the observable realities of everyday life. From transitory things that we miss, that we fail to notice, the existence of which we might even fail to be aware. We might have no inkling of them.

All Sundanese are familiar with the coconut tree. And many are acquainted with the names for the phases of its life. But only a keen observer, restless in calling on his intellect as well as senses, was able to use the transitions in the name of the coconut as it passes through its growth phases in order to metaphorically describe the order of the world, of the macrocosmos, more broadly. This could only be done by a person who constantly inquired with great meticulousness into his own existence as well as his life in the entire world. Hasan Mustapa was observant and perceptive, adroit and clear-sighted, while at the same time he never ceased sharpening his feelings and sensory perceptions in his daily life.

If we look into his other verses and writings, another undeniable perspective arises: Hasan Mustapa was knowledgeable and familiar with the daily life of the Sundanese in both its outer and inner aspects. This is clear from the lexicon and structures of his writings. These were not the ones commonly used amongst the religious scholarly elites. He also mobilised the lexicon and terminologies of agricultural life: he knew the names of trees, and their characteristics and benefits; he knew the rhythms and rituals of agricultural life; he was familiar with weaving terminologies which may have almost disappeared in contemporary Sundanese life (to the point that some of the Sundanese owners of weaving mills are more comfortable using a foreign language to describe their weaving apparatus); he knew the names of musical instruments, right up to the [modern musical genre] *ketuk tilu*, he knew the terminologies and methods of fishing, the names of the diverse parts of water-courses, the various species of fish: and he was especially knowledgeable of the lexicon of life in the Islamic school and all its sciences, for he was brought up on them, and was a product of that environment.

Much of this language is scarcely used in contemporary times, and the Sundanese lifeworld has been overtaken by change, carried away by the flood of time. More than other Sundanese of his generation, who also lived in a Sundanese lifeworld that was still 'intact', still 'original', Hasan Mustapa immortalised that life as well as its vitality in his writings. In truth, the customs of those times and their lexicon have disappeared without trace from everyday reality, leaving Hasan Mustapa's writings as a dead witness to convey those customs and its lexicon to the present generation and those to come.

The following is a metaphor for a person who places too much importance on external things, to the point where his life becomes unbalanced through neglect of the spiritual life. The figurative image used by Hasan Mustapa is characteristically Sundanese:

| | |
|---|---|
| *Mun aing suhud ka iwung,* | If I concentrate on (eating) the bamboo shoots, |
| *tandaning lali ka awi,* | that means I am forgetting the bamboo, |
| *susah keur nganyam ayakan,* | and weaving a sieve will be difficult. |
| *éléh ku ngeunah sakali,* | If overtaken by a singular pleasure, |
| *ngarasa kurang keur kurang,* | we will feel a lack at a time of need, |
| *butuh keur anyaman bilik.* | of the stuff we need to weave our walls. |

From *To end up sitting in melancholy: Kinanti*

Many metaphors refer to the world of agriculture, for Sundanese life of Mustapa's time was still an agrarian one. The villages and small communities had not yet been wrecked by the insecurity of today.

In the nineteen twenties, a book entitled 'Bandung Townhall' (*Balé Bandung*) (1925) was published in Bandung, containing the correspondence between Hasan Mustapa and Kiai Kurdi of Singaparna. These were not private letters such as those we commonly encounter. They discussed matters of religious belief and philosophy in a humorous way. The reason why this book was so popular, in my estimation, was most likely not because of the subject matter, but because most of the letters appeared in the forms of children's verse, rhyming allusions, and coarsely humorous verses etc. In the formal Sundanese poetry of the time, these were not much valued, in fact, they were not at all valued, although in daily life verse forms of this kind were still very much alive.

The forms used by Hasan Mustapa and Kiai Kurdi in their correspondence were not imported forms like the bulk of Mustapa's verse. They were the true Sundanese literary forms (poetry): children's songs like *ucang-ucang anggé*,[6] *umbieu-umbieu*, *oray-orayan*, *trang-trang koléntang*, *cok-cang*, *ambil-ambilan* etc., as well as the coarsely humorous verse, rhyming allusions, and so on.

Poetic patterns based on the repetition of the final syllable of a line are never used in Mustapa's verse [*dangding*], but in the rhyming allusions and coarse verses, the final syllable pattern becomes crucial, much like the Malay pantun:

| | |
|---|---|
| *Turub cupu buli-buli* | A locket with its lid |
| *eusina komala inten.* | contains diamonds and jewels. |
| *Daék sukur henteu paduli,* | If you want it or not, it's up to you, |
| *urang mah geus boga nu hideung santen.* | I already have a beautiful brown one. |
| *Takokak jeung daun pacing* | The *takokak* and *pacing* leaves |
| *akeupan buah rumanten.* | hug a *rumanten* fruit. |
| *Nu matak raka téh cicing* | What makes me sit in silence, |
| *ngeukeupan nu hideung santen.* | is cuddling my beautiful brown one. |

All the metaphors and symbols used by both Hasan Mustapa as well as Kiai Kurdi in their correspondence were present in Sunda, in its conceptual world, its literature, its philosophy, its history and chronicles, and in daily life. The symbols and metaphors included: Lady Sumbi, Princess Asri, Prince Mundinglaya Dikusumah, the

6 The titles here all refer to children's songs and game rhymes. They cannot be translated effectively because their semiotic function is to establish the rhyme of the song rather than to refer to describeable phenomena external to the text.

Virgin Sunti, the Lady of the Silent Feelings, The Sacred Mother, the King of Galuh, Pakuaji, the Kingdom of Pajajaran, etc.

In the first letter of the book, replying to a letter from Kiai Kurdi in which he apologised for not being able to see Mustapa because he had received his message too late, Hasan Mustapa said he just got back from a journey carrying 'white cotton fabric woven by Lady Sumbi' to east Priangan, but unfortunately no one wanted to even look at it. Kiai Kurdi replied 'Of course', for 'white cotton fabric woven by Lady Sumbi will not sell, even if woven by the Virgin Sunti, for people are used to batik made by others.' He continued, 'It will still sell in Singaparna, because the thread and the needle of the Lady of the Silent Feelings are still there, …pineapple leaves with the spikes filed off … used to stitch up the mountain and darn the universe, to make a hem for the horizon.'

In response to that answer, Hasan Mustapa 'wailed to the heavens', expressing his disappointment that people forget their own origins, and are tempted by foreign things. He likened it to swapping teak with cheaper wood. Mustapa compares the scream of his soul with Princess Asri's lament when Mundinglaya was tempted by strangers:

| | |
|---|---|
| *Deudeuh Akang Mundinglaya Di Kusumah,* | My beloved Mundinglaya Di Kusumah, |
| *tiwas-tiwas ti peuting kaimpi sumping,* | I long at night, dreaming of you coming, |
| *ti beurang katéang datang,* | in the day I imagine you visiting. |
| *bisi kasilih ku junti,* | I fear you will be replaced by strangers, |
| *ulah kabeunangan bagdja.* | And deprived of your happiness. |
| *Sugan téh kukupu hideung,* | I thought it was a black butterfly, |
| *sihoréng obat kabeuleum;* | turned out to be burnt gunpowder; |
| *Sugan téh Mundinglaya kukuh katineung,* | I thought Mundinglaya firm in conviction, |
| *sihoréng kabéngbat deungeun.* | but he was tempted by a stranger. |
| *Masing éling ka wiwitan,* | Remember your origins, |
| *mangka awas ka wekasan …* | be mindful of the end … |

This is the plea of someone asking us to return to the beginning, the yell of someone pleading us to go back to our origin, to return to the start, which manifests in our selves as conviction, as belief, as faith. One cannot persist in serving a master if one is tempted by the external colours and forms of other people, forgetting the authentic while it is replaced by something fake. He urges us not to be tempted by novelties that appear in passing.

At this encouragement, Kiai Kurdi replied further:

| | |
|---|---|
| *Cai asa tuak bari,* | Water tastes like spoiled palm wine, |
| *dileueut wayah janari;* | and is drunk after midnight, |
| *geura mulih ka sasari,* | please go back to your usual self, |
| *nya ati di sanubari.* | to your innermost feeling. |

Hasan Mustapa, who did not feel that he had moved away from his usual self, replied:

| | |
|---|---|
| *Euleung euy, euleung,* | I say, friend, I say! |
| *taneuh tela ledak dieu;* | the ground has cracked open here; |
| *nanjak jalan ka pareuntas;* | the road ahead is sloping up; |
| *Eureun euy, eureun,* | Let us stop, friend, let us stop, |
| *ti baheula gé di dieu,* | since long ago I have been here, |
| *teu nyaba ka alas peuntas.* | I've never been to the distant forest. |

After both felt affirmed in their feelings of being neighbours in the same village, of being unwavering to their true selves, and of choosing the authentic over the inauthentic, they resumed their correspondence, but now it became even more esoteric: both reach for conclusions, both allude to their meanings, both praise the other. Their play reaches deep into their inner feeling:

| | |
|---|---|
| *Euleung euy, euleung,* | I say friend, I say, |
| *hurang ulin di basisir,* | shrimps are playing by the beach, |
| *ka darat loba kayakas;* | many crabs head onto land; |
| *Eureun euy, eureun,* | Let us stop friend, let us stop, |
| *urang ulin di jero sir,* | we are playing deep in our feelings, |
| *ku surat jiga wewekas.* | through letters like funeral wishes. |

This inner feeling is a reflection that brings forgetfulness of everything. Like someone in a state of utter distraction:

| | |
|---|---|
| *Ucang-ucang anggé,* | Swing, baby, swing, |
| *ka Lintung jalan ka Lémbang,* | to Lintung on the way to Lémbang, |
| *ka Lémbang ka Cibiana;* | to Lémbang to Cibiana; |
| *Urang-urang hadé,* | Let us beware of ourselves, |
| *kaduhung beunang kagembang,* | distraction causes regret, |
| *kagembang kieu rasana.* | and distraction feels like this. |

The packaging through which Mustapa conveyed his messages might be different from the Islamic packaging that came from the desert, for all belief systems conform to the characteristics and conditions of their place of origin. The original Sundanese belief, they say, is 'secreted away in the cardamom leaves, buried next to the intersection, covered in shade by the Spanish Cherry, overshadowed by acanthus shrubs, hidden under dried leaves'. Even though one searches for it, 'it will not be found by the grasscutter, will not be uprooted by the weeder, will not be proven by the student of Islam, and will not be revealed by the sage'. It will only be revealed by 'the reciter of legends who is descended from creation'.

Everything that comes from outside, or is considered a visitor, must be compared with what is secreted away in that leaf. It is then put into Sundanese, is understood, and comprehended. So it is with the Qur'an, according to Hasan Mustapa, which must be harmonised and compared with the Qur'an that goes back to the Sundanese ancestors. He wrote in the *Padika Qur'an* (Method of the Qur'an) verse 100:

> … if a visitor should bring the Qur'an, harmonise it with the ancestral Qur'an; make it like the songs that a grandmother uses to admonish young people, to be friendly to a visitor, mindful of what will remain after the visit, saying:

| | |
|---|---|
| *Kembang kacang kembang kacang*<br>*barudak, geura beungkeutan;*<br>*Sémah nganjang*<br>*barudak, geura deukeutan.* | Flowers of the nut plant,<br>children, bind them!<br>A guest is coming;<br>children, go and meet him! |
| *Kembang kacang kembang kacang*<br>*barudak, geura pipitan;*<br>*Sémah nganjang*<br>*barudak, geura ciwitan.* | Flowers of the nut plant,<br>children, pick them!<br>A guest is coming;<br>children, go and pinch him! |
| *Kembang kacang kembang kacang*<br>*barudak, geura asakan;*<br>*Sémah nganjang*<br>*barudak, geura asaan.* | Flowers of the nut plant,<br>children, cook them!<br>A guest is coming;<br>children, go and feel him! |

> This must be done in case he leaves feeling upset, in case he complains while leaving. So find out for sure about each new guest, quickly meet them, pinch them and feel them …

Truly we must be prepared to confront one another, to challenge someone even if they be 'in the same line of descent' [*sajajaran pancakaki*]. If we look back to the past, we realise that where the Sundanese are concerned, they have had many experiences of confronting others. Our Sundanese ancestors of old showed their courage in facing various influences and 'visitors' from outside, from India, from Java, from Arabia, and the results have always shown that the Sundanese spirit has the ability to create a harmonious synthesis. The Sundanese spirit has always had the courage to endure these confrontations with resolve, convictions, beliefs and a conceptual world that are entirely different in character from those that come from outside. The results of these confrontations always show that the Sundanese spirit has not been swept away, has not been extinguished, and has not been overcome by 'visitors', but dynamically as well as harmoniously absorbs their influence, and makes it its own private property.

After examining Hasan Mustapa, both in his writings as well as the popular anecdotes about him, it is my opinion that Hasan

Mustapa, from the Islamic mystical-philosophic perspective, could only appear and thrive in the spiritual and cultural environment of the Sundanese, because he is a manifestation of the imaginative spirit that has been active and creative throughout traditional Sundanese literature (the bardic stories, the stories of Sangkuriang and Kabayan). Firmly and profoundly, he stands rooted in his place of origin, which is the Sundanese lifeworld, the world of Sundanese culture.

Cihideung, 17 February 1960.

Translated from Sundanese by Rabin Hardjibrata,
Hawé Setiawan and Julian Millie

**Sources referred to in the editor's footnotes**

Rosidi, Ajip
1973 'My experiences in recording "Pantun Sunda"', *Indonesia* 16, 105-111.
1989 *Haji Hasan Mustapa jeung Karya-karyana*. Bandung: Pustaka.
2011a *Wawacan*. Bandung: Kiblat/LBSS.
2011b *Guguritan*. Bandung: Kiblat/LBSS.

*Chapter 7*

# FORM AND SEMANTICS OF MUSTAPA'S VERSIFICATION

Hawé Setiawan

| | |
|---|---|
| *Satungtung catur micatur* | As long as we make utterance |
| *Basa meletik ti biwir* | and language rises from our lips |
| *Bagian kamanusaan* | we are a part of humanity; |
| *Panglandi tina rohani* | a name for something from our inner selves; |
| *Geusan medalkeun ku basa* | the site of forms arising in language, |
| *Diunikeun ku jasmani* | verbalised through our bodies. |

*The quail laments in its cage*
(Rosidi 1989: 113)

## Introduction

Reading the Sundanese verse of Haji Hasan Mustapa (1852-1930) is like wading into a fast-flowing river. No matter how much we feel attracted and want to reach out to it, we are at the same time held back by a fear of being swept away. Puzzling and enticing religious and philosophical speculations beckon us further and further inwards. In this essay, to avoid being drowned in the sheer volume and weight of Mustapa's work, I avoid the invitation conveyed by his religious speculation, and cling to the 'external' aspects of Haji Hasan Mustapa's poetry, that is, the poetic forms and tools that he infuses with the 'spiritual' message of his mysticism.

Sundanese verse, including the forms used by Mustapa, is bound by fixed rules that have been handed down from one generation to the next. In this sense, it is highly structured in forms prescribed by convention. But this does not reduce the significance of these structures and forms. Precisely because such constraints exist, we are drawn to examine the creative ability with which a specific writer navigates and makes use of convention. This is not the same as asking how high a bird can fly in its cage by flapping its wings. Rather, I wish to examine the kind of creative freedom this bound subject enjoys when it lets its song be heard. If the poetics of Sundanese verse are to be described in terms of a grammar, then the verse of Haji Hasan Mustapa clearly represents a distinct utterance within the framework of that grammar.

For a mystical poet such as Mustapa, questions of genre should not be the main issue. He did not create his verses for the sake of poetry itself, but rather for the flashes of insight and reflections that he wished to convey. At times, these flashes dragged poetic forms into new directions, for we see examples in his work in which poetic forms 'arise of their own accord', in the same manner as steam rises from the kettle when the water becomes hot. This is not so surprising in Mustapa's case, for he was an inspired and prolific composer of verse, producing more than 10,000 stanzas within a short period (Rosidi 1989: 88). This legacy will be more easily accessed by a reader with some familiarity with the techniques of Sundanese verse. This chapter provides this familiarisation with the genres Mustapa used, as well as his specific modes of working with them.

My analysis might fall short of the expectations of someone who fully appreciates Mustapa's mystical vision. Mystical experience can be understood or felt to the full by one who is open to that experience, and for such people, the poetic and linguistic tools are secondary things. For the searcher, form is never sufficient of itself. The definitions found in the dictionary, which contain only generally accepted meanings, are never sufficient for the conveyance of mystical experience, vision or feeling. But even so, an approach based on Mustapa's poetics is valuable. All poets, and mystical poets in particular, are impelled to seek idioms and create metaphors, or in other words, to overcome the limitations of everyday language and thus more or less recreate the language in his own way. Because of this, while not intending to neglect the importance of mysticism, this essay concentrates its attention on the processes of language use.

The western nomenclature for understanding verse in its historical aspect is quite useful here. The Sundanese have for a long time been writing in a wide diversity of verse forms, including free verse, and amongst these forms, the conventions of Sundanese versification used by Mustapa can be equated to some degree with 'classical forms'. The forms used by Mustapa are structured ones, and contrast with 'modern' verse forms for that reason. Although this comparison with the development of literature in Europe is of limited value, it nevertheless helps us appreciate how convention leads to a special notion of creativity in Sundanese verse also:

> The classical flow is a succession of elements whose density is even; it is exposed to the same emotional pressure, and relieves those elements of any tendency towards an individual meaning appearing at all invented. The poetic vocabulary itself is one of usage, not of invention: images in it are recognizable in a body; they do not exist in isolation; they are due to long custom, not to individual creation. The function of the classical poet is not therefore to find new words, with more body or more brilliance, but to follow the order of an ancient ritual, to perfect the symmetry or the conciseness of a

> relation, to bring a thought exactly within the compass of a metre. Classical conceits involve relations, not words: they belong to an art of expression, not of invention. The words, here, do not, as they later do, thanks to a kind of violent and unexpected abruptness, reproduce the depth and singularity of an individual experience; they are spread out to form a surface, according to the exigencies of an elegant or decorative purpose. They delight us because of the formulation which brings them together, not because of their own power or beauty. (Barthes 1968: 45)

Mustapa's verses do indeed draw our attention to a meeting point between creativity and 'the order of an ancient ritual' in Sundanese poetics, or in other words, to the 'symmetry or the conciseness of a relation' between elements of versification and mystical contemplation.

In what follows, however, I argue that the 'ancient ritual' was pushed and pressured by an individual possessed of a relentless creativity that saw him occasionally turn back on those forms to play with them. Mustapa did create new words. He produced them in striking combinations of recognisable elements. At times, this process resulted in new meanings, at others, it quite deliberately resulted in *no meaning*.

**Sundanese verse**

Sundanese verse (*dangding*) can be understood as belonging to the category of metrical verse. This is a traditional form of poetry that has fixed rules which, as will be set out below, impose limits on each of its lines. The lines of Sundanese verse, as is usual in metrical forms, are regulated by a 'metrical grid'. The four aspects set out in Fabb and Halle's study of metrical verse are useful here:

> ...every well-formed line of metrical verse consists not only of the phonemes and syllables that determine its pronunciation, but also of what we have called a metrical grid, i.e., a pattern, which though not pronounced, determines the perception of a sequence

> of syllables as a line of metrical verse, rather than as an ordinary bit of prose. Our further claim is that each grid is the output of a computation whose input is the string of syllables that make up the verse line: the grid is not pre-constructed and then attached to the line, but is generated separately from each individual line. Our third claim is that the computation consists in the ordered application of a licensed set of rules selected from a finite set of rules … (A set of rules is 'licensed' when it is observed by a poetic school or tradition.) Our fourth and final claim is that a verse line is well formed metrically if and only if its grid is well formed (i.e., the grid is the output of a licensed set of ordered rules) and if the syllables composing the line satisfy certain further conditions. (Fabb and Halle 2008: 11)

These rules can be divided into two kinds, namely those concerning metrics (*guru wilangan*), which relates to the number of syllables in each line and the number of lines in each stanza, and end-rhyme (*guru lagu*), which determine the vowel to be found in the final position in the line. But the rules of verse that bind *dangding* can in many ways also be understood as the rules of a musical composition, for Sundanese verse is basically composed for a reader who sings. The resulting form of poetry, which is also called *guguritan*, is bound by a set of basic rules relating to melody, as well as those connected with the number of syllables in each line, the number of lines per stanza, and the variations in final vowels.

It is not surprising that the tradition of Sundanese verse owes its preservation among other things to the support of the musical art known as *tembang*, in which verses composed in the same forms as those used by Mustapa are used as texts by singers. The term *dangding* itself is probably a word that originally imitated a sound. Whereas the term *guguritan*, 'composition' (from a base-word *gurit*, to compose, arrange), places emphasis on the act of writing or making a composition, the term *dangding* references the sound produced in this activity. In his well-known guide to Sundanese verse Satjidibrata uses the units *dang*, *ding* and others as sound tokens in his illustration of metrical patterns (Satjibrata 1953). The *dangding*, therefore, derives from the mnemonic phrases that enable one to recall the correct determination of vowel sounds.

On the basis of the rules governing their versification, the poetical forms are divided into 17 *pupuh* (stanza forms), each with its own name. And each is connected with a mood (*watek*). The stanza form of *Asmarandana*, for example, is the vehicle for expressing romantic desire. *Durma* is for battle. *Kinanti* is associated with longing and melancholy, *sinom* for moral instruction, and so on.

These songs are delivered by a reader, who is usually listened to by other readers in a gathering, specifically the readers of *wawacan*, that is, a sequence of *pupuh*. Sundanese composed *wawacan* with many purposes. Narratives and romances are popular, but so were religious works, and even instructional works for subjects like rice-farming.

This reveals the particular expectations associated with this form of poetry. When confronted with *dangding*, the experienced reader will not approach the task as if it were a situation of silent reading. First of all, the reader of *dangding* will recognise the melody of each *pupuh*, as well as the specific rules of its verse-form. This familiarity distinguished the reading process. At this point the intersection of this form of literature with oral tradition can be seen: because it is a written form that has a pattern and is also melodious, *dangding* is easy for the reader to memorise.

*Dangding* and *guguritan* have been influenced by similar forms in the Javanese literary tradition. In former times, in particular when Sundanese politics and culture were influenced by Java, knowledge and skill in the field of Javanese language and literature were regarded as signs of an educated person among the Sundanese. According to the *Bujangga Manik*, a work in Old Sundanese passed down from the 16th century, for example, the hero of the story, Bujangga Manik derives his superiority from the fact that he '*bisa carék Jawa*', that is, he was good at speaking Javanese (Noorduyn and Teeuw 2006). It is not surprising that the *geguritan*, being part of the linguistic culture of Java, entered the Sundanese region as part of a general flow of cultural influence and as a result, the verse forms of the *guguritan* or *dangding* become centrepieces of the treasury of Sundanese literature.

Since then, *dangding* has remained central in Sundanese culture. It is still today studied in schools, but does not have the influence now it held in the past. Sundanese verse has provided a means to express oneself in song that shaped the outputs of many Sundanese intellectuals in their respective times. For example, Wahyu Wibisana (1934 -2014), a well known Sundanese poet, began writing Sundanese verse when he was in fourth class at primary school. R.A.A. Kusumahningrat, alias Dalem Pancaniti, the Regent of Cianjur (1834-1862), wrote letters to his wife in verse form (Lubis 1998: 240-1). Similarly, Mustapa exchanged letters with his colleague Kiai Koerdi on matters relating to religion in verse form, creating a body of correspondence in poetry. A regent of the colonial period, R.A.A. Wiranatakoesoemah (1888-1965), compiled a book called 'The Story of the Honoured Prophet (peace and blessing be upon him)' (1941), in which is found a translation of several verses of the Quran in a verse form – a form of literary creativity later continued by Hidayat Suryalaga (1941-2010) with his adaptation of the holy scripture in the form of verse. Through the efforts of these writers and others, Sundanese versification has occupied a special place within Sundanese culture.

Even though the golden age of verse has passed, a number of Sundanese poets are still composing works in these forms alongside more contemporary forms such as free verse, novels and short stories. The days when people enjoyed listening to long narrative verses (*wawacan*) in *dangding* are gone, but nevertheless, since the 1950s, the more contemporary forms have been developing hand in hand with continuing adaptations of the traditional forms.

Mustapa has left a large corpus of verse. Responding to the commonly held belief that Mustapa's corpus consists of 20,000 verses, Iskandarwassid *et al* stated:

> At this point, the number of stanzas of verses known to have been written by Haji Hasan Mustapa is 10,812. Out of this number only 9,472 still exist, and are found in various places, such as the Wangsaatmadja collection, the Library of the University of Leiden, the Manuscript Section of the National Library, and the collections of private individuals. It is possible that there are more not yet discovered. Although there are nowhere near 20,000 stanzas, it is clear that there are more than 10,000. (Iskandarwassid et al. 1987: 23).

**Mustapa's poetics**

Mustapa described his literary language as 'polished language *(basa beunang ngahampelas*). Diction is an important element of that 'polishing' process, and I wish to focus on two elements of Mustapa's diction here. First, Mustapa used a number of Sundanese words that are not very familiar, at least for contemporary speakers of this language, but which demonstrate the poet's creativity in producing a kind of new idiom. Second, I wish to draw attention to Mustapa's use of Arabic. In certain cases, Mustapa's borrowings from Arabic are presented in Sundanese patterns of word formation.

Mustapa's use of the affix *–um–* illustrates his approach to neologisms. Words formed with *–um–* are frequently loan words from Javanese, and their meaning and forms are very varied (Coolsma 1985:111). Basically *–um–* is an infix, as in *gumilang* (from the base-word *gilang* meaning radiant), but if the base-word begins with a vowel, this affix is added as a prefix, as in *umangkeuh* (from *angkeuh* meaning stubborn, in error). The meanings or connotations contained in words formed with the infix *–um–* are: 1. A connotation of movement, as in *lumaku* (to walk); 2. A connotation of movement which is repeated or occurring in succession, as in *jumegur* (to boom more than once), which can be compared with *ngajegur* (to boom once); 3. A connotation that shows that the condition is not genuine or proper, as in *gumeulis* (vainly beautiful, from the word *geulis* meaning beautiful) (Kats and Soeriadiradja 1982:156-8).

In Mustapa's verse we find quite a few words formed with the affix *–um–*. Some of them are neologisms devised by Mustapa himself with specific intent, for example, *umaing* (egocentrism), *bumatur* (to distance a person), *uméta* (to continuously point elsewhere), *sumaha* (to frequently ask 'who?'), Mustapa achieved poetic emphasis with these words and others. Here is an example:

| | |
|---|---|
| *Umaing méakkeun batur* | My 'I'ness exhaust others. |
| *Bumatur méakkeun aing* | My otherness exhausts me. |
| *Umaing méakkeun éta* | My 'I'ness exhausts that. |
| *Uméta méakkeun aing* | My thatness exhausts me. |
| *Umaing méakkeun saha* | My 'I'ness exhausts whom? |
| *Sumaha méakkeun aing* | My whoness exhausts me. |

*The quail laments in its cage*, (Rosidi 1989: 101)

In this example Mustapa pushes recognisable Sundanese forms into novel forms. Listeners are confronted by a strangeness that is simultaneously highly familiar. The words *umaing*, *bumatur* and *uméta* are recognisable for listeners because the roots are very commonly used in daily communication, as is the *–um–* infix. But these new creations are simultaneously strange and alien, for they are unprecedented combinations. The recognisable gives rise to foreignness.

Mustapa adapted the *–(n)ing* suffix with similar creativity. This suffix derives from Javanese language. It generally indicates possession or attribution. The prior term suffixed with *(n)ing* is possessed by or an attribute of the latter. Here is an example:

| | |
|---|---|
| Rumrumaning nagasari | The scent of the coconut blossom at its most fragrant |
| | (Mustapa 2009: 89) |

The line works with the common word *arum*, meaning fragrant. Mustapa doubles the element *rum* and adds *–(n)ing*. I doubt *rumrumaning* appears elsewhere in Sundanese writing. The musical effect is striking. Once again, the effect is metrical. But the poetic effects are greater than that. The suffix ties the two substantives together in a special relationship. It points to the realness and naturalness of the possession or attribute.

Mustapa's use of tools like this are a distinctive feature of his work. They appear time and time again. In Mustapa's diction, the language provides an almost infinite range of possibilities for novel poetic combinations. The aural orientation of his work encouraged him to explore the plasticity and flexibility of poetic resources.

**Arabic borrowings**

For most of his early life, Mustapa studied Islamic materials in the Arabic language. He then utilised much of that learning in his own expressions, which are of course written not in Arabic, but in his mother tongue, Sundanese. As is the case with most non-Arabic

Islamic writing, Arabic nevertheless appears frequently in Mustapa's writing in citations of the Qur'an and hadith. In this sense, Mustapa belongs to the global tradition of vernacular interpreters of Islam. But Muṣtapa is interesting for the ways in which he repackaged Arabic lexical items in Sundanese morphology and syntax. Mustapa's works are full of Arabic terms that are transformed according to Sundanese patterns of word formation.

I interpret Mustapa's perception of this process as follows: he wished to introduce Sundanese to key Islamic concepts by using the original Arabic lexical items, but at the same time, he wished to mitigate the foreignness of these terms by pushing them into Sundanese morphological conventions. The word *kauluhiyahan* appears frequently in *The Teachings* (see Chapter Two). Mustapa formed this noun by adding the Sundanese affixes *ka–* and *–an* to the Arabic noun *uluhiyah* (divinity, divine power). Does the affixation effect a semantic distinction? It does. The formation of nouns in this way expands the root meaning. It refers to not only divinity, but also to things that belong to and are associated with divinity. While some Sundanese may interpret *uluhiyah* as a technical Islamic term, when draped in Sundanese affixes it is recognisable as more than an abstraction, but as a real presence in Sundanese life.

The title of the *The Teachings of Our Islamic Inheritance* displays a similar morphological creativity. The Sundanese title of the work is *Gelaran Sasaka di KaIslaman*. The work *kaIslaman* is formed by adding the suffixes *ka–* and *–an* to the base word. It means more than Islam, drawing attention to all things connected with Islam (Islamicness).

Concentrated poetic creativity can be read in Mustapa's in-text translations. The example below is constructed around the Muslim creed *La ilaha illa Allah* (Arabic: There is no God other than Allah). The italicised text is Sundanese, the regular text is Arabic:

| | |
|---|---|
| La ilaha illallahu | There is no God other than Allah |
| *pokpokan nu beurat lain* | *An utterance that is not difficult, no!* |
| illallah *nu beurat enya* | Other than Allah *is difficult, yes.* |
| Allahu *méh taya lain* | Allahu *just means there is no other.* |
| hu *bitu ngan kari enya* | Hu *explodes leaving only the real.* |
| *hakéki ngan kari budi* | *The essence remains only as our deeds.* |

*The quail laments in its cage* (Rosidi 1989: 104)

The Arabic text of the creed would have been highly familiar to all Mustapa's listeners/readers. But here, Mustapa fragments it and reorients so as to produce a highly poetic and sufistic interpretation. Lines 2 to 5 oscillate between the affirmation (Arabic: *isbat*) and denial (Denial: *nafi*) that are the essence of the creed's structure and meaning (they alternately end with no/yes/no /yes: Sund. *lain/enya/lain/enya*). But the most striking aspect of the stanza is Mustapa's sonorous pairing of the Arabic case-marker '*u*' with the Sundanese *bitu* (to explode). Working with familiar materials in both Arabic and Sundanese, the effects are striking and confusing for many Sundanese listeners and readers. Mustapa's verse is full of fragments of Arabic phrases reassembled in forms that were simultaneously familiar and new to his listeners and readers.

**Defying interpretation**

A number of Mustapa's verses present challenges because they do not seem to allow for coherent interpretation in the context at hand. They point in directions that are semantically irreconcilable. We can compare such sequences with the *sampiran* (first half of a pantun) in Classical Malay poetry, in which a sonic and rhyming pattern is established in the opening lines. The value of assonance is high in these lines, and they do not convey any sensible reference.

This reference is provided in the second two lines, which resolve the semiotic problem, usually with an aphorism or words of wisdom that replicate the sound-patterns of the earlier assonance. We can compare them also to the *rajah* (introductory invocation) in the Sundanese epic tradition (*carita pantun*). The example below, excerpted from *The humming of a well-again person*, presents visual imagery as well as auditory effects:

| | |
|---|---|
| *Japati hiber ka bumi*<br>*macokan kembang dalima*<br>*hayam jago ngéplék jawér*<br>*rubak dada lebar jangjang*<br>*kalayang ka tanah wétan*<br>*diburu ku hayam tukung*<br>*koléang kana taweuran.* | The dove flies to the earth<br>and eats the pomegranate flower.<br>The cock's comb falls to the side,<br>its breast is wide, its wings are broad.<br>Flying to the eastern lands,<br>followed by a hairless chicken,<br>coming to land on the roof. |
| *Waliwis hiber ti peuting,*<br>*eunteupna kana bangbayang,*<br>*diboro ku hayam katé,*<br>*koléang kana suhunan,*<br>*barina kokoréakan,*<br>*kurulung si beurit jantung,*<br>*eusina kumaha dinya.* | The teal flies in the night,<br>coming to land on the long roof.<br>Pursued by a small chicken,<br>coming to land on the roof,<br>while sending out its call:<br>A song called 'The Brush Rat' is heard.<br>The meaning is up to you. |

*The humming of a well-again person*
(Rosidi 1989: 126)

These two stanzas are full of alliteration, which suggests a resolution later in the stanzas. But the resolution never comes. The last line in the quotation above ('the meaning is up to you') indicates Mustapa's perverse sense of humour. It appears that he is making a kind of *sampiran* without stating or emphasising any content. The 'shell' is given without any 'content'. A reader/listener with experience in these genres might expect a resolution based in didacticism or everyday wisdom. But instead, Mustapa resolves the lines by asking the reader to make her own significance for the preceding 'nonsense'. This is a sort of poetic game in which Mustapa plays with the expectations aroused in his readers by his use of conventional genres.

A more explicit example is found in *The quail laments in its cage*:

| | |
|---|---|
| *Sindir sapada ti indung* | A stanza from my mother |
| *hiji ti bapa pribadi* | and one from my father. |
| *nu sapada sisindiran* | One of them is an allusion |
| *pangasuh aing keur leutik* | and was my nurse when I was a child. |
| *eusina wallahu 'alam* | The meaning? Only Allah knows. |
| *moal sacangkang saeusi* | The shell does not match its content. |

*The Quail laments in its cage* (Rosidi 1989: 91)

After establishing strong alliteration in the first two lines, Mustapa draws back from clarity of meanings with 'The meaning? Only Allah knows / The shell does not match its content'.

In other words, Mustapa's verse includes 'empty spaces' devoid of referential meaning. These spaces enable him to move his works away from certainty and clarity. If these empty spaces are placed at the beginning of the verse, then their function is like the *rajah pamuka* (introductory formulas) in a *pantun* story, through which the reader can experience a kind of psychological conditioning, before entering into the profundities of mystical speculation. And if the empty spaces are placed in the middle of a series of lines of verse, then their function is like an interlude.

As well as creating empty spaces, Mustapa is often absorbed in the musical potential of his verses, arranging words to foreground musicality, and sacrificing interpretation with great inhibition. In lines such as this, it is as if the words are freed from the bonds of meaning, and returned to their primordial forms. The following stanza, which appears in similar forms in other works, is from *The quail laments in its cage*:

| | |
|---|---|
| *Ngalantung batur sakurung* | My other self went strolling |
| *kurang pakurang pakuring* | Lacking lessen self-forming |
| *kuring pakurang pakurang* | Self lessen lessen |
| *kurang pakurang pakuring* | Lacking lessen self-forming |
| *kuring pakuring pakurang* | Self self-forming lessen |
| *kurang pakurang pakuring* | Lacking lessen self-forming. |

*The quail laments in its cage* (Rosidi 1989: 94)

With these examples, Mustapa brought a unique vision to the Sundanese poetic tradition. He worked with a very firm foundation in that tradition (idiom, metaphors, versification), but exercised a talent for creatively appropriating words and their sounds. Against a background where verse was generally utilised as a vehicle for tales or accounts of things real and unreal, Mustapa used Sundanese verse as a poetical template for presenting his inner experiences and understandings relating to Islamic mysticism.

Of course the deliberate mobilisation of poetic form to obscure and frustrate semantic clarity points strongly to Mustapa's religious vision. His poetic style opened the way for interpretations that denied everyday reality and turned his readers towards the world of mysticism. His most widely known stanzas are those which convey paradoxes, absurdities or fruitless quests. The following two examples from *The quail laments in its cage* are frequently cited in contemporary West Java:

| | |
|---|---|
| *Sapanjang néangan kidul*<br>*kalér deui kalér deui*<br>*sapanjang néangan wétan*<br>*kulon deui kulon deui*<br>*sapanjang néangan aya*<br>*euweuh deui euweuh deui* | As long as I search for the south,<br>north again, north again.<br>As long as I search for the east,<br>west again, west again.<br>As long as I search for being,<br>nothing again, nothing again.<br>*The quail laments in its cage*, (Rosidi 1989: 97) |
| *galantung méméh ngalantung*<br>*ngalinjing méméh ngalinjing*<br>*néangan méméh néangan*<br>*nepi ka méméhna indit*<br>*datang saméméhna iang*<br>*indit saméméh mimiti* | Strolling before going for a stroll,<br>nervously pacing before nervously pacing,<br>searching before going on a search,<br>arriving at the point of departure,<br>arriving before departure,<br>departing before setting out.<br>*The quail laments in its cage*, (Rosidi 1989: 98) |

The expression *nepi ka méméhna indit*, 'Arriving at the point of departure' defies everyday interpretation. This stanza commits us to a kind of (hermeneutic) circle, in which the starting point in the line drawn is at the same time the point of arrival.

**Conclusion**

The reader interested in the mystical meanings of Mustapa's verse might find the above account dry. It is of course plain that (Islamic) mysticism forms the subject-matter of all his verse. But nevertheless, that mysticism is achieved through poetic effects. This is what I have tried to draw attention to in this essay: Mustapa's mysticism is a product of a literary technique and sensibility that grew within a tradition of writing, and the rules of Sundanese versification provided him with resources that he was able to adapt with stunning creativity.

And there is much to be said for highlighting the elements of Mustapa's verse independently of the mystical tradition. Mysticism is not attractive to all Sundanese, and by concentrating on Mustapa's verse technique, we open a space for Mustapa's legacy to serve as a rich collective point of reference not just for Sufis but for the Sundanese community at large. After all, Mustapa's works are expressed in literary conventions that have been at the core of Sundanese cultural self-identification for many centuries. And furthermore, Mustapa himself did not demand that we view him as a mystical figure. He was not an advocate for the religious establishment, and his poetic statements invite us to consider him as a figure with much to say to all segments of West Javanese and Indonesian society:

| | |
|---|---|
| *Dinyarana kuring santri* | People think I am a santri |
| *sapédah bisa ngajina* | just because I can read the Qur'an. |
| *dinyarana alim kabot* | People think I'm a great scholar |
| *pédah getol ngawurukna* | just because I instruct. |
| *sinyarana bijaksana* | People think I am wise |
| *sapédah mulus rahayu* | just because I live clean and prosper, |
| *puguh sagala turunan* | and my entire lineage is clear |
| [...] | |

| | |
|---|---|
| *Barodona alam nyantri* | The *santri* world has its stupid ones, |
| *tacan kitab tacan Qur'an* | who can't yet read scriptures or Al-Qur'an, |
| *tacan daraék masantrén* | who do not wish to study |
| *tacan agama drigama* | and know neither religion nor law. |
| *kaula éra paradah* | I feel shame at |
| *sirung ngamomoré* | the seedling that is ignorant |
| *dapuran kamanusaan* | of the thicket of humanity. |

*The humming of a well-again person*
(Rosidi 1989: 126-127)

Translated by Julian Millie

## Sources cited

Barthes, Roland
1968 *Writing Degree Zero*, translated by Annette Layers dan Colin Smith. New York: Hill and Wang.
Coolsma, S.
1985 *Tata Bahasa Sunda*. Jakarta: Djambatan.
Fabb, Nigel, Morris Halle
2008 *Meter in Poetry: A New Theory*. Cambridge: Cambridge University Press.
Iskandarwassid, Ajip Rosidi, and Josep C.D.
1987 *Naskah Karya Haji Hasan Mustapa*. Bandung: Proyek Penelitian dan Pengkajian Kebudayaan Sunda (Sundanologi).
Kats, J. & Soeriadiradja, M.
1982 *Tata Bahasa dan Ungkapan Bahasa Sunda*. Jakarta: Djambatan.
Lubis, Nina H.
1998 *Kehidupan Ménak Priangan: 1800-1942*. Bandung: Pusat Informasi Kebudayaan Sunda.
Mustapa, Haji Hasan
2009 *Asmarandana nu kami*. Edited by Ajip Rosidi. Kiblat/Pusat Studi Sunda: Bandung.
Noorduyn, J. and A. Teeuw (eds and translators)
2006 *Three Old Sundanese Poems*. Leiden: KITLV.
Rosidi, Ajip
1989 *Haji Hasan Mustapa jeung Karya-karyana*. Bandung: Pustaka.
Satjibibrata, R.
1953 *Rasiah tembang Sunda*. Second edition. Djakarta: Balai Pustaka.
Wiranatakoesoema, R.A.A.
1941 *Riwajat Kangdjeng Nabi Moehammad s.a.w.* Bandoeng: Islam Studieclub.

*Chapter 8*

# THE SOLITARY MAN

## Hasan Mustapa's spirituality in the present

Asep Salahudin

In an article published in West Java's most widely read newspaper, *Pikiran Rakyat* (24 January 2009), Julian Millie commented on the striking difference between the legacies and commemoration of K.H. Hasyim Asy'ari (1871-1947), the famous Islamic scholar from Jombang Pesantren in East Java who founded the *Nahdlatul Ulama*, Indonesia's largest Islamic organisation, and the mystic and philosopher from West Java, Haji Hasan Mustapa. The former is very well known in Indonesia because of the vast following of that organisation, and because of his status as a national revolutionary hero. By contrast, there are few who know anything about the latter figure. Mustapa was no revolutionary hero, and no organisation of any kind counts him amongst its founders. It might appear that he was not active in those contexts that generate respect and popularity amongst Indonesian Muslims.

Millie could have taken the analysis deeper. Mustapa was truly a solitary figure. Not in his range of social connections, which was broad and varied, but in his religious outlook and expression. Mustapa's solitariness, his freedom from institutions and ideological dependencies, is the subject of this chapter. I approach this solitariness as a natural mode of existence for a 'searcher' of Mustapa's type. But I wish to press this theme further and argue that this solitariness is what makes it so important for the Sundanese to remember Mustapa and his work in the present. In contemporary West Java, the Sundanese need to commemorate Mustapa as an exemplar whose ideas and teaching have much to offer.

**A Solitary Man**

Haji Hasan Mustapa's lack of popularity in fact reflects the way of life that he himself chose. He had no interest in *ngamuridkeun* (taking pupils), or in setting up Islamic colleges, boarding schools or being the spiritual guide of a mystical movement. It was not that he avoided such institutions and activities; his closest friends included such people heavily involved in them, such as his study-mate, Abah Sepuh, the founder of the Suryalaya Pesantren in Tasikmalaya, and spiritual guide of the Qadiriyah *Naqsyabandiyah* movement. Furthermore, people close to him in Bandung established a study group around his works entitled the *Galih Pakuan* (The Heart of Pakuan). But Mustapa's inner condition was something different. He was happier to be a solitary man, and was not inclined to leadership. He was not a 'solidarity' person, capable of gathering people together and forming a mass organisation with thousands of members.

A solitary man is a kind of person who experiences the 'ecstasy' of spiritual achievement not in the midst of a throng of followers (brothers), but in deep reflection, in solitude. It is this character that allowed him to become a unique individual who revealed his spiritual experiences in a series of lonely words: the fascinating *guguritan* and *dangding* (classical Sundanese verse) which have resisted the ravages of time, even though they are difficult to comprehend. Mustapa understood his writings as being somewhat distant from the busyness unfolding around him:

> Ari kaula mah teu ngaku pangkat bujangga, sumawona rucita ku basa Arab, atawa basa Latin tapi nyampak rucika tedak sorangan, moal jongjon kajongjonan paramé-ramé, pacéntal-céntal
>
> I do not claim the rank of poet, let alone to be skilled in Arabic or Latin, but I do claim the skill to use my private words, not letting myself be tempted to join in with the hurly-burly or to hurl reproaches
>
> (Kartini et al 1985: 80-81)

Another characteristic of the solitary man is epistemological freedom. He is never content to remain within the bounds of just one field of knowledge, but constantly exercises his individual reason, embarking on a never-ending pilgrimage of the mind and a journey of the spirit. How could he possibly 'take pupils' while he himself is possessed by a feeling of dissatisfaction? Mustapa was haunted by his own longing to pursue truth, as is evident in his poem *The Quail Laments in its Cage*:

| | |
|---|---|
| *Sapanjang néangan kidul* | As long as I seek the south, |
| *Kalér deui kalér deui* | north again, north again. |
| *Sapanjang néangan wétan* | As long as I seek the east, |
| *Kulon deui kulon deui* | west again, west again. |
| *sapanjang néangan aya* | As long as I seek existence, |
| *euweuh deui euweuh deui* | the void again, the void again. |
| [...] | |
| *Ngalantang néangan tungtung* | Wandering in search of the end, |
| *Kawit deui kawit deui* | the beginning again, the beginning again. |
| *Sapanjang néangan tengah* | As long as I seek the middle, |
| *Sisi deui sisi deui* | the edge again, the edge again. |
| *Sapanjang néangan awas* | As long as I seek clarity, |
| *Huam deui huam deui* | obscure again, obscure again. |

| | |
|---|---|
| *Ngalantun timu panemu* | I set out to discover the answer, |
| *Nimu deui nimu deui* | discovering again, discovering again. |
| *Sapanjang néangan ngaran* | As long as I seek a name, |
| *Lain deui lain deui* | denied again, denied again. |
| *Sapanjang néangan padang* | As long as I seek illumination, |
| *surem deui surem deui* | darkness again, darkness again. |
| | *Kinanti: The Quail Laments in its Cage* (Rosidi 1989: 97) |

This dissatisfaction was a feature of Mustapa's thought even in his youth. As a student he was already sceptical about opinions which in his view could not be proved. When the other students followed the words of their teachers, Haji Hasan Mustapa on the other hand would think deeply and look for his own answer. In the collection of Mustapa's saying and teachings made by Wangsaatmadja, we encounter this statement by Mustapa:

> *Geura kaula geus heubeul teu leukeun ku nu kapibiheung deungeun: lakar deungeun ngaranca gé batur-batur; barisa ngaji teu boga pancering iman, nu sok leungit ku mikir nu lain-lain* [...] *tara matangankeun meureun, cukup ku lampahing hirup*
>
> I have for long not been concerned with other peoples' suspicions: other people are, after all, other people; they can read the Qur'an but have no foundation in their faith, for it disappears when their thoughts go to other things [...] they never inquire into the 'maybe', but are satisfied with their life experiences.
>
> (quoted in Kartini et al 1985, 110)

**Giving service to the ego**

It is not a coincidence that Haji Hasan Mustapa made the Sundanese verse forms known as *guguritan* and *dangding* the vehicles for conveying his ideas and spiritual experience. These genres enable a kind of '*sapienza poetica*' (poetry of wisdom), in the sense used by Levi-Strauss (1972), because only by means of this form of poetry could the complexity and depth of his reflections be conveyed, and his solitariness be channelled in the best way. It could not have been done with prose, in which words and expressions attract less attention to themselves *per se*, and make meaning on a more superficial level.

In verse, Mustapa was able, for example, to express his solitariness as a religious value. I am referring here to his constant reference to I/ego. In many verses, the Sundanese first person singular *aing* is ambiguously used: is Mustapa referring to himself, or to the ego (*sang uing*) as a concept? For Haji Hasan Mustapa, when this *sang uing* has achieved purity of spirit, it will be able to find a place at the side of the Divine Essence, or *Sang Maha Aing* [The Supreme Self], which he expressed in his writing as follows:

| | |
|---|---|
| *Nagara alam jatnika* | In the domain of sufficiency, |
| *nya jirim kadua jisim* | the body is paired with the soul, |
| *nya raga kadua nyawa* | the body is paired with the spirit, |
| *nya abdi kadua gusti* | the servant is paired with the master. |
| *tunggal barang sahiji* | Coming together in one, |
| *hiji surup hiji timbul* | one recedes the other appears, |
| *bulan sirna ku beurang* | the moon vanishes upon daylight |
| *sréngéngé ku ti peuting* | and the sun vanishes with evening. |
| *katunggalan iraha peutinganana* | But when is the twilight of singularity? |
| | Kartini et al (1985:112) |

| | |
|---|---|
| *Bukurna nu dipibingung* | The thing that causes confusion |
| *pahili ku barang hiji* | is the replacement [of plurality] by singularity. |
| *nyawa kaleungitan rasa* | The spirit loses its feeling, |
| *lawas kalindih panglandi* | for so long pushed aside by names. |
| *marukan lain manéhna* | People say 'that is not the one', |
| *enya gé di lain-lain.* | and even the authentic is denied. |
| | Kartini et al (1985:113) |

For Haji Hasan Mustapa, it is this failure to comprehend this 'quality of I' that traps Sundanese people in particular into falling into error, as can be seen in his saying:

> *Geura prak agus ngawula ka éling aing, ngawula ka élmu aing, ngawula ka iradat aing, ngawula ka déngé aing, nguwula ka awas aing, ngawula ka kalan aing, moal enya ngawula lamun aing teu boga ma'ani.*

> Young man, you must give service to the remembrance of the I, give service to the knowledge of the I, give service to the will of the I, give service to the hearing of the I, give service to the vision of the I, give service to the speech of the I, but this will not be genuine service if the I has no substance.
>
> *The Teachings of Our Islamic Inheritance* (Rosidi 1989: 271)

In this example, the things to which one must give service (knowledge, will, hearing, vision and speech) are in fact Divine attributes for which the believer strives. Naturally, formulations such as this were not without risks. At its simplest, the risk was that not many people would comprehend the products of his thought. A society that was not accustomed to thinking hard would find it difficult to be attracted to the expressive power of his poetry, and to comprehend the significances of a passage such as this one. Haji Hasan Mustapa was fully aware of this risk, and considered the thought-world of the Sundanese at that time to be unused to comprehending texts that veiled in symbols and metaphors. He once wrote: 'My people hold to the [genres of] allusion, wordplay, and rhyming, but rarely do they give serious thought to journeying beyond their horizons'. Or as he wrote in one of his verses: 'The time has not come / for people to arrive at my knowledge' (Kartini et al 1985: 118).

But there were also groups, conservative ones in particular, which were not familiar with metaphorical and figurative language, and attributed mistaken meanings to his verses, and even accused him of disbelief. These critics started from the position that they themselves held a monopoly of truth in homogenous forms. Mustapa did not respond to the anger of the conservatives. In fact, it is quite likely that these critiques compelled him to move deeper into his figurative and metaphorical expressions of Islam.

Although the echoes of his voice can only faintly be heard in the present, this solitary man is a fascinating subject for further study. In the past, scholars as Snouck Hurgronje, Hazeu, Holle, Brandes and Rinkes had admiration for Haji Hasan Mustapa's thought. Nowadays, considerably fewer are interested. In particular, for the Sundanese themselves, Mustapa's call is heard by only a few. Many only know him as a street in Bandung. Some even mix him up with the popular literary figure, Abdullah Mustapa. For many Sundanese, perhaps the name signifies nothing other than the fried potato snack known as *Mustapa*. Hasan Mustapa is a symbol for Sundanese life that has been swept away by the stream of pragmatic hedonism.

**Conversations with the ancients**

Although Mustapa completed his studies in Mecca and even became a popular teacher there, he was never attracted to the Saudi Arabian scripturalist school of thought that came to prevail not long after his final departure from there. Instead, he carried on an 'intellectual correspondence' with the mystics of the Middle Ages such as Syaikh Muhyi al-Din ibn 'Arabi through the book 'The Meccan Openings' (*al-Futuhat al-Makiyyah*), 'Abd al-Karim al-Jili through 'The Perfect Man' (*al-Insan al-Kamil*), al-Ghazali through the book 'The Revival of the Religious Sciences' (*Ihya 'Ulum al-Din*) and Ibn Fadhillah al-Burhanpuri, who wrote 'The Gift Addressed to the Spirit of the Prophet' (*al-Tuhfa al-Mursala ila al-Ruh al-Nabi*). By doing this, he was following traditions already followed for centuries by Islamic scholars of West Java and the Indies: the classics of sufism had been studied by these scholars since long before Mustapa's time.

The great teacher of mysticism, Ibn al-'Arabi (1165–1240), exerted a particularly strong influence on Haji Hasan Mustapa. The essence of Ibn al-'Arabi's verse is the clearing of a space for opening the possibility of uniting God and humankind, which he expresses in the term *wahdat al-wujud*, which refers to the 'unity of existence' of the Divinity and creation. Reynold A. Nicholson interprets Ibn al-'Arabi's concept of *wahdat al-wujud* (Unity of Being) as follows, 'Co-relative terms are only names for various different aspects of the one Reality, each aspect logically requiring the existence of another aspect, and able to be exchanged one for another. According to this view, God (in fact) is mankind and mankind is God, or God (in thought) is not mankind and mankind is not God' (Rumi 1925-1940: 121).

It is a truism that in the writings of Ibn al-'Arabi and other sufi thinkers we encounter a preference for multiple possibilities as opposed to singularity. This preference is manifest in all of Mustapa's work. Mustapa was a searcher who could not except that the search could ever terminate in certainty:

| | |
|---|---|
| *Jung nutur-nutur suhud*<br>*kalangkang ti sanubari*<br>*mapay talapakan rasa*<br>*di mana nya mukti sari*<br>*di mana Alloh kaula*<br>*bisi pahili papanggih* | Apply yourself with diligence<br>in the shadow of your feelings,<br>tracing the imprint of those feelings.<br>Where is the true sufficiency?<br>Where is my Allah?<br>I fear I will meet its replacement |
| *Kadungsang-dungsang kasandung*<br>*manggih lain manggih lain*<br>*rék nanya ka saha*<br>*keur pada ngalain-lain*<br>*teu kaur asa piasa*<br>*asa enya asa lain*<br>[...] | and stumble in despair,<br>finding something else, something else.<br>To whom should I ask<br>While all are in denial?<br>The feeling of certainty does not come,<br>perhaps yes, but perhaps no. |
| *disidik-sidik aringgis*<br>*wantu mapay nu néangan*<br>*kapanggih aringgis lain.* | I am fearful of checking too carefully,<br>for when the seeker meets with his goal,<br>the discovery brings up other concerns. |

Rosidi (1989: 17)

His implicit message was that there is no monopoly on truth. Truth cannot be captured in formalistic visions of religion, but is heterogeneous, and involves the summoning of diverse possibilities.

Not surprisingly, this position attracted disapproval during his lifetime. His learned critics took exceptions to formulations such as this:

| | |
|---|---|
| *Da aing kudu jeung batur* | The I must be with others. |
| *da batur kudu jeung aing* | Others must be with the I. |
| *da aing kudu jeung saha* | The I must be with who. |
| *da saha kudu jeung hiji* | The who must be with one. |
| *da hiji kudu jeung dua* | One must be with two. |
| *da dua kudu jeung hiji* | Two must be with one. |
| [...] | |
| *ceuk aing Allah mah batur* | The I says Allah is another. |
| *ceuk batur Allah mah aing* | The other says Allah is I. |
| *ceuk aing Allah mah éta* | The I says Allah is that. |
| *ceuk éta Allah mah aing* | That says Allah is I. |
| *ceuk aing Allah maha saha* | The I says Allah is who. |
| *ceuk saha Allah mah aing* | Who says Allah is I. |

*The quail laments in its cage*, Rosidi (1989: 99-100)

### The fruit of the sugar palm

In the hands of Haji Hasan Mustapa, mystical poetry was fused with a Sundanese spirit. Sunda and Islamic esotericism became one, just like sugar and its sweetness. This cannot be separated from his firm assertion about the dialectic connection between Islam and the local Sundanese culture, which he felt should be mutually enriching, not mutually negating. Like his sufi predecessors, Hasan Mustapa treated language as a medium to search out new possibilities of meaning that were unpredictable, dynamic and open. His Sundanese background provided materials to be used in the project of being Islamic. As he expressed it:

> *Baheula ku basa Sunda ahirna ku basa Arab. Jadi kaula nyundakeun Arab nguyang ka Arab, ngarabkeun Sunda tina Basa Arab.*
>
> At first [in one's life] we use Sundanese, and finally Arabic. So I have Sundanised Arabic, searching in Arabic, and then Arabised Sundanese using the Arabic language

From *The Noble Qur'an* (Rosidi 1989: 394)

Statements like this, as well as his overwhelming preference for Sundanese language and idioms, assert that Islam does not have to break with local tradition, but should accommodate that tradition as an integral part of the religion itself. A pious person does not lose touch with his cultural roots, just as God once 'borrowed' the Arabic language with all its cultural wealth in order to provide a vehicle for His ideas (in the Qur'an). Being religious does not mean one must become an Arab with all the cultural attributes that surround this. On the contrary, being a true Sundanese is precisely a mirror of the process of pilgrimage to the heart of religiosity itself.

And so it can be understood that the metaphors that Hasan Mustapa uses are idioms that grow within the thought-world of Sundanese society. Mustapa compares the bamboo shoot with the bamboo, and the sugar palm with its fruit (*caruluk*), in order to depict the intimate connection (*awor*) between the servant (*kaula*) and his Lord (*Gusti*). Similarly, he peoples his writings with mythical figures from Sundanese legend, such as Mundinglaya di Kusumah, Hariang Banga, Ciung Wanara, Sunan Ambu, Prabu Siliwangi, Ratu Galuh, or Dayang Sumbi. Mustapa brought these stories into his Islamic writing to 'replace' those of the legendary Islamic figures. Furthermore, performance genres of the Sundanese are frequently invoked. The figurative and veiled language of the *wayang* puppetry, for example, was constantly appropriated for its multi-layered imagery (e.g. A Sinom for the Use of the Youth, *Sinom Pamaké Nonoman*)

In the hands of Haji Hasan Mustapa tradition was not something static, but was truly brought to life again filled with new meaning, including Islamic tradition. By filling his mystical poetry with metaphors which drew on the everyday experience of his audience, Hasan Mustapa succeeded in moving beyond a simple dialectic between religion (Islam) and culture (Sundanese culture), beyond the borders of formalism, and into the heart (*mataholang*) of religiosity and tradition.

**Islam's indigenisation**

In the 1980s Abdurrahman Wahid for the first time launched the idea of the 'indigenisation' (*pribumisasi*) of Islam, which showed how Islam as a normative teaching originating from God was accommodated to culture, which originated from man, without either of them losing their identity, so that it was no longer necessary to have an agenda for purifying Islam or for making it conform with the religious practices of Muslim society in the Middle East (Wahid 2001). 'Indigenous Islam' tended to display an ideology of cultural cooptation that ensured the wide spread of the religion. In actual fact, if we look carefully, we find that long before that, the same awareness had already grown in Haji Hasan Mustapa's soul, though naturally in a different idiom.

This is seen, for example, in the way Haji Hasan Mustapa explained the necessity for Islam to hold a creative dialogue with local (Sundanese) tradition. At the time when Islam entered the Sundanese region, its arrival did not involve a process of marginalisation with regard to the local culture, which had existed there for hundreds of years, but rather one of being obliged to accommodate a living culture. In the end Islam is not identical with Arab culture, even though its holy book itself is formulated in the Arabic language.

Mustapa's refusal to make culture and religion into opposing categories is an example of great value in the present. The Sundanese lands have traditions of tolerance and openness, but our recent record has not been a satisfying one. Organisations that monitor levels of religion-based conflict such as the Moderate Muslim Society and the Setara Institute frequently point out West Java, along with Aceh, as the Indonesian province with the highest levels of conflict. Many violent jihadists have been known to originate from West Javanese communities. This situation is in part caused by religious interpretations that search for oppositional others, othering them through religious positions based on the imperative of purifying religion from harmful elements.

By contrast, Mustapa's Islamicness was not something to be purified of foreign elements, but an experience that was refracted through the Sundanese realities in which he had been raised. The end result is a religious vision that reaches out with respect for difference. Mustapa's Islamic vision avoided formalism and homogeneity and embraced multiculturalism. His use of Sundaese metaphors such as those mentioned above indicate the closeness of the Lord and the believer. In Mustapa's vision, a Sundanese foodstuff is a superb vehicle for conveying spiritual truths. The realities of Sundanese life are not extrinsic to Islam, but are in fact materialisations of the same spiritual essence.

In giving meaning to indigenous Islam, Islam is liberated from puritanism, radicalism, and the quest for authenticity. At the same time local forms of religious understanding are preserved without losing the normative identity of Islam. Indigenous Islam supposes a creative dialogue between the normativity of the holy book and the dynamics of local culture, not with the aim of suppressing each other, but rather as an endeavour to open up the possibility of producing a new tradition with is able to enrich the outlook of existing traditions. Indigenous Islam liberates itself from the claim that is often made by puritan Islam, which holds the view that the Qur'an as source of orthodoxy is a comprehensive scripture, so that every kind of matter, even ones of a technical or specific nature, can be found in it, whereas in fact the Qur'an does not pretend to be a 'vade mecum', either biographical or encyclopedic. The only comprehensive thing about it lies in the act of interpretation, which has a dynamic nature and is continually changing.

This creative process of matching Islam with local culture has frequently given rise to misunderstandings and even tensions among Islamic scholars, and Mustapa is no exception. He was accused of heresy and disbelief, as he reveals in the admission:

| | |
|---|---|
| *Béja majarkeun kaula* | People say that I |
| *Geus leungit élmuning santri* | have lost my scholarly knowledge |
| *Geus ngaruksakeun agama* | and have harmed the religion, |
| *Jadi kapir jadi zindik* | becoming an unbeliever, a heretic, |
| *Jindikna jadi mungkir* | because I deny |
| *Kana tutur lampah rasul* | the examples of the Prophet |
| *Kana salat puasa* | as well as worship and fasting. |
| *Ana malik kula nyeri* | When I reply, hurt by their words, |
| *Kahuruan ngajawab jeung handuruan.* | my scorching answer echoes loudly. |

(Kartini et al 1985: 117-118)

But in the end Haji Hasan Mustapa, as a solitary thinker, accepted with resignation the disagreement of those other scholars with the words:

| | |
|---|---|
| *Kiwari tacan arusum* | The time has not yet come |
| *Nepi kana pamaké kami* | for people to reach my knowledge. |
| [...] | |
| *Heulaanan kuring mundur deui* | For the moment I will step back again |
| *Tacan téga ka barudak urang* | still caring for our young ones |
| *Basana sérab pangilo* | who say they are blinded by my reflection |
| *Sapédah kula kitu* | because of my nature, |
| *Matak risi nu sisip budi* | disturbing those already in stress |
| *Budi daya kula* | on account of my ways. |
| *Geus tepi ka kitu* | It has come to that point, |
| *Dongkap ka masya allohna* | to the point where I say 'Whatever Allah wills'. |
| *Kajeun teuing hararemeng galih* | So many consider me strange |
| *Moal matak doraka* | but I will not commit wrong. |

Kartini et al (1985: 118-119)

In current times, the homogenising pressure of Arabic culture is strongly felt in Indonesian Islam. A century ago Mustapa was resisting this trend, not out of dislike for things Arabic, but for the same reasons underpinning Abdurrahman Wahid's indigenisation concept: Islam would be more deeply experienced by Indonesians when materialising in cultural forms with which they felt comfortable:

> *Pondokna waé, ngawalatrakeun pangaji Kuranul Adim, Alloh jeung para Nabina sing walatra kahartina kasurtina, sugan sabasa-sabasana. Jadi di urangna pangheulana hutbah mending ku basa Sunda. Barangtangtu panglaérna jampé wudu, jampé adus, telekin ku basa Sunda.*
>
> In short, spread the study of the Inimitable Qur'an, of Allah and the Prophets in a way that their meaning and wisdom will spread, adapted into the languages of those [to whom it spreads]. Amongst us, therefore, it is better to prioritise sermons in Sundanese. Without doubt the most familiar things such as the prayer for ablution, the cleansing prayer, and supplications on death are those that are in Sundanese.

(Kartini *et al* 1985:86)

The Sundanese nationalist Ajip Rosidi was to make the same point a century later (Rosidi 2005).

The emphasis Mustapa placed on *feeling* not only underpinned his mystical concepts, but also held linguistic implications. For him, Sundanese was a linguistic medium that possessed a *feeling* (*rasa*) that corresponded with the feeling of Islamic speculation. Needless to say, this correspondence was shaped by Mustapa's upbringing in Sundanese-speaking environments, and by the value he identified in its genres for achieving meaningful communication with other Sundanese.

The connections Mustapa makes between feeling and the material aspects of life have been well captured by Kartini et al (1985: 60), who made a list of the idiomatic expressions concerning feeling referred to by Mustapa in the final pages of *The Teachings of Our Islamic Inheritance*, namely:

1. *Rasa teu benung ku bĕja* (feeling cannot be conveyed by words);
2. *top élmu ngarah rasana* (seize knowledge in order to savour its taste);
3. *ngawula nurutkeun rasa* (to serve according to feeling);
4. *aya rasa moal sarasa* (a feeling will never feel the same);
5. *rasa rumasa* (feeling full of feeling);
6. *rasa dipalsu pangrasa* (feeling falsified by the perception of someone else);
7. *niat kumaha rasa* (intention according to how one feels);
8. *lamun geus tibalik rasa tangtuna tibalik basa* (if the feeling has been turned around, the language too will be turned around);
9. *sarasana sarasana* (each one has his own perception).

(Kartini et al 1985: 60)

Mustapa's work forms a stunning corpus for the study of language and feeling. The latter was a constant pre-occupation of his religious view, but at the same time, he used Sundanese with unprecedented skill and creativity to make these writings. While insisting that language should be sublimated beneath feeling, he used Sundanese to make texts resonant with feeling. Here are the final words of his major work, *The Teachings of Our Islamic Inheritance*:

> *Jawaban lain ku basa tapi jawab ku rasa nyaéta teu ku rasa panarima nyatana mapay hidayat, hidayat ti Gusti Alloh, mapay sirotol mutaqim ulah kairid ku lali.*
>
> The response [to the dichotomy of arrogance and humility] is not made in language, but through feeling, that is through the feeling of acceptance, namely the following of guidance, the guidance from Gusti Allah, and following the *straight path* instead of the path of forgetfulness.
>
> (Rosidi 1989: 290)

**Conclusion**

In a time when religious borders appear to becoming more significant as tools for promoting separation, Haji Hasan Mustapa provides an image of a cosmopolitan man whose Sundanese identity served as an ideological template for welcoming diverse social experiences. He welcomed deep and personal contact with Arab culture as well as Dutch colonial society. But he also had deep contact with Javanese and Maduresе culture, such as he experienced during his cultural tour with his close friend Snouck Hurgronje through Java and Madura in 1889, as is documented in the notes published Van Ronkel. He also did not hesitate to spend a lengthy period acting as colonial official in Aceh.

In times when dogmaticism, fanaticism and exclusivism become templates for avoiding contact with 'the other', we can learn from Mustapa's example of social flexibility. For him, this was something recommended by religion:

> *Kula ayeuna ngawakcakeun jalan karahayuan, yén urang sugria manusa kajajadén taya nu boga. Pusaka nyaah ka sasama, jadi rapih pada sili pihapékeun diri, rumasa pada dadasar sabar tawekal.*

> I am now outlining the way of prosperity, namely that we are all created beings owned by no one. Our inheritance is to love others, to be in harmony through supporting each other, and to together feel that patience and acceptance are basic principles for doing so.
>
> (Kartini *et al* 1985: 24-25)

It is very important that we devote attention to the task of bringing mystical poetry in the style of Hasan Mustapa back to life. We find ourselves now in a situation where national and Sundanese culture have recently come to be dominated by thinking and movements in Islam that give more prominence to formalistic and symbolic aspects compared to the substance. These movements bring out the Arabist-fundamental side rather than the spirit of its Sundaneseness, forming symbolic dichotomies between the *blangkon* (indigenous headdress) and the *surban* (Middle Eastern turban), or between the *rebana* (tambourine) and the *suling* (flute). The rise in empty religious symbolism will only cause a decline in the substance of morality and religious spirit. On the other hand, a meaningful adherence to religious belief will strengthen the ideals of religion itself as well as inspiring social and cultural change in the direction of a truly civilised way of life.

Translated by Stuart Robson

## Sources cited

Kartini, Tini, Ningrum Djulaéha, Saini K.M. and Wahyu Wibisana

1985 *Biografi dan Karya Haji Hasan Mustafa*. Jakarta: Pusat Pembinaan dan Pengembangan Bahasa.

Levi-Strauss, Jean Claude

1972 *Structural Anthropology*. London: Penguin Books.

Rosidi, Ajip

1989 *Haji Hasan Mustapa Jeung Karya-karyana*. Bandung: Pustaka.

2005 'Islam dalam Kesenian Sunda', in *Sundalana 4: Islam dalam Kesenian Sunda* Bandung: Pusat Studi Sunda.

Rumi, Jalaluddin

1925-1940 *The mathnawi of Jalalu'ddin Rumi*. Commentary by Reynold Nicholson. 3 vols. London: Luzac.

Wahid, Abdurrahman

2001 *Pergulatan Negara, Agama dan Kebudayaan*. Jakarta: Desantara.

*Chapter 9*

# HASAN MUSTAPA AS SUNDANESE WRITER

Ruhaliah

I write this chapter based on my experience as a philologist appointed by the Centre for Sundanese Studies (PSS) to produce the transliterations of Mustapa's verse that were published in five volumes in 2009 (Mustapa 2009a-2009e). Over a number of years, it was my task to transform Mustapa's verse from manuscripts written in Arabic script into readable Sundanese text in Latin script. Alongside my work as an academic in the field of Sundanese literature, this experience of transliterating microfilm copies of Mustapa's works has left me with privileged insight into this man and his writing activities.

The difficulties I encountered in this activity gave me insight into the reasons for which the works of this towering figure are not well known to the Sundanese public. In fact, there are other Sundanese writers, with outputs of lesser distinction, whose works are better known. In this chapter, I address this problem by focusing on Mustapa against the background field of Sundanese writing. I choose this approach for the reason that even though Mustapa is perhaps the most celebrated of Sundanese writers, his position in the Sundanese writing landscape is not a simple one. He fits in rather uneasily into the map of Sundanese genres and writing cultures. This sense of otherness has not helped the acceptance of his work. By locating Mustapa in the broader field of Sundanese writing, I explore the failure of his legacy to attract attention. Furthermore, Mustapa's work has thrown up challenges of a philological nature, and these are also relevant in explaining the narrow circulation of his work.

An early qualification: Mustapa is not to be understood by a survey of his work. We need to look also at the man himself. The man did things in his own way. He paid very little attention to publication or preservation of his work. In fact, most of it was put into written form by others. After dictating a work, he appeared to take no interest in its publication or dissemination. And even those transcription copies have not survived well, for many were destroyed or guarded jealously to the point where they fell out of view. Although his output is massive, the figure of Hasan Mustapa is very distant from the ideal of the professional or career writer. These facts are contexts for his low profile amongst readers, but also testify to the difficult task faced by scholars and philologists wanting to approach his corpus.

**Genres**

Mustafa wrote in a diversity of genres and forms. This diversity was shaped by the unique range of his life experience, social interactions and professional engagements. In his life, he dealt closely with the Sundanese elite into which he was born, with the *Jawa* colony in Mecca, with Dutch colonial officials, with Acehnese elites, with members of the Indies' religious elites (*ulama*), with Bandung's intelligentsia, as well as with village society. The structures and conventions in which his creative output emerged reflect this social and political diversity, in its themes as well as the genres and forms in which it materialised.

So, although Sundanese writing before Mustapa was mostly in verse, we find in his *ouvre* many prose works on a broad variety of themes. The works produced in an official capacity, such as the famous *Treatise on the customs of the Priangan people and other Sundanese* (1913), or his reports on the situation in Aceh (see Ali in this volume), are in prose. These 'official' writings reflect his position as *hoofd penghulu* (Peak officer in the colonial religious bureaucracy), and relate to contemporary developments of political and social importance. He also wrote major prose works on religion, such as *The Teachings of Our Islamic Inheritance*, translated in this volume. He produced prose works of *tafsir* (Qur'anic interpretation, e.g. Mustapa 1937). Many of his prose works display Mustapa's preference for the adoption of a contrived dialogical structure such as questions and answers, or as a conversation between interlocutors (e.g. Mustapa 1924).

Mustapa's verse legacy is huge. Some of these are written in four-line stanzas resembling the Malay pantun (Sund: *sisindiran*), or four line mono-rhyming verse (Sund: *kakawihan*). But his preferred vehicle was the metrical/melodic combinations known variously as *dangding* and *guguritan*. *Dangding* is a system of rules for verse composition which has constraints affecting poetic form and melody (see Setiawan in this volume). A *guguritan* is a shorter work, usually of lyrical, non-narrative nature, written in *dangding* (Rosidi 2011). Mustapa's *guguritan* reveal Islam as his central preoccupation. Many of them express a highly personal mystical scheme that draws on canonically Islamic works as well as local conceptions. Without doubt, Mustapa was influenced by the Javanese models for this kind of expression, known as *suluk*.

Mustapa was rigorous in sticking to the metrical and rhyming rules of the stanza forms he used. In this sense, his verses display great conformity with Sundanese poetic models. But in other senses, he adapted these models for his own purposes. For example, each of the stanza forms of the *dangding* are associated with emotional states or modes. Each stanza form has its character (*watek*). This was disregarded by Mustapa. As Rosidi has pointed out (1983: 59), he was not concerned that the content of the verse should match the mood with which the particular pattern is associated.

The final genre to be mentioned here is correspondence. During the almost three years of his stay in Kota Radja, for example, Mustapa sent a steady stream of reporting letters to C. Snouck-Hurgronje in Arabic. More letters were sent during Mustapa's Bandung period. These letters are preserved in the Leiden University Library. A notable work of Mustapa entitled *Balé Bandung* (1925) contained his correspondence with Kyai Kurdi (see Rosidi in this volume).

During Mustapa's life, the first Sundanese autobiographies began to appear (Drewes 1985). Even though Mustapa never wrote his own biography, frequent references to his own life are found spread throughout his writings. Some of the more substantial of these are discussed by Rosidi (1989: 33-61).

**The corpus**

Mustapa was not at all concerned with retaining or documenting his own wo.rks. His grandson Endi stated to Ajip Rosidi that not one manuscript was found in his house after his death (Rosidi 1989: 4). Rather, his writings found their ways into various holdings. The collection in the Leiden University Library is notable. The Indonesian National Museum has a small holding of materials by Mustapa. A significant holding is located in the collection of the family of M. Wangsaatmadja in Bandung. Some manuscripts are in private ownership in Bandung. The Islamic school of Suryalaya also holds at least one manuscript containing a work by Mustapa (Rosidi 1989: 31). (According to Abah Anom, the leader of the Suryalaya pesantren who died in 2011, Mustapa's son Muhammad Subki had been a friend of Abah Sepuh (d. 1956), the founder of the school).

The majority of extant manuscripts of Mustapa's work belongs to two groups distinguished by their provenances. These groups reflect two phases of Mustapa's life, and require some background knowledge of Mustapa's relationships with his two 'secretaries' or 'scribes', Wangsadiradja and M. Wangsaatmadja. The former made copies of Mustapa's works while Mustapa was chief Islamic official (*hoofd penghulu*) of Bandung, while the latter commenced working as Mustapa's secretary in 1923, long after Mustapa's retirement in 1918, and worked for him until 1930 (Kartini *et al* 1985: 38-39). These relationships relate to two groups of manuscripts, and lead us also to the two most complete secondary works about Mustapa's work, namely Kartini et al (1985) and Rosidi (1989). These two works drew upon sources from these two groups respectively.

I start with Kartini et al (1985). According to this source, after Mustapa's death his then secretary M. Wangsaatmadja retained a chest of manuscripts by Mustapa. In 1960, Prof. Dr. Husein Djajadiningrat, then the director of the National Museum in Jakarta, requested that the works be typed for storage and preservation purposes. The copies filled eighteen volumes, and were made in duplicate. The titles of these volumes all commence with *Aji Wiwitan* (Sund: 'Original Teaching'). One set of eighteen volumes is missing (cf. Rosidi 1989: 11-13). The remaining set, held by the family of Wangsaatmadja, lacks one volume. These works, along with fourteen publications of Mustapa's works, formed the basis for the work done by Kartini and her colleagues in preparing their 1985 book.

Kartini and friends note that there are queries over the authorship of the *Aji Wiwitan* series: some appeared to have been written by Wangsaatmadja. After 1923, it appears Mustapa no longer wrote the works himself, but dictated them to Wangsaatmadja, and then left him to organise them into texts.

The other group of manuscripts was first brought to light in a substantial way in 1989 by Ajip Rosidi, who had been collecting works by Mustapa through a process of borrowing, stenciling and retyping, since the late 1950s, mostly borrowing them from members of the *Galih Pakuan* (see Solomon 1986). In 1984, Ajip Rosidi was funded by the Toyota Foundation to travel to Leiden University, where he hoped he would encounter works by Mustapa. Rosidi attributes ten bundles of Sundanese writing to Mustapa, all of which were written by the hand of Wangsadiradja, the first secretary of Mustapa. These manuscripts had reached Leiden Library through the collection of Mustapa's friend, Christiaan Snouck Hurgronje. A number of these works were edited and published by Iskandarwassid, Ajip Rosidi and Josef CD (Mustapa 1987), and Rosidi's comprehensive anthology of works by Mustafa was published in 1989. It included excerpts from the Leiden collection as well as selections from books, manuscripts and correspondence.

Ajip Rosidi had brought back from the Netherlands seven rolls of microfilm containing works by Mustapa, all of them written in the hand of Wangsadiradja. In 2002, at Ajip's request, I commenced making transliterations of three of these, which contained seven titles. In 2009, these transliterations were published by Kiblat in five volumes (Mustapa 2009a-2009e). The titles of these books are excerpted from the first lines of the works concerned.

As is clear from the above, not all of Mustapa's work is in manuscript form. There are a number of print publications, appearing through the efforts of a number of dispersed, small-scale projects with limited scope and distribution. Some appeared during his life, the most notable being his *Treatise on the customs of the Priangan people and other Sundanese* (Moestapa 1913), which Mustapa probably wrote at the request of his mentor Christiaan Snouck Hurgronje. A number of small books were published during Mustapa's lifetime at the instigation of Wangsaatmadja. The study group known as the 'Heart of Pakuan Foundation' (*Yayasan Galih Pakuan*), financed by the then Bupati of Bandung R.A. Wiranatakusumah, published a number of works after his death.

Mustapa's work can be obscure even to Sundanese speakers, so it is not surprising that it has not attracted much attention from translators. The Dutch translation of *Treatise on the customs...* (Moestapa 1946) was commenced by Mehmed Sastrahadiprawira and completed by R.A. Kern. An Indonesian translation was produced by the Culture Foundation of Padjadjaran University (*Lembaga Kebudayaan UNPAD*) (Mustafa 1996). The major translation of his verse into Indonesian is Mustapa (1987). Finally, mention needs be made of Josef CD's translation into Sundanese of Mustapa's defence, written in Arabic, to the attacks upon him of 1902-1903 (Rosidi 1989: 438-467).

### Mustapa as a Sundanese writer

Mustapa is not easily located as a writer. I explore this difficulty here by discussing the three currents of Sundanese writing on which he drew. On one hand, these currents reveal Mustapa as a Sundanese writer who was a product of his environment. At the same time, he can't be comfortably placed within any one of these currents, and the discussion below reveals him as something of an outsider to the major literary movements in West Java.

The genealogical elites of nineteenth century Sundanese society were involved enthusiastically in literary production. They adapted the Islamic romances and apocrypha that were so popular around the Islamic world, as well as lengthy renditions of Sundanese myths and legends. This affinity of the elite with literary production is encountered in many societies of the Netherlands Indies. When Karel Frederick Holle, the plantation owner and adviser to the Dutch government on Sundanese matters, took charge of publishing reading materials for Sundanese readers in 1861, the works he produced were frequently written by members of West Java's aristocratic families, such as Muhammad Musa (Limbangan) and members of his circle (Berge 1998; Moriyama 2005). In this sense, Mustapa, born of the minor nobility in Garut, was not exceptional as a Sundanese writer.

The Islamic romances, pious narratives and Sundanese myths gained broad popularity as works to be performed in ritual settings. Mustapa himself wrote affectionately of the Sundanese peoples' preference for reciting these works in the seven days after birth, during which a newly-born child was to be protected from evils, or during pregnancy (Moestapa 1913: 19, 28-29). But Mustapa had no inclination towards contributing to this corpus. Although he used conventional Sundanese genres, and although references to Sundanese myth and legend are frequent in his work, he showed no desire for perpetuating the literature of the days of yore. Mustapa reached out into the present, which for him, involved actively participating in diverse social spaces. In other words, Mustapa wrote about the Sundanese present, using the time-honoured literary forms of the Sundanese to do so.

The second current of Sundanese writing that enables us to contextualise Mustapa is the chronological successor to the one just mentioned. In the early twentieth century, new forms of writing signalled processes of change resulting from the expanding influence of colonial modernity in West Java (Rusyana 1979, Setiawan 2001). The earliest literature and journalism in Sundanese were written by people working in 'new' roles such as journalists, teachers, editors, activists and civil servants (examples are D.K. Ardiwinata, Yuhana, Muhammad Sanusi, Mohammad Ambri etc).[1] Works by these figures form the foundation of what is now remembered as modern Sundanese literature, and some of their works are still in print.

Although Mustapa was a contemporary of some of these writers, he cannot be considered within the space of modern Sundanese writing. He never wrote a novel. But more importantly, he never submitted his writing to the networks of publicity in which these writers participated, and which were so important in the emerging awareness of 'imagined communities' that Benedict Anderson has identified (1983). In fact, Mustapa appears to have been disinterested in the publication of his own work (with the exception of the work he prepared for publication at the behest of the Colonial government, i.e. Moestapa 1913). He even prohibited his scribe Wangsaatmadja from selling his work (Rosidi 1983: 75), with the result that very little of his work was available to a reading public. For these reasons, Mustapa was an outsider to the literary modernity being created by the best-remembered writers in Sundanese of his time. He remained apart

1 Biographies of these figures are found in Rosidi (ed.) (2000).

from the evolutions of mainstream Sundanese writing. Although he had moved beyond the days of yore, he did not quite step into 'the modern'.

The final current of writing to be mentioned here consists of the scientific, speculative and pedagogical genres of Islamic learning. Mustapa had deep experience of many Islamic genres. In his early education as well as his time in Mecca he studied the literature of the Islamic sciences, most of it written by Arabs, but some by scholars of Indies societies. He would also have known of the sufi literature in which Indian and Persian scholars made adaptations of canonical Islamic ideas. Cirebon, Banten, Tasikmalaya and Garut were locations at which these works were copied and taught. Mustapa's verse indicates he was also familiar with the indigenous, speculative literature (*suluk*) in which Indies Muslims adapted ideas from the giants of Islamic mysticism.

Mustapa fits quite comfortably into this trajectory of writers from Indonesian societies who adapted the corpus of the Islamic sciences, and most notably Islam's sufi current, into localised cultural forms. The most prominent and earliest writer of this category was the Acehnese Hamzah Fansuri (d. 1527), who wrote in Malay. But these authors face marginalisation from the mainstream Islamic canon in the present. By creatively adapting orthodox Islamic ideas into localised spiritual lexicons, they create reasons to be excluded from the centre of Islamic life, where suspicions arise about the 'correctness' of their teachings. The sufi authors typically promoted Islamic concepts that the protectors of orthodoxy regarded as dangerous and misleading for general Muslim audiences. As a result, in the greater landscape of Indonesian literatures, this is a marginal field, specially in comparison with the 'modern' writing such as novels and newspaper articles mentioned above. Still today, very few Islamic interpreters from the pre-independence past have survived in public memory. Hamzah Fansuri exists at the periphery of public knowledge, and so does Mustapa.

Based on these reflections, what is Mustapa's position in the history of Sundanese writing? Perhaps the most adequate categorisation is that he was unique. He was not a person to be located within any category. Critics and commentators have recognised this uniqueness. Not a few have described Mustapa as *mahiwal* (Sund: idiosyncratic). As a person who did not fit into the categories and factions that prevailed in his time. Ahmad Gibson Albustomi has located him 'at the crossroads' of religious and cultural authority, not fitting easily into either domains (Albustomi 2012: 81-84).

**His writing practice**

In what remains, I wish to convey some of my experience in transliterating Mustapa's work for the five volumes published by *Kiblat* in 2009. My reasons for this are to illustrate the writing culture in which Hasan Mustapa produced his output. This cultural milieu belongs to the past, but provides a necessary context for understanding his corpus.

Up until the early decades of the twentieth century, Islamic writing in the Netherlands Indies used Arabic script with minor changes to suit local phonemic realities. This script is sometimes called *pégon*. Mustapa wrote a number of works in this script using his own hand, but many of his works were dictated to his secretaries, who later transliterated a number of works for publication. Having done this, the original manuscripts were frequently destroyed (Rosidi 1989: 31).

The manuscripts generally carry a record of the date of writing (*titimangsa*), and also a record of the amount of stanzas written in the particular stanza patterns being used.

The script used in Mustapa's writing is without doubt an impediment to those wishing to study his work. At the time Mustapa was writing, *pégon* was commonly used in religious and literary contexts. Even at that time, however, it was rapidly being replaced by Latin script, and nowadays few Sundanese feel comfortable reading their language in that script. The writing in Mustapa's corpus is small and can be unclear, and the ink has faded in some parts. Numerous illegibilities are encountered, and no help is provided by punctuation: R.A. Kern, the co-translator of Mustapa's famus book on Sundanese custom, commented, 'Mustapa wrote his work in Arabic characters without punctuation' (Moestapa 1946: X).

There is also a problem arising from the possibility of multiple readings. We are dealing here with a writing system in which many vowels are not expressed, leaving the reader to 'fill in the gaps'. Frequently, the vowels are written hastily or incorrectly above or below their consonants. Furthermore, it is at times difficult to distinguish between certain consonants. Not surprisingly then, it can be difficult to distinguish between multiple possibilities: *jeujeuhan-jajahan; bukti-bakti; urat-urut; lebur-leyur; tangtung-nangtung.* Imagine the difficulties encountered in transliterating a paragraph such as the following, where varying vowel sounds must be identified in similar or identical consonantal structures. This stanza is excerpted from Rosidi's publication of *The Quail Laments in its Cage*:[2]

2 Mustapa did not intend that stanzas such as this and others like it should convey coherent semantic content in a linguistic sense.

| | |
|---|---|
| *Pulang anting luntang lantung* | Coming and going without any destination. |
| *teu nungtungan pulang anting* | No end to the coming and going. |
| *pulang dianting dipalang* | Prevented from returning with an earing. |
| *palang dipulang dipaling* | A barrier returned and then stolen. |
| *paling dipalang dipulang* | A thief is repulsed then returned. |
| *pulang dipulang dipaling* | A return is to be brought back by theft. |

(Rosidi 1989:93)

The appendix to this chapter carries a reproduction of one page of Mustapa's writing from Cod. Or. 7881, a manuscript stored in the library of Leiden University. That codex contains a number of Mustapa's works, and is written in the adapted Arabic script sometimes called *pégon*. The page reproduced is the first page of his work, *I have the consolation of the jewel: Kinanti*. The full text can be read in the edition made by Iskandarwassid et al (Mustapa 1987: 176-211). Following that, the appendix includes a transliteration of the first seven stanzas from the page into Latin script, along with an English translation. This appendix is included as a specific aid for those interested in the process which must be performed before Mustapa's material can be made available to wider publics, and to convey an impression of the writing culture in which Mustapa was active.

**Concluding discussion**

In some ways, Hasan Mustapa's work clearly belongs to the past. The writing culture in which he was active is no longer found today. In contemporary times, Roman script is used for almost all Sundanese writing. Manuscripts have lost their functional value in the days of print publication. The copying of manuscripts by hand occurs quite rarely. The structuring of texts in the conventional verse forms (*dangding*) is now considered an elite form, rather than the accessible mode of communication it constituted in Mustapa's time. Paper is becoming a less important part of publication and circulation. And so on.

Against this background, it is enormously gratifying that people continue to find meaning in Mustapa's work. Individuals and institutions have made contributions to Mustapa's legacy, even when he himself appeared not to care for it. Wangsaatmadja and the Heart of Pakuan Foundation perpetuated his memory through their meetings and publications. R.A. Wiranatakusumah published some of these. Ajip Rosidi has shown dedication for a long period to the cause of documentation and spreading his work. Monash University and UIN Sunan Gunung Djati collaborated on the holding of a seminar about Mustapa in 2009. The publisher Kiblat has produced some useful volumes. Leiden University has held an important collection of Mustapa's works in secure storage for a long time. Without this support, Mustapa's disregard for his own creative output might have led to the obliteration of his name from the legacy of Sundanese culture and the Islamic traditions of Indonesia.

## Appendix

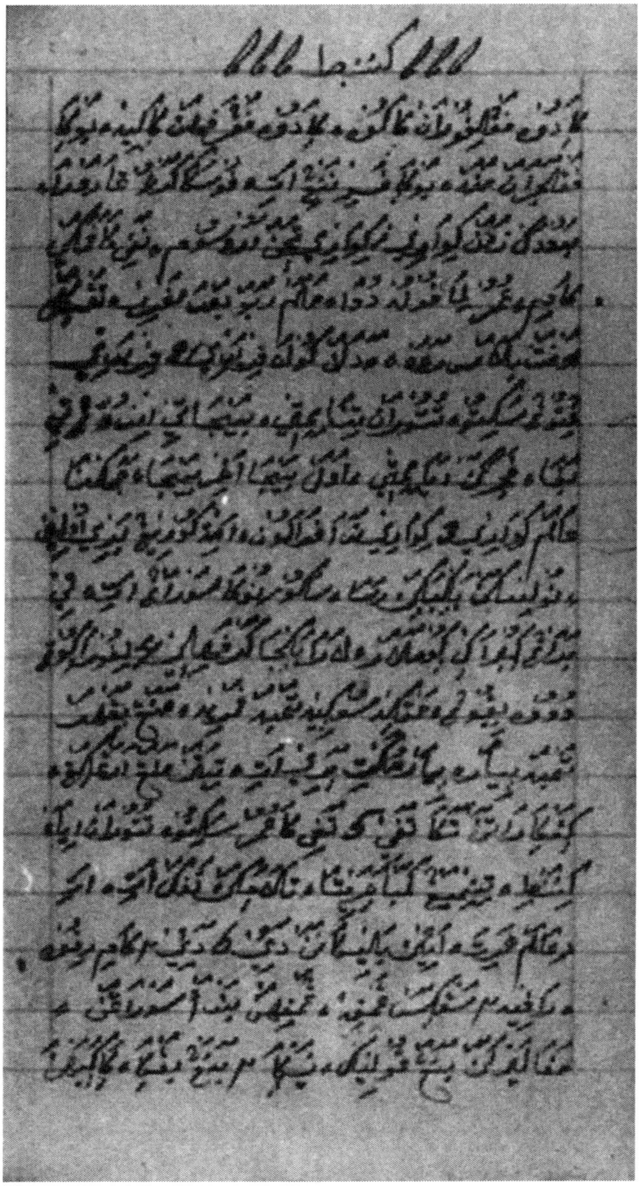

**Image D:** Opening page of *I have the consolation of the jewel: Kinanti*
Codex Or. 7881, stored in the library of Leiden University, contains a number of works by Mustapa, including *I have the consolation of the jewel: Kinanti.*

*I have the consolation of the jewel: Kinanti*

| | |
|---|---|
| *Gaduh panglipuran galuh*<br>*gaduh pangrapihan galih*<br>*boga panglejaran manah*<br>*boga pangsirnaning ati*<br>*pusaka keur nu ngarora*<br>*barudak jaman kiwari.* | I have the consolation of the jewel.<br>I have the calming of the emotions.<br>I have the relaxing of the soul.<br>I have the clearing of the heart.<br>An heirloom for the young,<br>for the youth of today. |
| *Kiwari tacan arusum*<br>*nepi ka pamaké kami*<br>*umur lima puluh dua*<br>*malem Rebo ba'da Magrib*<br>*tanggal opat belas Rewah*<br>*wedalan kula pribadi.* | The time has not yet arrived<br>for me to make use of my knowledge.<br>I am fifty-two years old.<br>It is Tuesday night after evening prayer<br>on the fourteenth of the month of Rewah,<br>the date of my birth. |
| *Pribadi ngitung sakitu*<br>*tuturan tina mimiti*<br>*béja ti indung ti bapa*<br>*pajarkeun aya mimiti*<br>*awal béja ahir béja*<br>*jamakna alam kiwari.* | I worked that out myself<br>from what was said from the beginning,<br>said by my mother and father.<br>They said there was a beginning.<br>Beginnings and endings are words,<br>that is what it is like nowadays |
| *Kiwari neda paralun*<br>*amit kuring bari ulin*<br>*nuliskeun bagbagan rasa*<br>*sakur nu kasorang ati*<br>*ti barang gubrag gumelar*<br>*lara bagja keur pahili.* | Now I seek your leave.<br>I playfully ask permission<br>to write on the topic of feeling,<br>on all my heart's experiences<br>from the time of my birth,<br>good and bad, one after the other. |
| *Lipur agung wuwuh bingung*<br>*manggih sugih tambah pamrih*<br>*meunang beunghar tambah nyiar*<br>*nyiar mukti nyiar ati*<br>*ti batan meunang aranggang*<br>*ganggarateun teu katepi.* | Too much enjoyment enhances confusion.<br>Gaining wealth increases desire.<br>Gaining riches makes one search for more.<br>The search for status is a search for contentment,<br>but instead of achieving distant things,<br>things that are close remain out of reach. |
| *Tepi ka umur sakitu*<br>*tuturan ieu kinanti*<br>*tinimbang kemba carita*<br>*talacakra* (?) *tapak ati*<br>*ati di alam harita*<br>*lain balikaneun deui.* | Upon reaching such an age,<br>my goal in this *kinanti* is to give<br>rather than keeping it to myself<br>an impression of my heart<br>as it was back at that time<br>but not to return to it once more. |

| | |
|---|---|
| *Deui-deui kami ripuh* | I continue to be burdened, |
| *rapih-rapih sanggeus ngampih* | but have found ease after going within |
| *ngampihan banda sorangan* | and taking stock of my own things, |
| *mapalérkeun beunang ngulik* | appreciating the things I have gained, |
| *néga-néga beunang bangga* | overlooking the things I strived for, |
| *gagabahna ...* | not caring... |

From Mustapa's work, *I have the consolation of the jewel: Kinanti* (Leiden Or. 7881).

Translated by Julian Millie

## Sources cited

Albustomi, Ahmad Gibson
2012 *Filsafat manusia Sunda: Kumpulan esai HHM, Teosofi dan filsafat*. Bandung: SkylArt.
Anderson, Benedict
1983 *Imagined communities: Reflections on the origin and spread of nationalism*. London/New York: Verso.
Berge, Tom van den
1993 *Van kennis tot kunst, Soendanese Poezie in de Kolniale Tijd*. PhD Thesis, Rijksuniversitieit Leiden.
Drewes, G.W.J.
1985 'The Life-Story of an old-time Priangan Regent as told by himself', *Bijdragen tot de Taal-, Land- en Volkenkunde* 141: 4, 399-422.
Kartini, Tini, Ningrum Djulaéha, Saini K.M. and Wahyu Wibisana
1985 *Biografi dan Karya Haji Hasan Mustafa*. Jakarta: Pusat Pembinaan dan Pengembangan Bahasa.
Moriyama, Mikihiro
2005 *Sundanese print culture and modernity in 19th-century West Java*. Singapore: NUS.
Moestapa, Hasan
1924 *Balé Bandoeng: Nja Éta Pakoempoelan Atawa Soesoeratanana Antara Djoeragan Hadji Hasan Moestapa Hoofd Panghoeloe Bandoeng Pangsioen sareng Kiai Koerdi Goeroe Pasantrén Soekawangi Singaparna*. Bandoeng: Drukkerij Sin Bin.
1937 *Petikan Koer'an katut Adab Padikana*. Comite Mendakna.
Mustafa, Hasan
1996 *Adat istiadat Sunda*, translated by Maryati Sastrawijaya. Bandung: Alumni.
Mustapa, Hasan
1913 *Bab adat-adat oerang Priangan djeung oerang Soenda lian ti éta*. Batawi: Kandjeng Goepernemen.
1946 *Over de gewoonten en gebruiken der Soendaneezen: Uit het Soendaasch vertaald en van aanteekeningen voorzien*. 's-Gravenhage: Nijhoff

1987 *Naskah Karya Haji Hasan Mustapa.* Transliterated and Translated by Iskandarwassid, Ajip Rosidi, and Josef CD. Jakarta: Proyek Penelitian dan Pengkajian Kebudayaan Nusantara, Bagian Proyek Penelitian dan Pengkajian Kebudayaan Sunda (Sundanologi), Departemen Pendidikan dan Kebudayaan.
2009a *Dangdanggula Sirna Rasa.* Edited by Ajip Rosidi. Bandung: Kiblat/Pusat Studi Sunda
2009b *Kinanti Kulu-Kulu.* Edited by Ajip Rosidi. Bandung: Kiblat/Pusat Studi Sunda.
2009c *Sinom Barangtaning Rasa.* Edited by Ajip Rosidi. Bandung: Kiblat/Pusat Studi Sunda
2009d *Sinom Wawarian.* Edited by Ajip Rosidi. Bandung: Kiblat/Pusat Studi Sunda
2009e *Asmarandana Nu Kami.* Edited by Ajip Rosidi. Bandung: Kiblat/Pusat Studi Sunda.

Rosidi, Ajip
1983 *Ngalanglang Kasusastran Sunda.* Jakarta: Pustaka Jaya.
1989 *Haji Hasan Mustapa jeung karya-karyana.* Bandung: Penerbit Pustaka.
2000 (ed.) *Ensiklopedi Sunda: Alam, manusia, dan budaya termasuk budaya Cirebon dan Betawi.* Jakarta: Pustaka Jaya.
2011 (ed.) *Guguritan.* Bandung/Kiblat/LBSS

Rusyana, Yus
1979 *Novel Sunda sebelum perang.* Jakarta: Pusat Pembinaan dan Pengembangan Bahasa/Departemen Pendidikan dan Kebudayaan.

Setiawan, Hawé
2001 'Perumusan konsepsi kesusasteraan Sunda pascakolonial', in Ajip Rosidi, Edi S. Ekadjati and Chaedar Alwasilah (eds), *Konferensi Internasional Budaya Sunda (KIBS) Prosiding, Jilid 1.* Bandung: Yayasan Rancagé, 117-134.

Solomon, Wendy
1986 'Text and personality: Ajip Rosidi in search of Haji Hasan Mustapa', *Indonesia Circle* 41, 11-27.

*Chapter 10*

# ETHNIC ISLAMIC LEGACIES IN THE INDONESIAN PRESENT

Julian Millie

A number of the preceding chapters have commenced by affirming that Hasan Mustapa was a man of remarkable qualities. Those remarkable qualities are without doubt critical to our discussion of Mustapa in the present, but they are not the focus of this chapter. My intention here is to shift the focus away from the qualities of the man, and onto something equally as complex, if not as remarkable, and that is the ways in which he is remembered and commemorated in the present. Remembrance and commemoration are understood here in a wide sense, including not only acts specifically dedicated to remembrance, but also other less explicitly commemorative processes by which Mustapa's name, life and work might be given meaning in the present (research, study, publication, representation, quotation, imitation, performance etc.). The shift in focus of this chapter is important because understanding the contemporary meanings of Mustapa and other figures like him requires a perspective beyond the deeds and qualities of the figure concerned. It requires an inquiry into the processes, institutions and practices through which remembrance is achieved, and the social and political meanings of these. Almost all the actors behind remembrance of Mustapa have been and are members of a sub-national ethnicity of the Republic of Indonesia, and they understand him to belong within a sphere of Indonesian life that is highly significant and sensitive, Islam. For those reasons, an inquiry into Mustapa's commemoration enables a perspective on how Islam and ethnicity shape public action in the Republic of Indonesia.

Contemporary remembrance of Mustapa is almost as complex as the man himself. At the meeting where the original impetus for making this book arose, in Bandung in 2009, the participants had no trouble identifying impediments to Mustapa commemoration, but we had difficulty in specifying the causes and motivations behind the practices of Mustapa remembrance that are actually occurring. We agreed that a major factor impeding Mustapa commemoration in the present is that he does not fit into the most prominent categories within which other ethnic Muslim figures from the pre-independence period have been acknowledged in the Indonesian present. Two categories stand out above others. The first consists of Islamic figures who are remembered through embodied practices. In embodied practices, text-based objectifications of Islamic knowledge are secondary to bodily practices such as attendance, gesture, vocal participation, commensality, bodily performance, comportment and dress. The practice of visiting graves is a prominent example. Many Indonesians commemorate saints and deceased Muslim notables by visiting their graves. The practice of *haul* (anniversary) is another example. A *haul* is a celebratory commemoration consisting of group prayers and other performances, typically held in Islamic schools on the anniversary of the death of the founder of the school. Mustapa is not remembered in these ways, for he kept his distance from the

Islamic organisations that emerged during his lifetime, and was not affiliated with any institution that might nurture his memory over a long period.

Mustapa is an even poorer fit with the second category, which consists of the heroes of the independence struggle (see generally Schreiner 2002). Since 1958, Indonesia's national heroes have been appointed through a bureaucratic process currently located within the Ministry of Social Affairs, and heroes of the independence movement are prominent amngst them. This process has transformed a number of Islamic figures, who before the establishment of the Republic in 1945 were subjects of the Netherlands East Indies self-identifying as nationals of various indigenous groups, into heroes of the post-colonial state. The exemplary figure of this kind is the Javanese Hasyim Asy'ari (d. 1947), appointed as a national hero in 1964. This man resonates with two major constituents of Indonesian civic identity: respect for the revolution as the birth of the nation, and secondly Islam. Historical remembrance of Asy'ari focusses heavily on two fatwa he produced in 1945, in which he stated that it was obligatory for Muslims to oppose the colonial forces, and that Muslims killed while doing so would die as martyrs (Amiq 1998). A recently-released bestselling novel (Irawan 2012) and subsequent feature film have bolstered his identity as revolutionary hero in the public imagination. For reasons discussed below and in the preceding chapters, especially Mufti Ali's, Mustapa cannot be remembered in this way.

Understanding Mustapa remembrance in the present requires us to look beyond embodied remembrance and national heroes, to other less obvious commemorative practices, processes and institutions within contemporary Indonesian society. Importantly, this effort requires that we engage with the Republic of Indonesia as much as with the Sundanese ethnicity. In an intuitive sense it seems natural to constrain our understanding of Mustapa's significance to the Sundanese ethnic group, after all, all the scholars attending the 2009 conference, other than myself, were Sundanese, and Mustapa's work continues to be published primarily in Sundanese, a language not understood by non-Sundanese Indonesians. Yet the processes through which Mustapa is remembered are, in important ways, national phenomena. The new Republic brought with it novel conditions for interpreting sub-national Islams, as well as new spheres, techniques and media for their representation and reification. These have affected all Indonesia's ethnic groups, not just the Sundanese. This inquiry into remembrance of Mustapa provides a striking case study of how regional Islamic legacies generally are shaped by the enabling conditions emerging after the Indonesian Republic.

There is another advantage in shifting the analytical perspective from Mustapa the Sundanese subject to the processes by which he is remembered in the present: it enables the analysis to move beyond the idea that Islam's ethnic distinctiveness is a matter of qualitative difference. There is no denying that it is helpful to understand sub-national Islamic diversity in Indonesia as something that materialises in qualitative differences; the practices and traditions of Javanese, Acehnese, Sundanese, Minang and Madurese Islams can without doubt be distinguished through contrasting attributes identified in the ethnographic record. But the examples of Mustapa remembrance explored in this chapter, as well as the examples from other ethnicities cited here in passing, signal the importance of institutional processes and commemorative practices to the construction of ethnic Islamic distinctiveness. Regional Islamic legacies should not be understood merely as continuations of qualitatively contrasting Islamic practices established in the period before the dawn of the national stage. Legacies such as Mustapa's display novel forms and meanings that are generated within the contexts of Indonesian modernity.

Now is a suitable time to reconsider the meanings of Indonesia's ethnic Islamic legacies, for both Islam and ethnicity have recently surged anew in Indonesian identity formation. The global Islamic resurgence has seen Indonesia become a more Islamic society than previously, at least in public life, and Indonesia's post-Suharto decentralisation has increased ethnicity's importance in political life. The actors behind commemoration of Mustapa, and those from other ethnic groups engaged in commemoration of figures within their respective legacies, are creating a map of Islamic Indonesia that foregrounds sub-national identity, and does not neatly conform to the national pattern. This encourages us to pay attention to ethnicity as a structuring influence on Islamic memory in the Indonesian present.

In what follows, I first give a general overview of the commemoration of ethnic Islamic legacies in contemporary Indonesia. Following this, I narrow that discussion to the specifics of Mustapa and his work, noting the conditions that have enabled remembrance of his name, life and work. The remainder of the Chapter observes two modes of remembrance through which Mustapa is given meaning in the present, based in the main on our discussions of 2009 and the preceding chapters of this book. These are the scholarly work performed on cultural patrimony by Sundanese scholars, and the mobilisation of Mustapa's name and work in public contest.

## A new public Islamic stage

The Republic has not caused the disappearance of ethnic and local Islamic distinctiveness. Embodied observances shaped by local convention, such as the grave-visiting and anniversary (*haul*) commemorations mentioned above, have remained authoritative for many. Local forms of celebration, supplication and commemoration have proved durable. At a glance, people appear to continue to do what their ancestors did. But the understandings and subjectivities that underpin this practice are not pure continuations of past models. Citizenship has provided new foundations for Muslims' reflexive understandings of their social and political environments, and the national public constitutes a compelling frame within which people understand the circulation of Islamic meanings. To a significant degree, these developments have reduced the authority and prestige of sub-national Islamic custom and practice.

For Indonesian Muslims oriented towards public action (in politics, social action, cultural expression etc), the emergence of the nationalist movement brought a novel public forum in which ideas and actions were to be rationalised, justified and contested.[1] Novel supra-local networks were a core element of this new forum, clearly described in John Bowen's (1993) study of the early twentieth-century Gayo Highlands. Local mosques became key nodes in networks of Muslim reformists interested in accommodating Islam to the needs of emergent political realities. This process saw Islamic authority shifting away from local settings. A different yet related process was the new state's construction of Islam in forms suitable to the new political collective. After independence the state threw its authority

1 Illustrative sources on Islamic society during and after the transition to the Republican period include Benda (1958), Atkinson (1983), Geertz (1973), Noer (1973).

behind a new definition of the role of religion in public life (Geertz 1973). Sukarno installed a rationalised monotheism amongst the ideological foundations of the state, known as the *Pancasila* (five principles) doctrine. The state's concern for the religious content of Indonesian life was reflected in emerging bureaucratic infrastructure: the establishment of a Ministry of Religious Affairs was an expression of the state's 'responsibility' for developing Indonesian society as a monotheist one (Kipp and Rodgers 1987).[2]

Other developments – mentioned here only in broad outline – reveal the intensifying concentration of Islam authority in national rather than sub-national forms, symbols and institutions. Islamic education, for example, has evolved in ways that recognise the desirability of national ideals of citizenship subjectivity (Noer 1978). Language change is also relevant. In the late 1920s the nationalist movement adopted *Bahasa Indonesia* as national standard, and that language quickly became icon of and medium for Indonesian modernity (Anderson 1966). While regional languages enabled communication high in affect and intimacy, Indonesian was often preferred in religious contexts because it pointed strongly to the progress and opportunity offered by the modern republic (Keeler 1998, Millie 2012).[3] Media technologies have enabled the emergence of national

---

2 Islamic law provides a notable example of the homogenising Islamic impetus brought by the Republic. Some Islamic scholars argued that Indonesian conditions required a compilation of Islamic legal stipulations that suited those conditions (Feener 2001). The national system of Islamic courts has also brought normalisation (Nurlaelawati 2010).

3 The connection between ethnic Islamic legacies and print publication is a complex one. The rise of Indonesian as a medium for Islamic communications has not necessarily caused a decline in Sundanese publication. In a fascinating overview, Zimmer (2000) claimed that Sundanese writings in the genre of *tafsir* (interpretation) flourished from the mid-twentieth century, precisely the time at which the national language began to be spoken widely as the national standard. A plausible explanation for this is that the national standard was not taken up in

cultural markets, constructing an appreciation for a common national culture transcending ethnic boundaries.

These changes saw the emergence of new varieties of Islamic intellectuals and leaders. To some extent, these weakened the positions of 'traditional men of learning' who had been so dominant in locally specific settings. As Eickelman has written of Morocco, 'the notion of an all-important "modern" category of intellectuals that accompanied the heyday of modernisation theory in the 1950s reinforced the tendency to treat clerics [meaning scholars with authority based in traditional pedagogy] as a residual or disappearing category on the margin of significant political activity' (Eickelman 1985: 13). Indonesia has not precisely replicated the processes Eickelman encountered in Morocco, for Islamic traditionalists in Indonesia have succeeded in remaining closer to political power than their Moroccan counterparts. But the general point is applicable: when Indonesian communities started to look to the national stage as the site where important things were happening, Islamic leaders rooted in local contexts remained precisely that: Islamic leaders rooted in local contexts. They retained many of their substantive roles within their communities, but Muslims in those communities commenced to look over their heads to recognise new authority in figures on the national stage.[4]

---

the settings of Islamic education with the swiftness it was received in other public contexts. A second possible explanation is that regional concern about language loss has encouraged the preparation and financing of Islamic works in Sundanese.

4 The ethnic composition of Indonesia's first generation of national Islamic elites is an important topic for further research, for this generation featured a disproportionate representation from a single group, the Minangkabau of West Sumatra. Prominent Islamic political figures of the early generation included Haji Agus Salim (1884-1954), Haji Abdul Malik Karim Amrullah (1908-1981) and Mohammad Natsir (1908-1993), all of whom belonged to the Minangkabau ethnicity. These figures, widely remembered in contemporary Indonesia, form a useful comparison with Mustapa, for

The conditions of possibility for regional Islams have also been shaped by an affinity, central to the Republic's national ideology, between the modern state and a rationalised monotheism (Geertz 1973; Atkinson 1983). This affinity harmonised with a purifying, Islamic reformist sensibility that saw local specificity as an impediment to the development of a public Islam that would benefit the national community. In other words, the religious part of Indonesia's state ideology overlaps strongly with the purification agendas of Islamic reformists, to the point where it might appear that being a modern citizen properly required a Muslim to distance her self from ethnic specificity in Islamic practice. Academic studies, for example, sometimes support the arguments of Islamic reformists by implying that Islamicness is sullied or diluted by the particularity of cultural affiliation. Instead of approaching the Islamic spectrum as a range of variants of equal Islamic value, academic analysts have often characterised regional variants as syncretic. Clifford Geertz exemplified this when he wrote 'It is very hard, given his tradition and his social structure, for a Javanese to be a real Moslem' (1960: 160). This assertion worked in two directions. First, Javanese Islam was characterised as 'less Islamic'. Second, it meant that the santri (i.e. devout, scripturally literate) Muslims of Java could not belong to their 'tradition and social structure', for in becoming 'real Muslims' they would have to turn their backs on the authentic conventions of their regions. Approached in this way, it seemed the authentic Javanese Muslim could not exist. This dichotomy between pure and syncretic Islam has to some degree obscured and marginalised

---

they originated from an ethnicity whose 'otherness' beside the national identity is less substantial than that of the Sundanese. Unlike the Sundanese, Minangkabau speak a language very similar to modern Indonesian (see Hadler 2008).

the heritages of Islamic interpretation and translation expressed in regional languages and conceptual repertoires.

**Effacement of ethnic Islamic particularity**

In a world where the division of the globe into sovereign states has become such an indispensable framework for understanding it, Indonesia's sub-national Islamic identities and legacies have to a degree been effaced by and appropriated into national discourses. Ethnic distinctiveness tends to vanish, for example, when Indonesia's Muslims are contextualised in supra-national settings. Categories such as 'Indonesian' de-differentiate ethnicity. The constructions made of Southeast Asian Muslims who travelled to the Holy Land in the pre-national period are a case in point. Snouck Hurgronje (1931: 215-216) described how students coming to Mecca from the geographical spread between 'Siam and New Guinea' were all categorised as originating from an imagined entity: the *bilad al-Jawah* (The Lands of the Jawa). This imagination was shaped by Arab perceptions of the closeness of the Southeast Asians' geographical origins, their similar appearance, and their shared use of Malay (known in the context of the Hijaz as the 'Jawi language') as lingua franca (Laffan 2003). This identification effaced the ethnic contexts in which these scholars were born and raised, and to which many of them, including Mustapa, returned after their stay in Mecca.[5]

Historians have performed a similar dedifferentiation. In grappling with peripatetic Muslims and networks of learning, historians have – perhaps unavoidably – retrospectively attributed ethnic subjects with generic ethnicities that overlook ethnic particularity. The paradigmatic work of this kind is Azyumardi Azra's (2004)

5 Laffan (2003) suggests this identification was an early stage in the conceptualisation of the supra-local collective that later became the Indonesian state.

important work on the 'transmission of reformism'. Azra's goals were to provide a badly-needed correction to a historical record which had retrospectively excluded 'Malay-Indonesians' from participation in global Islamic networks, and to correct the impression that Islam in the archipelago is not 'real Islam' (Azra 2004: 2). The book traces the movements to and from the world's Islamic centres by Islamic scholars from maritime Southeast Asia, and traces the networks that emerge through patterns of citation and translation. Even though Azra is writing about Islam in the pre-independence period, the transnational contacts he identifies are not between scholars of the Islamic centres with those of the ethnic nations of the Indies. Rather, he represents the contacts as having occurred between the Middle-East and a group labelled as 'Malay-Indonesian Muslims'. Through this nomenclature, we observe how strongly the shadow of the contemporary nation state looms over Azra's work, and how it moves sub-national identities to the margin. 'Malay-Indonesians' is a compound that pays respect to the two dominant nation states of post-independence maritime Southeast Asia. This identity is projected back in time in a way that obscures the ethnic complexity of the people and places concerned. Azra's work is not the only example. Johns' celebrated article (1961) on Sufism and the spread of Islam labels Muslims of the Indies between the fifteenth and eighteenth centuries as 'Indonesians'. These retrospective views reduce the relevance of ethnic contexts in the history of Indonesian Islam.

The work of Azra and Johns confronts us with pressing questions: in an era when national citizenship is so influential in reflections on identity and belonging, is it possible to give adequate respect to sub-national identity in the past and present? Considering that ethnicity has been so radically reconfigured after the onset of the nation state, should special efforts be made to respect ethnic particularity in the present? Or can ethnic particularity be ignored? These questions invite political and philosophical reflections that cannot be accommodated here. What is clear, however, is that contemporary Sundanese, and Muslims from other Indonesian ethnicities, are not following the groupings preferred by Azra and Johns. Their work frequently valourises ethnic identity. In the remainder of this chapter, I argue that these meanings should be recognised simultaneously as products of Indonesian nationhood as well as counter-narratives to the Republic's effacement of ethnic Islamic distinctiveness.

**Problems of Mustapa remembrance**

Mustapa's name is familiar to many people in contemporary Bandung because of the major thoroughfare named after him (P.H.H. Mustapa Street). Their understandings of the street's name, however, reveal something important to this discussion. Residents of Bandung tend to connect this street's eponym with the category of national hero. This was illustrated in an exchange I experienced while travelling along P.H.H. Mustapa Street in a taxi. I asked the driver whether he knew who Hasan Mustapa was. The taxi-driver informed me that Mustapa had been a *kyai* (Islamic teacher/leader) based in the Cipasung religious school in Tasikmalaya. Mustapa had been a hero, he informed me, in the national struggle for independence.

That he should say this was not surprising. As noted at the beginning of the paper, ethnic Islamic leaders of the past are transformed into national heroes through state recognition of their role in the revolutionary struggle. Public recognition of such figures is high. If Indonesians do not remember these people by name, they have a high recognition of the genre, which includes a small number of West Javanese Islamic leaders.[6] Against this background, it is not surprising that my taxi-driver would assume that the Islamic figure after whom a major street had been named was a hero of the nationalist struggle.

As the brief biography in Chapter One above indicates, Mustapa fails the tests for inclusion into this category. In fact, comparison between Mustapa and the figure mentioned in the opening paragraphs of this chapter, Hasyim Asy'ari, creates a striking symmetry. Asy'ari's celebrated fatwa urged Indies Muslims to fight against colonialism (Amiq 1998). Mustapa's 1894 fatwa urged the Acehnese to end their resistance to colonial rule (see Ali in this volume). The comparison is perhaps unfair to Mustapa, as Asy'ari isues his fatwa during the extraordinary period of the national revolution. But other sources indicate that Mustapa's support for the colonial government was unusual for his time. The Dutch scholar R.A. Kern (1875-1958), who partially translated Mustapa's 1913 ethnography into Dutch, intended to give approval to Mustapa with the following appraisal, but it certainly would condemn him in the judgement of anti- or post-colonial readers:

> In Muslim lands there is traditionally a tension between religious teachers and worldly authority, and in Java the *kyai*s keep their distance from the government. In their efforts to fully observe the law of Islam, they countenance no concessions from it. In their impressions, the wickedness of the present is to be ever more distinguished from the golden era of the first caliphs. Reality has never corresponded with this imagery. They look past the fact that

6 These were Zainal Mustafa (1907?-1944) of Pesantren Sukamanah (Tasikmalaya), and Abdul Halim (1887-1962), of Pesantren Santi Asromo (Majalengka). The taxi driver might also have been mindful of the figure of Ruhiat bin Abdul Ghofur (1911-1977), a revolutionary leader who was the principal of the Cipasung pesantren in Tasikmalaya.

> the law, because of its practical unfeasibility, for the most part can never be dominant, dedicating themselves to its study, and overlooking and condemning all that belongs to the *adat* [custom]. Hasan Mustapa forms an exception: he held a fondness for the ordinances of his fatherland, studying and learning them, while also striving to reconcile the *adat* with the spirit of the religious books. He further distinguished himself in that he opposed the objections which many Muhammadan scholars derived from their books of learning towards a sincere relationship and heartfelt cooperation with a European government. This aspiration distinguished him long before it was thought possible that he should hold any position in government service, and he was therefore correctly recognised in general as of unimpeachable quality. This disposition was also the reason that in 1892 he was named as the government's Islamic functionary in Kuta Raja, a position that he held between 1893 and 1895. (Moestapa 1946:VIII)

Van Koningsveld's (1985) critique of Snouck Hurgronje's conduct towards Muslims in Mecca and Java provides an indirect critique of Mustapa. The core of that critique was that the Dutchman feigned his Islamic faith in order to gain access and make relationships that were of value in his political duties. Van Koningsveld describes how his careful cultivation of connections established in Mecca and West Java enabled Snouck Hurgronje to be welcomed into familial networks of influential Muslim figures. Mustapa arranged one of Snouck Hurgronje's two marriages to Sundanese women, namely his second marriage in 1898 to the 13 year-old Siti Sadijah, the daughter of Mustapa's friend Kalipah Apo. After returning to the Netherlands, the Dutchman did not acknowledge these marriages or his children in West Java, yet the marriages enabled him to play a historically unparalelled 'linking role' between the European and West Javanese elites (1985: 119). Van Koningsveld makes an uncomfortable observation:

> [...] both of Snouck's marriages were of fundamental importance to the political history of the Netherlands-Indies between 1890 and 1906. Through them he secured for himself an intimate position within the religious feudal elites of West Java. (Koningsveld 1985:120)

**Two modes of commemoration**

Although Mustapa fails to register in key modes through which Indonesians have commemorated ethnic Islamic legacies, he is nevertheless remembered in the present. In the remainder of this chapter, I draw attention to two significant domains of activity in which Mustapa and his work are given meaning in the present. The first is the work carried out by academics dealing with the cultural patrimony of the Sundanese ethnicity. For scholars in disciplines such as philology and literary studies, Mustapa's written legacy in an important resource in which authentic expression of collective values are to be found, and the conventions and protocols of these disciplines provide methods for giving representation to these legacies in ways that are acceptable in the present.

The second contemporary process by which Mustapa is given meaning in the present is through mobilisation of his name and work in public contest. Some Sundanese activists and scholars take issue with the homogenisation and narrowing of publically permissible Islamic meanings that is taking place in Indonesia by citing and referencing Mustapa and his work in public contest. In this way, they align themselves against Indonesian proponents of an Islam purified of 'cultural accretions', arguing for an expanded public Islam open to the texture of regional diversity. Mustapa's work is mobilised as an authentic regional Islamic expression. This process, as I argue below, is not limited to Mustapa's legacy, but has been advocated by Islamic activists across Indonesia.

**Regional cultural patrimony**

Chapter Six above was written by the critic, poet, editor, researcher, cultural activist and playwright Ajip Rosidi (b. 1938). This man is the patriarch of the study of Sundanese culture, especially of its written genres, and has worked hard to ensure that contemporary Sundanese have access to high quality resources for the study of their culture. He has been an innovator in developing new forms for the preservation of regional cultures in Indonesia. A striking example is his *Sundanese Encyclopaedia* (Rosidi *et al* 2000). This work of 716 pages was the first encyclopaedia of an Indonesian ethnicity. Another form has been the literary prizes he has established for writing in Sundanese. Since the early 1950s this Sundanese autodidact has been the most industrious and insightful interpreter and documenter of Mustapa and his work (see Solomon 1986). He published his 1989 book on Mustapa, the standard work in the field, after a 1988 visit to the Netherlands sponsored through a Toyota Fellowship. More recently, he edited poems by Mustapa that were published in five volumes by Kiblat in 2009 (Millie 2014). His services to Mustapa's legacy are many.

Rosidi's studies of Mustapa reveal a dominant motivation: Mustapa's legacy constitutes cultural patrimony for the Sundanese. For Rosidi, the legacy left by Mustapa (and those of other Sundanese cultural figures) materialises the continuity between contemporary Sundanese and their ancestral culture. In a frequently reprinted work in which Rosidi attempts to define the national character of the Sundanese, Mustapa is one of five figures selected as an exemplary source for understanding that character (Rosidi 1984). From this perspective, Mustapa's corpus sheds light on what it means to be Sundanese in the present. Practices such as editing, translating and publication provide the tools for materialising the connection between Mustapa, his work and the Sundanese people in the present.

Respect for Mustapa as bearer of Sundanese patrimony also emerges in the chapters by Hawé Setiawan and Ruhaliah, specialists in Sundanese literature and philology respectively. These writers share Rosidi's conviction that the literary corpus of Sundanese writers is an artefact of Sundanese identity. Setiawan is a journalist, poet, critic, curator and lecturer residing in Bandung, where he teaches at Pasundan University, the university run by the 'Sundanese Association' (*Paguyuban Pasundan*). Like Rosidi, he is intimidated by Mustapa's religious content, but resolves this problem by focussing on the literary potential of Mutapa's work, and especially on the Sundanese (by way of Java) stanza forms in which Mustapa wrote his works. Ruhalia teaches at the Indonesian University of Education, Bandung, and is a member of a small circle of philologists working on Sundanese literature, epigraphy and archaeology. Her chapter is underpinned by her experience working in a typical regional patrimony project: she was funded to transliterate manuscripts of Mustapa's work brought by Ajip Rosidi from the Netherlands after his Toyota fellowship.

Terms like 'scholarship' and 'research' do not adequately express the motivations underpinning the work of Rosidi, Ruhalia and Setiawan. Cultural patrimony is a very serious thing for them, and they do not approach their ethnic legacies with a disinterested ethic of scientific neutrality. Their work is an expression and negotiation of ethnic affiliation. And in contemporary times, the work they do in the disciplines of philology and literary studies are considered appropriate practices for giving expression to that affiliation. Academic work of this kind is prestigious, and furthermore, relatively large amounts of private and state funds are channelled into these processes. And most striking of all, the patrimony work they perform on Mustapa's legacy is being repeated across Indonesia by scholars of other ethnicities. Pre-Islamic legacies are finding representation and circulation through academic work carried out by subjects belonging to the ethnicity concerned. A flood of editions, translations and analyses of the writing of Hasyim Asy'ari have appeared recently, for example. I have not made a thorough account of the origins of the authors of these works, but it seems that nearly all of them are produced by East Javanese scholars (e.g. Zuhri 2010; Hadziq no date). Javanese academics are continuing to circulate the life and works of the Javanese guru Ahmad al-Mutamakkin, also known as Kiai Cebolek (1645-1740) (e.g. Bizawie 2002; Achmad and Tajuddin 2014). The life and work of the cleric and literary figure Raja Ali Haji (1808-1873) is kept in circulation by academics and institutions of Indonesia's Riau province (see for example Haji 2002; Junus 2004). The celebrated *kyai* from Madura, Cholil Bangkalan (1820-1925) is commemorated by scholars from East Java (e.g. Bakhri 2015).

I am not stating here that the motivations for these commemorations are precisely the same as those motivating commemorations of Mustapa's legacy. What is striking is how academic processes (citation, edition, commentary, documentation, analysis), which have high legitimacy because of the public value associated with education and research, enable ethnic advocates to give representation to pre-Republican Islamic legacies in a pattern that replicates the subnational rather than national map of Indonesia.

**Public Islamic contest**

West Javanese Islamic society is varied and vibrant, displaying a range of Islamic styles, practices and interpretative traditions. Yet as noted already in a number of chapters in this book, diversity is frequently the subject of conflict in the public Islamic sphere. Activist groups advocate a narrow orthodoxy, at times aggressively, arguing that this is for the public benefit. The resulting conflicts have made people wary about making contributions to public discourse on Islamic topics. Ahmad Gibson Albustomi and Asep Salahuddin, the writers of Chapters 3 and 8 respectively, have been willing to enter the fray of public exchange, arguing for an expanded public understanding of Islam. They see Mustapa's legacy as a source of Islamic concepts that are beneficial for contemporary Sundanese society because they legitimise Islamic diversity. In both cases, their assertions are aimed against rival religious positions in Sundanese society. In other words, they mobilise Mustapa's life and works in public contest.

Asep Salahudin (b. 1972) teaches at the Sunan Gunung Djati State Islamic University in Bandung, but is also vice-rector at the university campus located at the Suryalaya *pesantren* (Islamic school), located in Tasikmalaya, West Java. This school has been the West Java home of the sufi brotherhood (*tariqah*) known as the Tarekat Qadiriyah wa Naqsyabandiyah (TQN), and was founded by the Sundanese cleric popularly known as Abah Sepuh in 1905. According to some sources, Abah Sepuh was a friend of Hasan Mustapa (Sunardjo 1995: 30). The *pesantren*'s library houses writings by Mustapa (Rosidi 1989). The school is visited by many Sundanese who perceive it to be an inheritor of West Java's sufism-inflected Islamic tradition.

In a stream of articles published in the popular press as well as in scholarly media, Salahudin has put Mustapa to work in public contest. In a typical article (2012), he promotes Mustapa's theology and philosophy as antidotes to contemporary problems. He points out West Java's recent record on religious radicalism: not a few suicide bombers and radical movements have their origins in the province. But according to Salahudin, the Sundanese have for centuries developed a characteristic theology at the core of which lies moderation (Ind: *moderasi*, Sund: *siger tengah*). Salahudin cites a number of excerpts from Mustapa's work to show that it is an authentic expression of that theology of moderation. In a 2008 article, also highly typical of his work, he reproduces Mustapa's metaphors concerning the fruit of the aren palm (*caruluk*). He proposes that these are authentic Sundanese Islamic mediations, unlike the 'formalism' and 'Arabisms' of 'those who claim to be the sole owners of singular truths'. In Salahudin's championing of Mustapa, sub-national Islam becomes an authentic, ethnically-specific resource that metonymically represents diversity more generally.

The headings of Salahudin's articles scream out challenges to his opponents: 'The Roots of Sundanese Philosophy', 'The Inner Cosmology of the Sundanese', 'The Metaphysical Vision of the Sundanese'. All these connect Mustapa to religious variants such as inner and self-spirituality, pre-Islamic cosmology, local Islam, metaphysics and philosophy. These spiritual concepts cut across attempts to constrain sunni Islam within a homogenous orthodoxy, and Salahudin's writings are indeed aimed directly at opponents for whom those words signal abhorrent religious forms.

Like Salahudin, Ahmad Gibson Albustomi (b. 1965), known widely as 'Kang Gibson', has been a frequent contributor of articles about Mustapa to the West Javanese press. Kang Gibson has completed something that is rarely attempted: a comprehensive work of *tafsir* (interpretation) of a work by Mustapa. That work, *The Teachings of Our Islamic Inheritance*, as well as an abridgement of Gibson's interpretation, are included in this volume (Chapters Three and Four). In a recent collection of his articles (Albustomi 2012), Kang Gibson uses Mustapa to support his contributions to public contest about religion in West Java. Once again, these disputes are in large part about diversity, and Mustapa's 'philosophy', with its preference for ever shifting meaning and figurative richness, is represented as an authentic and inclusive Islamic positioning that is ideal for a pluralistic West Java. In contemporary West Java, Gibson argues, local realities have been written out of Islamic experience, causing a decline in the quality of public Islamic life. Mustapa's message is being overlooked.

There are Indonesian precedents for the work of Kang Gibson and Asep Salahudin. As noted by Asep in this book, writings by the former president Abdurrahman Wahid (1940-2009) contain many mobilisations of regional Islamic traditions intended as forceful contributions to contemporary disputes about Islam, politics and culture in Indonesia (a complete collection is Wahid 2006). He was an advocate for a historical process he called *pribumisasi* (indigenisation). According to this concept, regionally and locally specific Islamic cultures were resources by which Islam had developed so successfully in a pluralistic Indonesia. Indonesia's regional diversity is seen as a vehicle for revelation that simultaneously fragments and strengthens the message of revelation. Another similar initiative is the contemporary movement known as 'Archipelagic Islam' (*Islam Nusantara*), which advocates for the value of indigenous Islamic forms and concepts. This initiative is in large part a response to what its proponents believe to be an over-valuation of Arabic models (Ubaid and Bakir 2015). Along with the contemporary treatments of Mustapa's legacy, these movements point to an emerging national pattern: regional traditions are being mobilised as authentic alternatives in public Islamic contests.[7]

### Coteries

Mention must be made here of another form of commemoration stimulated by Mustapa's legacy. This one has less of a connection with national realities, but is relevant here because it draws attention to the continuing relevance of Mustapa's religious vision for coteries of 'seekers', by which I mean Muslims searching for spiritual fulfilment in forms contrasting with the widely accepted routines of worship and observance. The earliest of these, emerging after his death in 1930, was the 'Remembrance Committee' (*Comite Mendak*) which organised commemorations of Mustapa's death and organised the publication of works by Mustapa. R.A. Kern described this group as a:

> ...study group of educated Sundanese, no *kaom*-members amongst them, who have taken it upon themselves to study his unpublished writings.[[8]] For the present, they restrict themselves to the study of the poems. They study both the form and content of the poems. (Moestapa 1946: IX)

7 Asep Salahudin and Kang Gibson mobilise Mustapa to argue for an expanded range of public understandings of Islam, but it is incontestable that regional Islamic legacies could also provide legitimacy to advocates arguing for conservative and narrow Islamic visions. I have not encountered such programs, but neither has this research sought them.

8 By *kaom*-members, Kern is referring to the Islamic specialists residing in the area around the great mosque of Bandung. The term references high levels of Islamic piety and knowledge. Kern is here emphasising that Mustapa's appeal was most strongly felt outside the mainstream of Islamic scholars.

Out of this group emerged the 'Bandung Heart of Pakuan Foundation' (*Yayasan Galih Pakuan Bandung*). Rosidi spent some time with the group during its final stages in the 1960s, by which time it included only three members who had actually met with Mustapa in person (Rosidi 1989: 5-8). In Rosidi's view, it was the esoteric dimensions of Mustapa's work that attracted the *Galih Pakuan*'s members. The figure of Wangsaatmadja, the second of Mustapa's scribes, is significant amongst this group. According to Ryzki Wiryawan (2014: 46-68), Wangsaatmadja was a Sundanese theosophist, a member of the '*Galih Pakuaan Theosophical Lodge*', who had been included amongst the speakers at the 1916 congress of the Netherlands Indies Theosophical Movement (NITV).

A second coterie emerged around 1996 on the campus of Bandung's Sunan Gunung Djati State Islamic University. A group of students including Ahmad Gibson Albustomi, Iip Yahya, Bambang Q. Anees, Deden Effendi, Rosihan Fahmi and Dedi Slamet Riyadi formed a discussion group under the leadership of the playwright and poet Hidayat Suryalaga (1941-2010). This man had been a student of the Sundanese martial arts expert and politician Ema Bratakoesoema, a member of the *Galih Pakuan* (1901-1984). Originally, this student group was called the 'Pasamoan Sophia' (The Philosophical Gathering). In their understandings, Mustapa's ideas could be approached as authentic Sundanese philosophy. Kang Gibson's interpretations of Mustapa were partly shaped in these discussions.

These two groups share a common trait: their members were educated elites seeking a spiritual/intellectual experience that transcended the routines of everyday Islamic life in West Java. The Sundaneseness of Mustapa's imagery is central to both coteries, for their members are not only attracted by Mustapa's Islamic vision, but also have the linguistic skills and cultural empathy required to make serious study of his writings.

**Final words**

There is no doubt that the Republic of Indonesia brought a public stage on which ethnic Islamic legacies have appeared only at the margins, except when appropriated by the national discourse. Nevertheless, the discussion above indicates that the national era has seen the invigoration of ethnic Islamic legacies in new ways. Two important modes of commemoration emerged from our discussions: the remembrance of Mustapa through academic work as cultural patrimony, and the mobilisation of his work in public Islamic contests. Both these activities are byproducts of national modernity. Expert research in state-funded institutions is of course enabled by the Indonesian education system, by the objectification of knowledge that it implements, and by its infrastructures for research publication. Public Islamic contest is enabled through the mediated circulation of ideas through publics. In other words, post-independence Indonesia has caused Mustapa and his legacy to signify in ways he could not possibly have predicted during his life.

It is particularly striking that Mustapa is re-emerging in public discourse at a time when Indonesians are having heated exchanges about the role of Islam in social and political life. In joining the contest on a national stage which has tended to push culturally-inflected Islam to the margins, Asep Salahudin and Kang Gibson use Mustapa to force the cultures of sub-national Islam onto that public stage. Mustapa's authenticity is very important in this process, for it amplifies the public resonance of these men's writings.

Mustapa's identity as a celebrated Sundanese cleric, and his use of Sundanese language and writing genres, give his Islamic conceptions an authenticity that other concepts might lack. Ideas like cosmopolitanism, liberalism, pluralism and religious equality have their supporters, but for many Indonesians, they appear as unconvincing, foreign conceptions. It is not surprising that Asep Salahudin and Gibson do not express their public interventions through a western-derived lexicon of citizenship and social inclusion. Instead, they turn to the authenticity of a regional Islam. Through their work, it is clear that Mustapa's Islamic legacy, as well as those of pre-independence Islamic figures within other ethnicities of Indonesia, have exciting potential on the national stage.

## Sources cited

Achmad, Ubaidallah and Yuliyatun Tajuddin
2014 *Suluk Kiai Cebolek dalam konflik keberagaman dan kearifan lokal.* Jakarta: Prenada.

Albustomi, Ahmad Gibson
2012 *Filsafat manusia Sunda: Kumpulan esai HHM, Teosofi dan filsafat.* Bandung: Skylart.

Amiq
1998. 'Two fatwas on jihad against the Dutch colonization of Indonesia: a prosopographical approach to the study of fatwa', *Studia Islamika: Indonesian Journal for Islamic Studies* 5:3, 77-124.

Anderson, B.
1966 'The Languages of Indonesian Politics', *Indonesia* 1, 89-116.

Atkinson, J. M.
1983 'Religions in dialogue: The construction of an Indonesian minority religion', *American Ethnologist* 10, 684–96.

Azra, Azyumardi
2004 *The origins of Islamic reformism in Southeast Asia: networks of Malay-Indonesian and middle eastern ulama in the seventeenth and eighteenth centuries.* Leiden: ASAA/KITLV.

Bakhri, Mokh. Syaiful
2015 *Mahaguru pesantren: Syaichona Cholil Bangkalan.* Jakarta: emir/Penerbit Erlangga.

Benda, Harry J.
1958 *The crescent and the rising sun: Indonesian Islam under the Japanese occupation, 1942-1945*. The Hague: W. van Hoeve.
Bizawie, Zainul Milal
2002 *Perlawanan kultural agama rakyat: Pemikiran dan paham keagamaan Syekh Ahmad al-Mutamakkin dalam pergumulan Islam dan tradisi (1645-1740)*. Yogyakarta: Samha.
Bowen, John R.
1993 *Muslims through discourse: Religion and ritual in Gayo society*. Princeton: Princeton University Press.
Eickelman, Dale F.
1985 *Knowledge and power in Morocco: The education of a twentieth-century notable*. Princeton University Press: New Jersey.
Feener, R. Michael
2001 'Indonesian movements for the creation of a "national *Madhhab*"', *Islamic Law and Society* 9:1, 83-115.
Geertz, Cliford
1960 *The religion of Java*. Chicago: University of Chicago Press.
1973 'Internal Conversion in Bali', in Clifford Geertz, *The Interpretation of Cultures: Selected Essays*. New York: Basic Books, 170-189.
Hadler, Jeffrey. 2008. *Muslims and Matriarchs: Cultural Resilience in Indonesia through Jihad and Colonialism*. Ithaca: Cornell University Press.
Hadziq, Muhammad Ishomuddin
No date, *Kumpulan kitab karya hadlratus Syaikh K.H. Muhammad Hasyim Asy'ari*. Tebu Ireng: Al-Maktabah al-Masruriyyah Al-Tebu Irengi.
Haji, Raja Ali
2002 *Tuhfat Al-Nafis: Sejarah Riau-Lingga dan daerah takluknya 1699-1864*. Tanjung Pinang: Yayasan Khazanah Melayu.
Irawan, Aguk
2012 *Penakluk badai: Novel biografi KH. Hasyim Asy'ari*. Depok: Global Media Utama.
Johns, Anthony
1961 'Sufism as a Category in Indonesian Literature and History', *Journal of Southeast Asian History* 2:2, 10-23.
Junus, Hasan (ed.)
2004 *Sejarah perjuangan Raja Ali Haji sebagai Bapak bahasa Indonesia*. Pekanbaru: Unri Press.
Keeler, Ward
1998 'Style and authority in Javanese Muslim Sermons', *The Australian Journal of Anthropology* 9:2, 163-178.
Kipp, Rita Smith and Susan Rodgers
1987 'Introduction: Indonesian religions and their transformations', in Kipp, Rita Smith and Susan Rodgers (eds), *Indonesian Religions in Transition*. Tucson: The University of Arizona Press, 14-25.

Koningsveld, P. Sj. Van
1985 'Snouck Hurgronje: moslim of niet?' *Tirade* 29, 98-128.
Laffan, Michael Francis
2003 *Islamic nationhood and colonial Indonesia: The umma below the winds*. London: RoutledgeCurzon.
Millie, Julian
2012 'The languages of preaching: Code selection in Sundanese Islamic oratory, West Java', *The Australian Journal of Anthropology* 23, 378–396.
2014 'Arriving at the point of departing: Recent additions to the Hasan Mustapa legacy', *Bijdragen tot de Taal-, Land- en Volkenkunde* 170:1, 107-112.
Moestapa, Hadji Hasan
1946 *Over de gewoonten en gebruiken der Soendaneezen*, translated by R.A. Kern. 'S-Gravenhage: Nijhoff/KITLV.
Noer, Deliar
1973 *The modernist Muslim movement in Indonesia 1900-1942*. Oxford: Kuala Lumpur.
-1978 *Administration of Islam in Indonesia*. Ithaca: Cornell Modern Indonesia Project.
Nurlaelawati, Euis
2010 *Modernization, Tradition and Identity: The Kompilasi Hukum Islam and Legal Practice in the Indonesian Religious Courts*. Amsterdam: Amsterdam University Press.
Rosidi, Ajip
1984 *Manusia Sunda: Sebuah Ésai tentang Tokoh-Tokoh Sastera dan Sejarah*. Bandung: Kiblat.
1989 *Haji Hasan Mustapa jeung karya-karyana*. Bandung: Penerbit Pustaka.
Rosidi, Ajip, Edi S. Ekadjati, Dodong Djiwapradja, Embas Suherman, Ayatrohaedi, Nano S., Atik Soepandi, Komaruddin Sastradipoera (eds)
2000 *Ensiklopedi Sunda: Alam, manusia, dan Budaya termasuk budaya Cirebon dan Betawi*. Jakarta: Pustaka Jaya.
Salahudin, Asep
2008 'Suluk Haji Hasan Mustapa', *Pikiran Rakyat October 18, 2008.*
2012 'Belajar dari Haji Hasan Mustapa', in Hawé Setiawan (ed.), *Sosok pemimpin Sunda dalam gagasan dan pengalaman*, Bandung: Paguyuban Pasundan, pp. 63-86.
Schreiner, Klaus H.
2002 '"National ancestors": the ritual construction of nationhood', in Henri Chambert-Loir and Anthony Reid (eds), *The potent dead: Ancestors, saints and heroes in contemporary Indonesia*. Crows Nest: Allen and Unwin/ASAA, 183-204.
Snouck-Hurgronje, C.
1931 *Mekka in the latter part of the 19th century: Daily life, customs and learning of the Moslems of the East-Indian-Archipelago*, translated by J.H. Monahan. Leiden: Brill.
Solomon, Wendy
1986 'Text and personality: Ajip Rosidi in search of Haji Hasan Mustapa', *Indonesia Circle* 14:41, pp. 11-27.

Sunardjo, Unang
1995 *Menelusuri perjalanan sejarah pondok pesantren Suryalaya*. Suryalaya: Yayasan Serba Bakti.
Ubaid, Abdullah and Mohammad Bakir (eds)
2015 *Nasionalisme dan Islam Nusantara*. Jakarta: Kompas Media Nusantara.
Wahid, Abdurrahman
2006 *Islamku, Islam anda, Islam kita: Agama, masyarakat, negara, demokrasi*. Jakarta: The Wahid Institute.
Wiryawan, M. Ryzki
2014 *Okultisme di Bandoeng Doeloe: Menelusuri Jejak Gerakan Teosofi dan Freemasonry di Bandung*. Bandung: Khazanah Bahari.
Zimmer, Benjamin G.
2000 '*Al-'Arabiyyah* and *Basa Sunda*: Ideologies of translation and interpretation among the Muslims of West Java', *Studia Islamika* 7:3, 31-65.
Zuhri, Achmad Muhibbin
2010 *Pemikiran KH. M. Hasyim Asy'ari tentang ahl al-sunnah wa al-jama'ah*. Surabaya: Khalista.

# INDEX